CONTEXT AND M
QUALITATIVE RE

he returned on or before

CONTEXT AND METHOD IN QUALITATIVE RESEARCH

Edited by

Gale Miller and Robert Dingwall

SAGE Publications
London • Thousand Oaks • New Delhi

Chapters 10 and 11 Reprinted by Permission of Sage Publications, Inc.

First published 1997

SAGE Publications Ltd
6 Bonhill Street
London EC2A 4PU

SAGE Publications Inc
2455 Teller Road
Thousand Oaks, California 91320

SAGE Publications India Pvt Ltd
32, M-Block Market
Greater Kailash – I
New Delhi 110 048

British Library Cataloguing in Publication data

A catalogue record for this book is
available from the British Library

ISBN 0 8039 7631 3
ISBN 0 8039 7632 1 (pbk)

Library of Congress catalog card number 97-066251

Typeset by M Rules
Printed in Great Britain by Redwood Books, Trowbridge, Wiltshire

Contents

Notes on Contributors

David L. Altheide is Regents' Professor in the School of Justice Studies, Arizona State University.

Robert D. Benford is Associate Professor in the Department of Sociology, University of Nebraska, Lincoln.

Michael Bloor is Reader in Sociology in the School of Social and Administrative Studies at University of Wales, Cardiff.

Isobel Bowler is a Research Fellow in the Department of General Practice, University of Nottingham and an honorary research fellow in the School of Social and Administrative Studies at University of Wales, Cardiff.

Robert Dingwall is Professor of Sociology in the School of Social Studies, University of Nottingham.

Tom Durkin is Assistant Professor in Criminology and Sociology in the Department of Sociology, University of Florida, Gainesville.

Scott A. Hunt is Assistant Professor in the Department of Sociology, University of Kentucky.

John M. Johnson is Professor in the School of Justice Studies and the Women's Studies Program, Arizona State University.

Emmanuel Lazega is Associate Professor in the Department of Sociology at the University of Versailles and a researcher at CNRS-LASMAS, Paris.

Kath M. Melia is Professor of Nursing Studies in the Department of Nursing Studies, University of Edinburgh.

Gale Miller is Professor of Sociology in the Department of Social and Cultural Sciences, Marquette University.

David Silverman is Professor of Sociology in the Department of Sociology at Goldsmiths' College, University of London.

Philip M. Strong was Senior Lecturer in the Department of Public Health and Policy at the London School of Hygiene and Tropical Medicine, University of London.

Preface

This book was originally conceived at least in part as a mark of our respect for the scholarly contributions of two prominent British qualitative sociologists, David Silverman and Philip Strong, whose work had the conviction to challenge some of the fashionable theoretical and methodological stances of our time. In a succession of penetrating discussions, Silverman had laid out the case for methodological pragmatism, an acceptance that the practice of social research was both possible and essential in the modern world and that those involved in this craft should not be divided by artificial philosophical barriers. Strong also made methodological contributions of considerable significance. What we had come to admire in his writing, was his unblinking scepticism about Utopian thought in sociology and his desire to rehabilitate the discussion of liberalism in acknowledging that this was the foundation of most micro-sociological theory. The greatest good was not only unachievable but undesirable: with caution and modesty, the greatest evil might be avoided.

Sadly, Philip Strong died while this book was in preparation and his chapter is one of the last pieces that he ever wrote. With the permission of his former partner and executor, we dedicate the collection to his memory and to the programme that challenged and inspired so many of the contributors.

We have few other personal debts to record, except to thank the contributors and publishers for their patience and co-operation in the delays that seem inevitable when the editors are 4,000 miles apart. We are also grateful to Michelle Taylor for her assistance in consolidating and checking the bibliography and generally tidying up the manuscripts.

Gale Miller and Robert Dingwall

Introduction: Context and Method in Qualitative Research

Gale Miller

This book is concerned with the interrelations between context and method in qualitative research. The contributors are experienced qualitative researchers who both reflect upon and extend their research experiences. While they address practical methodological issues, the authors do not offer 'recipes' which detail the step-by-step processes of doing qualitative research. Rather, they stress the problems and possibilities associated with qualitative research, as well as the 'choices' available to qualitative researchers in organizing and completing their research projects.

The approaches to qualitative research considered here range from such traditional ethnographic techniques as participant observation and interviewing to newer orientations, such as conversation, dramaturgical and network analyses, and the new data-management options provided by recently developed computer-software packages for qualitative researchers. These, and other, approaches might be described as standpoints taken by qualitative researchers in engaging the socially organized settings that they describe and analyse. They are interpretive positions for observing social life, and for constructing relationships between researchers and the people they study. Different qualitative methods provide researchers with different possibilities for 'knowing' the social settings that they describe and analyse.

A major theme running through the book involves how research techniques and strategies are inextricably linked in qualitative research. Here, *technique* refers to the various procedures used by qualitative researchers in collecting and interpreting data about social settings. *Strategy* refers to the assumptions and concerns that qualitative researchers bring to each and every one of their projects. The usefulness of research techniques can only be assessed by considering researchers' strategic interests and aims which are then given concrete form and direction as researchers collect, record and interpret data. Thus, qualitative researchers' strategic goals are shaped and constrained by their data. It is for this reason that Silverman (1993) argues that qualitative researchers should resist becoming overly attached to any single research technique.

The authors also share an interest in using qualitative research to investigate issues involving the operation of institutions and organizations in society, and how they affect people's lives. These are long-standing concerns and are central to what might be called the *institutional studies tradition* in qualitative research, a tradition that includes some of the most influential studies in the history of the field (Fine and Ducharme 1995). It embraces such diverse studies as Blau's (1955) functionalist analysis of a government bureaucracy, Hughes (1971) and his students' symbolic interactionist studies of diverse work settings, Garfinkel's (1967) early articulation of ethnomethodology, and Smith's (1990) critical feminist analyses of organizational texts and of the social construction of mental illness.

The contributions of qualitative studies of institutions and organizations are many and varied. They have extended both general sociological theory and diverse middle-range theories. Examples of the latter include Glaser and Strauss's (1968) and Sudnow's (1967) studies of the social organization of dying, Becker's (1963) research on secondary deviance, Bittner's (1967) analysis of 'peace keeping' in police work, and Emerson's (1969) study of juvenile court processes as ceremonial activities. The institutional studies tradition in qualitative research also includes important contributions to discussions of social policy. One of the most important is Goffman's (1961a) *Asylums*, a study of the social organization of total institutions (such as prisons, mental hospitals and convents). Goffman's research raises profound questions about the (intended and unintended) consequences of treating human troubles as medical problems, and colonizing them within highly regimented, bureaucratic structures. Many aspects of the analysis remain relevant to contemporary policy debates.

The chapters that make up this volume contribute to the institutional studies tradition in qualitative research by addressing issues that have emerged from the authors' studies of diverse organizational and institutional relationships, activities and processes They include – but are certainly not limited to – studies of the mass media and information technology (Altheide 1995), criminal justice agencies (Johnson and Waletzko 1992), social movement organizations (Benford and Hunt 1992), medical settings (Bloor et al. 1988; Bowler 1993; Melia 1987; Strong 1979), counselling settings and practices (Silverman et al. 1992), law offices (Lazega 1992a), the social construction of litigation (Durkin 1994), and human service organizations (Dingwall et al. 1983; Miller and Holstein 1996). These and other qualitative studies speak to consequential issues affecting the opportunities offered to, and constraints experienced by, both members of contemporary institutions and others affected by their decisions and actions.

Focus of the book

The book is part of the burgeoning, cross-disciplinary literature on qualitative research in such fields as nursing, education, management, sociology and communications. These developments demonstrate a growing appreciation of qualitative research as a 'window' through which we might 'see' and comment on significant social issues. The issues include theoretical questions about how social life is organized, how institutions operate, and about the ways in which individuals and groups make sense of their lived experiences. But qualitative research may also speak to applied concerns. It may, for example, be used to develop new strategies for responding to people's troubles and to construct social policies that take account of the practical contingencies of people's lives. These uses of qualitative research are only suggestive of the ways in which qualitative methods might be implemented to address issues (and even solve problems) in a variety of disciplines and professions.

Whatever the research objectives, qualitative research involves the methodical study of socially organized settings, be they informal conversations among friends, the prosecution of cases in courtrooms, interactions in cyberspace, the assessment of others' mental health, the construction and interpretation of official statistics, or watching television. While the word methodical might be interpreted as an uninspired, plodding approach to research, I use it to convey a very different meaning. It refers, instead, to the ways in which qualitative researchers systematically – but artfully – invoke and use methodological techniques and strategies in formulating and solving research problems. Qualitative methods are resources that researchers use in observing and making sense of aspects of social life. Thus, the chapters that follow raise issues that are designed to enhance qualitative researchers' use of the methodological resources available to them in pursuing their research goals.

Perhaps the most fundamental assumption shared by the contributors to this volume is that qualitative research is an empirical enterprise. It involves the close study of everyday life in diverse social contexts. Two major objectives of qualitative research are to describe and analyse both the processes through which social realities are constructed, and the social relationships through which people are connected to one another. It is within, and through, these relationships and processes that organizations, institutions, culture and society emerge and are sustained. Social structures are, in other words, built from the 'bottom up'. They are interactionally constructed realities and patterns of social relationship that may be studied by using a variety of qualitative methods.

This is not to say that qualitative research is a simple matter of collecting and reporting the 'facts' that researchers observe. The relationship between qualitative researchers' observations of everyday life and analyses of it is complex, involving a variety of interpretive concerns and processes. The complexity of this relationship is evident in the various approaches to data collection and analysis taken by the contributors to this volume. They assume that qualitative research involves constructing accounts of the issues, events and relationships observed by researchers. Thus, the authors resist asking readers simplistically to choose between treating qualitative data as uninterpreted facts or as the exclusive product of researchers' perspectives and interests. Rather, they treat the relationship between the phenomena observed by qualitative researchers and the researchers' analyses of them as a topic for ongoing rumination and discussion. The discussion must speak to both the systematic (or scientific) and artful aspects of qualitative research.

Qualitative research might be further analysed as a dialectical process in which data and accounts emerge from researchers' management of the interconnections between the various aspects of their studies, such as the linkages between qualitative techniques and strategies and between choices stressing systematicity and artfulness. Central to this process is qualitative researchers' management of the interrelationships between the contexts of their studies and the methods that they use to observe, describe and analyse aspects of everyday life. Two contexts of qualitative research are emphasized in this book. They are the social settings within and about which qualitative research is conducted, and the audiences to which the research is reported.

These are not, of course, mutually exclusive considerations for qualitative researchers since one potential audience for their research may be the members of the settings under study. Still, the distinction is useful because it highlights two major aspects of the research process: systematically observing aspects of socially organized settings and delivering analyses of them (such as books, speeches and reports) to one or more audiences. These aspects of the dialectic of qualitative research are further considered in the next two sections.

Settings as contexts and contextualizations

Organizational and institutional settings are distinctive sites for observing and analysing social life. They are, for example, often formally organized social arenas involving distinctive social roles, political relationships, and even vocabularies for making sense of and responding to practical issues (Gubrium 1989; Miller and Holstein 1995). A major task of qualitative researchers, then, involves observing and specifying the unique and shared features of these socially organized settings, as well as analysing the implications of institutional structures and processes for people's lives and/or social issues. Achieving these research goals involves both developing a keen eye for observing everyday life (including aspects that others treat as 'trivial'), and developing an appreciation of how observers construct the settings that they describe and analyse.

Thus, one way in which context and method are related is through qualitative researchers' contextualizing practices which include both the data-collection techniques employed by qualitative researchers, and their strategic choices. Data-collection techniques matter because qualitative researchers' reports and analyses are built from, and limited by, their data. Interview-based research, for example, is very effective in generating data about respondents' concerns, feelings and/or perceptions, but cannot provide researchers with the direct and varied experiences (data) associated with participant observation. It is to be expected, then, that the descriptions of what appear to be the same social settings produced by interviewers and participant observers will differ because the data available to them for describing the settings are different.

The importance of qualitative researchers' data-collection choices may also be seen by comparing and contrasting interview- and participant observation-based data with the audio- and videotaped data used by conversation analysts in studying the sequential organization of social interactions which they may not have observed first-hand (Maynard 1989). In focusing on the details of a small number of social interactions, conversation analytic studies are less likely to provide information about the general issues often discussed in interviews or about the longer-term flow of events and relationships stressed by participant observers. But in revisiting their research sites over and over again, by replaying and transcribing their tape recordings, conversation analysts produce fine-grained analyses of the interactional organization of social settings that are not possible in studies based on interviews and/or participant observation.

While they are important, it is possible to overstate the significance of qualitative researchers' decisions about how to collect data. Equally significant are their strategic and analytic interests in doing the research. These interests help to define the objectives of qualitative research projects, and the meanings that may be assigned to qualitative data. An instructive example of how such interests influence the meanings of qualitative data is Gilbert and Mulkay's (1984) interview-based research on scientists' descriptions of their work and professional community. Gilbert and Mulkay (1984: 7) contrast their discursive strategy with the more typical qualitative approach to analysing interview data which rests on:

> the methodological principle of linguistic consistency; that is, if a 'sufficient pro-portion' of participants' accounts appear consistently to tell the same sort of story about a particular aspect of social action, then these accounts are treated as being literally descriptive. Only in those instances where the existence of incompatible accounts is treated as sociologically significant do analysts pay attention to the social generation of accounts; and, in such cases, reference to the social or personal context of participants' discourse is usually introduced into the analysis in order to explain away those accounts that weaken the analyst's conclusions, on the grounds that they are exaggerations, biased reports, ideology, lies, and so on.

Gilbert and Mulkay's research strategy, on the other hand, assumes that scientists' (and others') accounts cannot be judged as literally true or false: hence the question of linguistic consistency is irrelevant for their research. They focus, instead, on the variety of ways in which scientists describe their professional worlds, the social conditions associated with scientists' differing accounts, and the ways in which scientists 'resolve' the differences between their accounts. The image of science that emerges from this study, then, is distinctive even though the data under analysis are similar to those collected by other sociologists of science. Qualitative researchers' decisions about data-collection techniques are important, but they are only one part of the dialectical processes through which research is organized and done.

Other distinctive orientations to data analysis considered in this book are dramaturgical analysis, network theory, discourse studies and grounded theory. In choosing to analyse their data within one of these theoretical orientations, qualitative researchers define the contexts of their research and focus their attention on limited aspects of the settings. For example, dramaturgical analysis treats organizational and institutional relationships as 'theatre-like' encounters involving performances, scripts and actors (Goffman 1959). This focus may be contrasted with other qualitative orientations which involve very different assumptions about social relations in institutional and organizational settings, such as network analysis which involves building formal models or maps of the interconnections among setting members (Berkowitz 1982). Further, while dramaturgical analysts sometimes develop generalizations about organizational and institutional settings, their studies may also involve the analysis of only one setting. Grounded theory, on the other hand, requires that researchers adopt a comparative orientation to institutional settings because the objective of such research is to develop cross-situational generalizations (Glaser and Strauss 1967).

In sum, conceptualizing qualitative research methods as standpoints involves appreciating the interpretive implications of different qualitative research techniques and analytical frameworks. Qualitative methods are positions taken by qualitative researchers for observing institutional settings. Thus, both the descriptions of social reality that might be constructed by qualitative researchers, and the meanings that they might assign to the descriptions, vary depending on their observational and analytical positions. Treating methodological choices as standpoints also directs attention to how some of the most important interpretive possibilities of qualitative studies are established prior to data collection.

This is not to suggest, however, that qualitative researchers are always free independently to decide about the methods that they will use in doing their research. The processes of gaining access to research sites, and of building relationships with setting members, often involve negotiations about the techniques that researchers might use in collecting ('constructing') data. Organizational officials who initially review research proposals may, for example, reject some data-collecting techniques (such as participant observation and mechanical recording of social interactions) as too intrusive. Lower-level organization members may also influence researchers' options by directly refusing to participate in the research or by indirectly signalling their discomfort with some data-collecting approaches.

None of this, however, changes the above assertion that methodological choices are also interpretive choices. These possibilities only complicate the research process and highlight how members of social settings may participate in establishing how they are to be studied and what may be said about them. Setting members – like qualitative researchers – are an aspect of the dialectic of qualitative research which is an emergent – artful – process involving the assessment of one's options within concrete social contexts and choosing among the available options. Indeed, a choice sometimes faced by qualitative researchers involves whether the envisioned project can be done under the conditions specified by organizational and institutional officials. Sometimes these developments require that qualitative researchers rethink the objectives of their research, adjusting their projects to the circumstances presented by others. But recognizing the interpretive implications of methodological choices might also mean that qualitative researchers sometimes decline opportunities to do research in sites that are, under other conditions, very attractive.

Audiences, stories and credibility

The second major way in which context and method are linked in qualitative research involves the relationship between researchers' methodological choices and the audiences to whom they present their findings and analyses. The audiences might include professional colleagues, research funders, members of the institutional settings under study, dissertation supervisors, book publishers and/or government officials. These audiences may be differentiated by both their differing relationships with (and influence over) qualitative researchers, and their variable concerns about, and interests in, qualitative researchers' studies. Qualitative research has different meanings and implications for different audiences.

In orienting their research towards the concerns and interests of one or a few potential audiences, then, qualitative researchers construct social contexts for making methodological and analytical choices that shape what they can know and say about social settings. This is not to say that qualitative research can speak only to the interests of one audience at a time or that qualitative research findings cannot be interpreted differently for different audiences. It is to say, however, that audience considerations are implicated in qualitative researchers' methodological choices, even if the researchers are unaware of the implications and if they are not explicitly acknowledged in research reports. For example, anyone who has written a PhD dissertation knows how qualitative research can be influenced by the stated and presumed concerns of dissertation examination committee members who may approve or reject the research.

Treating audiences as contexts of qualitative research recasts recent debates among contemporary qualitative researchers about the authoritativeness of their descriptions, reports and analyses, particularly how qualitative researchers exercise power over others by representing their research as systematic and factual accounts of social life. The debate often turns on whether qualitative research is a scientific enterprise which involves reporting and analysing research findings, or is really a process of story-constructing and story-telling.[1] The latter view emphasizes how qualitative researchers' reports are always subjective – partisan – accounts which express only one of many interpretations that might be made about the settings and people under study.

Central to this debate is the assumption that qualitative researchers assert authority over their audiences, be they listeners or readers. Some argue that the researchers' authority is warranted because their accounts are based on procedures that are superior to other, less rigorous, approaches to observing and analysing social settings (Miller 1995). Critics of this position state, on the other hand, that qualitative researchers' descriptions of their research as scientific are rhetorical moves designed to privilege their interpretations and to undermine competing interpretations that might be described as un-systematic (Clifford and Marcus 1986).

This debate is significantly changed when we conceptualize the audiences of qualitative research as part of a dialectic involving researchers and audiences. So viewed, different audiences form social contexts or constituencies that may influence any and all phases of the research process, ranging from the initial formulation of the research problem to researchers' decisions about how to present their studies (Miller 1995). In particular, this change in focus reminds us of the ways in which audiences assess and pass judgement on qualitative researchers' work. Researchers can only assert authority over audiences if audience members grant credibility to the researchers' accounts, whether the accounts are presented as scientific findings or stories.

Analyses of qualitative research as a story-constructing and story-telling process, then, must attend to the expectations and assessment standards that audiences bring to their reading and/or hearing of qualitative researchers' stories. While these expectations and standards vary across audiences, many (I think the overwhelming majority) insist that qualitative researchers' accounts 'ring true' with their experiences and knowledge. They also often insist that researchers' portrayals of organizational and institutional settings include information that is potentially verifiable through subsequent observations of the settings, interviews with setting members, or similar procedures. Put simply, qualitative researchers are held to different standards by their audiences than are other story-tellers, particularly those who are said to tell fictional stories.

One way of conceptualizing how qualitative researchers and their audiences are interrelated is by analysing them as members of interpretive communities (Miller 1995). Such communities consist of the shared orientations to social reality and interpretive practices that like-minded readers and writers bring to their reading and writing of texts (Fish 1980, 1989). To say that interpretive community members are like-minded is not to say, however, that they are of one mind. Indeed, interpretive communities may involve diverse conflicts of interest and interpretation, but these conflicts are negotiated within contexts made up of community members' shared assumptions, concerns and interpretive practices. These conflicts may be contrasted with those involving members of competing interpretive communities in which the issues in contention are deeper and wider, sometimes involving disagreements about the

very circumstances under which the conflicts may be expressed and negotiated.

Qualitative researchers enter interpretive communities in deciding what to
study, how to study it, and in analysing their data. These decisions also
signal qualitative researchers' willingness to be held accountable to the standards of their chosen interpretive communities. This conceptualization of the
researcher–audience relationship is also helpful in responding to the competing advice and criticism routinely given to qualitative researchers about
their work. Some of this advice and/or criticism is very relevant and helpful,
some is less so, and some is simply irrelevant because it expresses the
assumptions and concerns of alternative interpretive communities (Miller
1995). A major and sometimes difficult task for qualitative researchers
involves assessing the relevance and usefulness of the criticisms and advice
directed towards them.

The chapters that follow, then, may be seen as invitations extended by the
authors to join (if only briefly) their preferred interpretive communities.
They do so by discussing their assumptions and concerns about qualitative
research, describing strategies and techniques for doing qualitative research,
and offering standards for assessing their own and others' qualitative studies of organizations and institutions.

Organization of the book

Organizing contributions written to stand alone into a single volume involves
a certain amount of arbitrariness, and that is certainly the case with this
volume. While each of the chapters in the book addresses one or more of the
issues raised above, they overlap in complex ways that make it difficult to
determine – in any definitive fashion – which pieces should be placed side by
side or which should go first and which should go last. A useful way of
thinking about the contributions to this volume involves focusing on four
major themes or questions about the interrelationship between context and
method in qualitative research. The questions ask (a) how might we assess
the validity and credibility of qualitative studies; (b) to what methodological
issues (both technical and strategic) should we attend in doing qualitative
research; (c) how might we use qualitative data to analyse organizations and
institutions; and (d) is qualitative research a moral discourse?

We begin with three chapters that focus on aspects of the issue of validity
and credibility in qualitative research. Silverman (Chapter 1) raises the credibility issue by, first, arguing for an ecumenical approach to research
methods, and then by illustrating how qualitative research on naturally
occurring interactions may be assessed. Melia (Chapter 2) addresses the
credibility issue by asking what is a useful story. She answers this question by
raising further questions about the usefulness of interviewing as a data-
collecting technique, and how researchers' analytical concerns influence the
stories that they tell. Bloor (Chapter 3) concludes this section by critically

examining the major techniques used by qualitative researchers in assessing the validity of their own and others' research. He neither rejects nor champions the approaches, but discusses their uses and limitations for assessing qualitative research.

The second part focuses on issues associated with doing qualitative research. We begin with Dingwall's (Chapter 4) discussion of the decline of participant observation (relative to interviewing) in qualitative research. He also makes a case for reviving participant observation studies by focusing on the ways in which social realities are constructed and acted upon in the course of everyday life. Bowler (Chapter 5) also discusses the advantages and disadvantages of interviewing and participant observation in her study of how South Asian women experience maternity services. She analyses the practical and cultural circumstances that qualitative researchers sometimes encounter in working with people from non-Western cultures. Miller (Chapter 6) retains Bowler's focus on the practical circumstances of qualitative research by arguing for an ethnographic approach to the study of organizational texts. He describes how such texts are embedded in the mundane social relations and activities of organizations, and how the practical meanings assigned to them are inextricably linked to organizational contexts.

Durkin's contribution (Chapter 7) shifts the focus by considering how qualitative researchers may incorporate computer-based analyses into their studies. He critically examines the opportunities and pitfalls of using computer software in qualitative research, and offers practical advice on how to choose computer software for qualitative research projects. Hunt and Benford (Chapter 8) conclude this section, and construct a bridge to the next section, by considering how the dramaturgical perspective may be used to analyse qualitative research on organizations and institutions. They discuss major aspects of the dramaturgical perspective, and challenge dramaturgical analysts reflexively to extend their studies by analysing their own roles and relationships from the dramaturgical standpoint.

The third theme stressed in the book involves developing analytical frameworks for analysing organizations and institutions using qualitative data. Lazega (Chapter 9) discusses how network analysis may be combined with qualitative methods to analyse organizational and institutional settings. He describes network analysis as a method for contextualizing the knowledge and behaviour of setting members, and shows how the approach may be linked to themes in symbolic interactionist theory. Dingwall and Strong (Chapter 10) also focus on the ways in which qualitative research may simultaneously address micro and macro issues. They do so by, first, critically examining the interactional literature on organizations, and then by outlining an interactional approach that focuses on language use and practical reasoning as organizing features of organizational and institutional settings. The integrative emphasis in Dingwall and Strong's chapter is also evident in Miller's (Chapter 11) which discusses how aspects of ethnomethodology, conversation analysis and Foucauldian discourse studies may be linked in qualitative research. Miller elaborates his argument by discussing how this synthesis of perspectives may help qualitative researchers in analysing power as a feature of organizational and institutional settings.

The final section considers how qualitative research is a moral discourse. That is, how it may be used to raise important moral issues about contemporary institutions and organizations, and how qualitative researchers' studies might contribute to the betterment of contemporary societies. Altheide and Johnson (Chapter 12) address these issues by analysing how ethnographers are 'justice workers', meaning that their studies are both the means of investigating ethical issues and of fostering greater justice in society. Equally important, Altheide and Johnson treat ethnographers' justice work as embedded in the activities, relationships and emergent issues of the qualitative research process. Strong (Chapter 13) extends this vision of qualitative research by describing how it may contribute to a new public ethic and liberal metaphysics, both of which focus on improving society while recognizing that our utopian dreams for a fully just world are unlikely to be realized. Finally, in the Conclusion, Dingwall argues that the Enlightenment project is not yet dead, and that a moral science of society is still possible. He challenges qualitative researchers to renew their heritage of social theory, rather than chasing after intellectual fashions of short-term consequence.

Note

1 See, for example, the special issue of the *Journal of Contemporary Ethnography* (vol. 21, April, 1992) on *'Street Corner Society* Revisited'.

PART I

VALIDITY AND CREDIBILITY IN QUALITATIVE RESEARCH

1

The Logics of Qualitative Research

David Silverman

In the Sociology Department where I work, we offer a graduate degree in Qualitative Research. This title was chosen to give a flavour of a degree largely taught by ethnographers who themselves mainly use qualitative methods. However, I feel that such a title may attract students more in terms of what it promises to avoid rather than by reason of what it offers.

'Qualitative research' seems to promise that we will avoid or downplay statistical techniques and the mechanics of the kind of quantitative methods used in, say, survey research or epidemiology. In fact, this is indeed the case – although we expect students to take a course in survey methods and to be aware of how the issues of validity and reliability so often posed by quantitative researchers are relevant to any kind of research (albeit in varying ways).

The danger in the title, however, is that it seems to assume a fixed preference or predefined evaluation of what is a good (i.e. qualitative) and bad (i.e. quantitative) research methodology. In fact, the choice between different research methods can depend upon quite pragmatic matters. For instance, if you want to discover how people intend to vote, then a quantitative method, like a social survey, may seem the most appropriate choice. On the other hand, if you are concerned with exploring people's wider perceptions or everyday behaviour, then qualitative methods may be favoured.

Other, less practical, questions arise when you choose between 'qualitative' and 'quantitative' methods. The researcher has to bear in mind that these methods are often evaluated differently. Table 1.1, which gives the terms used by speakers at a conference on research methods in the late 1970s, shows how imprecise evaluative considerations come into play when researchers describe qualitative and quantitative methods. In turn, these evaluative issues are linked to attempts to define mutually opposed 'schools' of social science.

In the 1970s, it was common to criticize what was called 'positivism' (Filmer et al. 1972). Unfortunately, 'positivism' is a very slippery and emotive term. Not only is it difficult to define but there are very few quantitative

Table 1.1   *Claimed features of qualitative and quantitative methods*

Qualitative	Quantitative
soft	hard
flexible	fixed
subjective	objective
political	value-free
case study	survey
speculative	hypothesis-testing
grounded	abstract

Source: Halfpenny (1979: 799)

researchers who would accept the label (Marsh 1982). Instead, most quantitative researchers would argue that they do not aim to produce a science of laws (like physics) but simply to produce a set of cumulative, theoretically defined generalizations deriving from the critical sifting of data. So, it became increasingly clear that 'positivists' were made of straw since very few researchers could be found who equated the social and natural worlds or who believed that research was properly theory-free.[1] Moreover, even the picture of the natural sciences as indelibly 'positivist' may be wide of the mark. For instance, post-Newtonian physicists may look askance at the suggestion that there is a stable point from which to derive universal laws.

Given the nebulous character of 'positivism', quantitative research seemed to offer an easier target. The critique of purely quantitative research has a long history, beginning in the 1950s. C. Wright Mills (1959) attacked the atheoretical character of much quantitative research, which he called 'abstracted empiricism'. Blumer (1969) noted how the attempt to establish correlations between variables depended upon a lack of attention to how these variables are defined by the people being studied. Finally, Cicourel (1964), influenced by Schutz and Garfinkel, drew attention to how the choice of a purely mathematical logic can neglect the commonsense reasoning used by *both* participants and researchers. Instead of attending to the social construction of meaning, quantitative research, it is claimed, uses a set of *ad hoc* procedures to define, count and analyse its variables.[2]

Such critiques can be seen to lay the foundation for a school of interpretive social science with a set of emphases different from more quantitatively oriented work. Unfortunately, these foundations were, to say the least, very shaky. In the first place, just as it is difficult to find a positivist 'enemy', the critics had established a 'straw man' to represent quantitative research. Quantitative researchers are rarely 'dopes'. So, for instance, epidemiologists and criminologists are only too aware of the problematic character of what gets recorded as, say, 'cause of death' or a 'criminal offence' (Hindess 1973). Equally, good quantitative researchers are highly conscious of the problems involved in interpreting statistical correlations in relation to what the variables involved 'mean' to the participants (Marsh 1982). In these circumstances, it might be better to avoid the term 'critique' and instead talk about *some* complaints made about *some* quantitative research.

Secondly, it is inaccurate to assume that quantitative and qualitative research are polar opposites. In *Interpreting Qualitative Data* (Silverman 1993; henceforth *IQD*), I sought to undermine the assumption that these two paradigms are incommensurable or, indeed, that they offer any worthwhile description of the major alternative directions of sociological research. For, of course, there are no principled grounds to be either qualitative or quantitative in approach. It all depends upon what you are trying to do. Indeed, often one will want to combine both approaches. For example, I recently tested a hypothesis by using simple tabulations on fifty-odd examples of HIV counselling 'advice packages' whose form can readily be identified and counted (Silverman 1996). This means that, if we want to understand the logic behind qualitative research, we need to recognize its points of continuity with, as well as difference from, more quantitative or 'positivistic' studies.

Thirdly, just as quantitative researchers would resist the charge that they are all 'positivists' (Marsh 1982), there is no agreed doctrine underlying all qualitative social research. Instead, there are many 'isms' that appear to lie behind qualitative methods: for example, interactionism, feminism, postmodernism and ethnomethodology (see Denzin and Lincoln 1994). This means that qualitative research can cover a vast range of research styles and can be used in studies without any conscious analytical perspective. For instance, in British market-research circles, 'qualitative' research is the latest fashion. It is seen to provide 'in-depth' material which is believed to be absent from survey research data. Above all, it is relatively cheap. However, all that is meant by qualitative research is open-ended interviews or 'panel' studies lacking a clear, analytical basis in social theory. As I argue in *IQD*, this makes any attempt to characterize qualitative research as a whole open to severe criticism (see also Atkinson 1995b). For instance, while Hammersley (1992a: 160) attempts to identify qualitative research with hypothesis-generation, more and more non-quantitative work happily *tests* prior hypotheses (for example, Silverman 1996; Strong 1979). Again, while many qualitative researchers would agree with Bryman (1988: 61) that their aim is to 'see through the eyes' of subjects, others would criticize such an aim as 'subjectivist' and even 'journalistic'.

We should learn from the now empty debate about 'positivism' that such analytical differences cannot be resolved by choosing sides from spurious polarities (for example, structure and meaning; quality and quantity). For instance, it is sometimes maintained that, while positivists are concerned with 'society', interpretive social science focuses on the 'individual'. But rather than choose one side of this polarity, we might look at how the individual–society opposition is actually used in everyday life.

As I suggested in *IQD*, we can find a striking example of how we all rely on the distinction between 'objective' and 'subjective' realities in Sacks's (1992) account of children's socialization. Sacks shows that participants search for underlying 'social structures' and try to understand the meaning of 'experiences'. What, then, is the status of social science research which itself chooses to focus on one or other of these realities? Such a question suggests that we need to look twice at the unthinking identification of the open-ended interview as the 'gold standard' of qualitative research. In *IQD*, I argue that some such interviewers depend upon a nineteenth-century, romantic ontology based on the primacy of 'experience' and are apparently ignorant of the linguistic turn explicit in de Saussure and the later Wittgenstein. This 'turn' reveals the 'public' character of apparently 'private' knowledge. As Sacks tellingly remarked, if we are really interested in the contents of people's heads, we should choose to be brain surgeons rather than social scientists.

In interviews, as Heritage (1984: 236) puts it, the mistake is to treat the verbal formulations of subjects: 'as an appropriate substitute for the observation of actual behaviour'. Unlike the research interview, observational data are of value precisely because they focus on naturally occurring activities. What do we lose if we base our analysis purely on such data? The first thing to bear in mind is that, to become data, observations have to be recorded in some way; for example, through field notes or pre-coded schedules. Moreover, while observational data should properly include descriptions of non-verbal aspects of social interaction – what Stimson (1986) calls 'the sociology of place and space' – much of what we observe in formal and informal settings will inevitably consist of conversations. However sophisticated are our field notes, they cannot offer the detail found in transcripts of recorded talk.

Drew and Heritage (1992) show how this has a direct impact on the kind of data we think are relevant. Most field researchers use such data as questionnaires, interviews, observation and diaries. They thus attempt 'to get inside the "black box" of social institutions to gain access to their interior processes and practices' (Drew and Heritage 1992: 5). However, such studies may suffer from two problems:

- The assumption of a stable reality or context (e.g. the 'organization') to which people respond.
- The gap between beliefs and action and between what people say and what they do (Gilbert and Mulkay 1983; Stimson and Webb 1975).

So, even though observational data can contribute a great deal to understanding how institutions function, its observations may be based upon a taken-for-granted version of the setting in question. For instance, Strong's (1979) powerful analysis of the 'ceremonial order' of doctor–parent consultations undoubtedly depends, in part, upon our readiness to read his data extracts in the context of our shared knowledge of what medical consultations look like.

Consequently, ethnographic work can only take us so far. It is able to show us how people respond to particular settings. It is unable to answer basic questions about how people are constituting that setting through their talk.

Detailed transcripts of conversation may thus overcome the tendency of tran-
scribers to 'tidy up' the 'messy' features of natural conversation. However,
without an analytical basis, even detailed transcription can be merely an
empty technique. Thus we need to ask: what sort of features are we searching
for in our transcripts and what approach lies behind this search?

To suggest how I would answer these questions, the rest of this chapter is
devoted to two practical illustrations from research based on the recording
and transcription of naturally occurring interactions. The first study I will
consider is Lucy Suchman's (1987) work on human–computer interaction.
Like conversation analysis (CA), I will show how Suchman's focus on the
sequential organization of verbal and non-verbal interaction can give us a
secure grip on the precise mechanics of organizational interaction. The
second study by Clavarino et al. (1995) is concerned with doctor–patient
interviews in the cancer department of an Australian hospital. It follows
Suchman in using recordings as data but its particular concern is with
addressing how detailed transcription can increase the reliability of qualitative data and the validity of its data analysis.

However, it should be stressed at the outset that, in selecting two studies
based upon recordings of naturally occurring data, I am *not* suggesting that
such a database, coupled with a CA method, is the *only* way to proceed in
qualitative research. First, such a firm position would undercut all that I have
said earlier about the risks of always choosing sides between the polarities
that tend to organize our thoughts. Secondly, much will depend upon what
we are trying to find out and what kind of data we are able to obtain.

So I have not selected these studies in order to recommend a panacea.
Indeed, my own research has used ethnographic as well as CA methods in
different cases. I simply intend to show the value of careful transcription in
qualitative studies which choose to focus on what participants are doing.
This value will, I hope, be seen in the way in which such CA-orientated work
can show how people create contexts for their interactions with each other
and with objects (like photocopying machines).

People's doings: communicating with the photocopier

Suchman (1987) is concerned with the interaction between people and
machines. She takes the example of a computer-based system attached to a
photocopier and intended to instruct the user in the photocopier's operation.
Her data derive from videos of four sessions, each of more than an hour,
involving first-time users of this 'expert system'. In each session, two novices
worked together in pairs. She is particularly concerned with how interactional 'troubles' arise and are resolved.

In Suchman's study the computer used in the photocopier: 'project[s] the
course of the user's actions as the enactment of a *plan* for doing the job,
and then use[s] the presumed plan as the relevant context for the action's
interpretation' (1987: 99; my italic). However, the problem is that 'plans'

have a different status for computers and users: 'While the [design] plan directly *determines* the system's behaviour, the user is required to *find* the plan, as the prescriptive and descriptive significance of a series of procedural instructions' (1987: 101; my italic). This is shown in Suchman's (1987: 107) model of how the computer is supposed to 'instruct' a user:

1 *Machine presents instruction*: User reads instruction, interprets referents and action descriptions
2 *User takes action*: Design assumes that the action means that the user has understood the instruction
3 *Machine presents next instruction*

Despite this rational model, much of the user's behaviour is unavailable to the system, for instance: 'the actual work of locating referents and interpreting action descriptions' (p. 107). This means that if an instruction is misunderstood by the user, the error will go unnoticed.

Predictably, Suchman's study reveals many conflicts between the design assumptions (DA) built into the machine and user assumptions (UA). Some examples of this, based on Suchman (1987: 148–167), are as follows:

> DA: Treat the question 'what next?' as a request for the next step – attended to by presentation of the next instruction.
> UA: Can ask 'what next' sometimes in order to know how to abort or repair an activity, e.g. where only one photocopy obtained instead of the five desired; 'while from the point of view of the design [they have achieved] precisely what they want to do, that intent is not a feature of *their* situation' (p. 165).
> DA: Repeat instructions either (a) where task needs to be repeated or (b) where user's action in response to the instruction is in error such as to return the system to a state prior to the instruction being given (a loop).
> UA: In the case of repeated instructions, (b) does *not* occur in human interaction. Instead, repetition of an instruction indicates that 'the action taken in response to the instruction in some way fails to satisfy the intent of the instruction, and needs to be remedied' (p. 148).
> DA: Users will follow instructions; where they do not, this will be detected by the machine. (But what happens when the faulted action goes unnoticed at the point where it occurs 'because what is available to the system is only the action's effect and that effect satisfies the requirements for the next instruction' (p. 167)?)
> UA: Can sometimes ignore instructions because of preconceptions about what is appropriate, based on prior experience.

Because of these kinds of conflicts between the assumptions of designers and users, Suchman concludes that users often fail to get what they want from the photocopier: 'Due to the constraints on the machine's access to the situation of the user's inquiry, breaches in understanding that for face-to-face interaction would be trivial in terms of detection and repair become "fatal" for human–machine communication' (1987: 170).

Like many studies concerned with the mechanics of organizational interaction, Suchman's findings are both analytically and practically rich. Among the practical implications of her study, we may note that:

- It reveals the character of practical decision-making in a way relevant to the design of expert systems.
- It suggests the constructive role of users' troubles in system design, i.e. troubles arise not by departing from a plan but in the situated contingencies of action. She notes how such systems may not seek to eliminate user errors but 'to make them accessible to the student, and therefore instructive' (1987: 184).

Analytically, Suchman's work is important because of its focus on the precise mechanics of organizational interaction. In particular, Suchman begins by using everyday interaction as a baseline and then sees how far human–computer interaction departs from it. This means that she refuses to accept the commonsense assumption that there is a stable organizational or institutional order separate from everyday interaction.

Suchman's work on human–machine interaction thus reveals what can separate conversation analysts from ethnographers. As Maynard and Clayman (1991: 406–407) argue:

> Conversation analysts . . . [are] concerned that using terms such as 'doctor's office', 'courtroom', 'police department', 'school room', and the like, to characterise settings ... can obscure much of what occurs within those settings . . . For this reason, conversation analysts rarely rely on ethnographic data and instead examine if and how interactants themselves reveal an orientation to institutional or other contexts.

Clearly, Maynard and Clayman's point should have a huge impact on how we study social institutions. So at least we can agree with the earlier critics of quantitative method that methodological issues cannot be reduced to merely technical matters.

Indeed, Suchman's focus on how rules function in human–computer interaction links with a very important debate in the human sciences about how rules function in everyday life. Suchman draws upon Gladwin's (1964) account of the navigation methods of a South-East Asian tribe – the Trukese – with no 'rational' Western theory of navigation. Instead, the Trukese navigate via various *ad hoc* methods (for example, responding to the wind, waves, the stars, the clouds, etc.). She asks how real is the contrast between Western and Trukese methods of navigation? Theories and plans don't *determine* the actions of either Western or Trukese navigators. Rather, Western navigators *invoke* a plan when asked to account for their navigation which, inevitably, depends on *ad hoc* methods (for example, accounting for disasters like the Exxon Valdez oil spill off Alaska).

This creates a problem in artificial intelligence systems that are 'built on a *planning model* of human action. The model treats a plan as something located in the actor's head, which directs his or her behaviour' (Suchman 1987: 3). As Suchman notes, plans neither determine action nor fully reconstruct it. Thus she argues that: 'artifacts built on the planning model confuse *plans* with *situated actions*' and proposes 'a view of plans as formulations of antecedent conditions and consequences that account for actions in a plausible way' (1987: 3). Conversely, she suggests, the successful navigation of the Trukese shows that: 'the coherence of situated action is tied in essential ways not to . . . conventional rules but to local interactions contingent on the actor's particular circumstances' (1987: 27–28). This implies that, in designing computers that can interact with humans, the system of communication 'must incorporate both a sensitivity to local circumstances and resources for the remedy of troubles in understanding that inevitably arise' (Suchman 1987: 28). This will mean that: 'Instead of looking for a structure that is invariant across situations, we look for the processes whereby particular, uniquely constituted circumstances are systematically interpreted so as to render meaning shared and action accountably rational' (1987: 67).

Why should we believe qualitative research?

What I have said so far can be organized into the following two assertions. First, as Suchman's discussion of rule-use reveals, analytical issues lie concealed behind apparently technical matters, such as the most appropriate research method. Secondly, these analytical issues are rarely properly identified with the tired old polarities of social science (for example, positivist/interpretive, quantitative/qualitative, structure/meaning, objective/subjective). However, if we argue for the pre-eminence of analytical issues in research, the implication might follow that the sole requirement for any research study is analytical integrity. This would mean that the validity of a piece of qualitative research could be settled simply by asserting its pristine, theoretical roots.

Along these lines, it is sometimes suggested that the assessment of the quality of qualitative data should transcend the conventional methodological approaches. The quality of qualitative research, it is argued: 'cannot be determined by following prescribed formulas. Rather its quality lies in the power of its language to display a picture of the world in which we discover something about ourselves and our common humanity' (Buchanan 1992: 133). If Buchanan is saying that the main question in field research is the quality of the analysis rather than the recruitment of the sample or, say, the format of the interview, then I would agree (see Mitchell 1983). However, Buchanan's opposition to 'prescribed formulas' can amount to something that might be called 'methodological anarchy' (see Clavarino et al. 1995).

I resist the 'anarchic' position on two grounds. First, it simply makes no sense to argue that all knowledge and feelings are of equal weight and value. Even in everyday life we readily sort 'fact' from 'fancy'. Why, therefore, should science be any different? Secondly, methodological anarchy offers a clearly negative message to research-funding agencies; namely, don't fund qualitative research because even its proponents have given up claims to validity. Moreover, in such an environment, can we wonder that qualitative research's potential audiences (for example, the medical professions, corporations, labour unions) take its 'findings' less than seriously?

However, even where questions of empirical validity are taken seriously, they are not easily settled. When presenting results, qualitative data analysts will suggest that certain patterns recur, that perhaps a particular sequence of events can be observed and that the patterns and events have the meanings ascribed to them; that is, that they are valid. In this process, there is some-times little capacity to determine the extent to which the interpretations of the data reflect the situations or events that occurred, whether other unre-ported data may contradict the findings, and the extent to which the findings reflect the personal qualities of the researcher. This not only creates a degree of uncertainty about the validity of the data but it also leaves unanswered questions about its reliability. Here the problem is serious because some categories or observations may be of a better quality than others, yet all are rendered uncertain by the failure of the researcher to establish their credibility.

To firm up the discussion, I will take the example of a recent research study in which I participated (Clavarino et al. 1995). In this qualitative study, we attempted to address directly the issues of the validity and relia-bility of our observations. Moreover, as will be seen below, we showed that different analytical traditions could give us different kinds of 'grip' on these issues.

Validity and reliability in a study of medical interviews

Our study sought to examine the basis upon which interpretive judgements were made about the content of a series of audio-taped doctor–patient inter-views between three oncologists and their newly referred cancer patients. It was during this interview that the patients were supposedly informed that their cancer was incurable.

The interviews were recorded, first, to provide insight into the nature of the interaction between the oncologist and the patient in the context of the disclosure of bad news. The second purpose was to determine whether or not it is possible to extract reliable information from such interviews. Two inde-pendent transcriptions were performed. In the first, an attempt was made to transcribe the talk 'verbatim', that is, without grammatical or other 'tidying up'. The second transcription was informed by the analytical ideas and tran-scription symbols of conversation analysis (see Heritage 1984; Silverman 1993). This provided additional information on how the parties organized their talk.

Using the first transcription, three independent coders, who had been trained to be consistent, coded the same material. Inter-judge reliability was then estimated. For instance, inconsistencies among coders may reflect some ambiguity in the data and some cross-over with the type of information being requested in another coding category. What the presence of multiple coders does do, however, is enable the researcher to detect instances of ambi-guity, inconsistency and simple coding errors.

In the first stage of the data analysis, the interviews provided the source for developing a coding scheme. Based upon the research objectives, a series of 24 issues were identified which reflected a range of factors relevant to assessing the quality of life of the patients. For reasons of space, we only deal with the topic of death and dying here.

In 21 of the 22 interviews, all three coders agreed that the patient had been told that the condition was incurable. For one case (W008), however, there was a discrepancy involving the interpretation of the interview data.

> W008 – male, aged 64 at entry to study, was diagnosed with small cell lung cancer one month prior to interview, the disease had spread by the time of initial diagnosis. This patient died almost exactly twelve months after diagnosis.

Two of the three coders believed that the patient had not been told that the condition was incurable. The discrepancy appears to have occurred primarily because the word 'incurable' was not used by the doctor. In addition, one of the two coders believed that there was some ambiguity attached to the doctor's statement in relation to the cancer. The following is a transcript of the relevant text:

[Ex.1, W008, p. 9] (D = doctor; P = patient; W = wife)

```
 1  D:  There's somewhere about 15% chance of being around in two years' time, with the
 2      disease under control. What that comes to long term is very hard to know. And with
 3      that, what we try and do is shrink this away, preferably totally away, and then
 4      probably also offer you some radiation to that area after that.
 5  P:  Mmm.
 6  D:  Uhm, and then watch, wait and see. And it really depends on what happens
 7      with time after that and how everything goes. It's very hard to be absolutely
 8      dogmatic about any predictions with these things. But despite all of those
 9      things, in the majority of people the disease does come back, even from the
10      beginning.
11  P:  Yes.
        . . .

14  D:  And if it does come back, we can try other drugs which may control it for a little
15      while, but generally all that you can try and do is control the symptoms.
16  P:  Yes Mm.
17  D:  Uhm, the first time gives us the best chance for a longer survival, hopefully
18      long term, but the odds are generally against that. But if [our emphasis] we do
19      nothing for these sorts of diseases, it kills you within a couple of months.
20  W:  The breakdown could be that quick could it?
21  P:  Mmm
22  D:  Well actually it's quite spectacularly fast.
```

In Extract 1, one coder believed that the doctor's use of the word 'if' (line 18) may have created some ambiguity in the mind of the patient. Given the degree of intercoder agreement where the information in the transcript is apparently unambiguous, this 'if' together with the lack of the word 'incurable', created disagreements between coders. Based upon these coding practices and this initial transcription, we can only clarify this ambiguity by

observing that the wife's comment (line 20) seems to reveal an understanding of the seriousness of the disease. Can a re-transcription, according to CA
standards, tell us how this doctor and patient heard each other's talk?

We might initially think that this is a fruitless path to follow. After all, CA
insists that it has no entry into people's 'minds' and, therefore, makes no
claims to show us what people are thinking. However, CA does claim to
reveal what people are *doing* and to reveal that doing in observable stretches
of talk-in-interaction. Here is our re-transcription of the relevant passages.
Extract 1* begins slightly before Extract 1 and ends earlier:

Ex.1*
[D talking about poor prognosis if 'the disease has spread outside the chest']

```
 1  D:  Now for the more limited disease like yourself
 2  P:  mm=
 3  D:  =those odds are improved
 4  P:  mm
 5  D:  such that there's somewhere about 15 per cent chance (0.5) of being around in two
        years' time
 6  P:  mm=
 7  D:  =with the disease under control.
 8  P:  mm
 9  D:  What that comes to long term is very hard to know.
10  P:  Mm
11      (0.6)
```

[D outlines treatment possibilities] . . .

The major difference between 1 and 1* is that 1* records considerably more
'mms' from P. Such 'mms' can be heard as 'response tokens' which indicate
to other speakers that one is monitoring their talk by identifying a potential
turn transition point but returning the turn to another. The positioning and
presence of such response-tokens (RTs) can be interpreted as having a significant bearing on how parties monitor each other's talk. Do these
response-tokens suggest ambiguity about how P is monitoring D's talk?

As Peräkylä and Silverman (1991) have suggested, in an information-
delivery format where a professional, like this doctor, delivers information to
a client, minimal response-tokens from the information-recipient will allow
the information-deliverer to continue through multiple turns. The absence of
response can be treated by the information-deliverer as indicative of lack of
uptake by the information-recipient.

Notice first how P provides two RTs (both 'mm') at lines 2 and 4. These
two RTs are positioned during a turn from D which implies a relatively
favourable prognosis ('limited disease', 'improved odds'). Hence, so far,
we have no reason to suggest that P is hearing D's talk as indicating that his
condition is incurable. However, on lines 6, 8 and 10, we also find RTs from
P even when it turns out that this means only a 15 per cent chance of survival in the context of 'long-term' uncertainty. None the less, D has not so

far suggested 'incurability' and, therefore, P's RTs are not indicative that he has receipted anything more than items like '15 per cent chance' and 'uncertainty'.

However, following D's outline of various treatment possibilities, the position clarifies:

Transcript 1* (continued)
24 D: But er despite all of those things, in the majority of people the disease does come *back*
25 (0.8)
26 D: even from the beginning.
27 P: Yes.
28 D: And (0.4) if it does come back, we can try other drugs which may control it for
29   a little while
30 P: mm um
31 D: but generally all that you can try and do is control the symptoms.
32 P: Yes mm.
33 D: Uhm, the first time gives us the best chance for a *longer* (0.5) survival,
34   hopefully long term
35 P: hhm
36 D: but the odds are generally against that.
37 P: Yes um (0.4)
38 D: But if we do nothing for these sorts of diseases, it kills you within a couple of months.
39 P: Yes.

After D has offered a statement which approximates to 'incurability' ('in the majority of people the disease does come back'), the continued re-transcription (line 25) reveals a 0.8 slot which P does not use to receipt this information. Now it appears that P can be heard actively to avoid receipting the category 'incurability'.

Presumably, D monitors P's (lack of) response in the same way because he continues by upgrading his statement ('even from the beginning'). Now, if P were still to say nothing, his silence would be distinctly noticeable possibly marking (to D) some psychological category like 'denial'. However, at this point, P *does* provide an RT ('yes', line 27). Its presence here, immediately after D has conveyed 'bad news', and in an upgraded form ('yes' rather than 'mm') strongly suggests that P has receipted the seriousness of his condition.

Both this 'yes' and P's 'yes mm' after further 'bad news' (line 32) are available in the original transcript (Ex.1). However, the re-transcription gives additional evidence of P's receipt of what D is saying about his incurability. On lines 37 and 39, P is heard to say 'yes' after D has said that 'the odds are generally against [long-term survival]' and that 'if we do nothing for these sorts of diseases, it kills you within a couple of months.' P, as well as his wife, receipts a bad prognosis.

However, we might also note that, despite the clearly 'bad' implications of what D is saying, D does not directly say 'you will die.' There is an element of ambiguity present here and we may speculate that D's failure to come out and directly say to P that his condition is terminal functions to manage different kinds of response to 'bad news'. By not being totally 'up front' about

P's prognosis, while none the less making an 'honest' statement, highly implicative of 'bad news', D preserves P's 'choice' about how to respond.

To recapitulate: our aim was to determine whether we could improve the reliability and validity of qualitative analysis.[3] First, we sought to identify and to explain differences between trained raters using rough transcripts. Next, drawing upon the transcription symbols and concepts of conversation analysis, we sought to reveal subtle features in the talk, showing how both doctor and patient produced and received hearable ambiguities in the patient's prognosis. This involved a shift of focus from coders' readings to how participants demonstrably monitor each other's talk. Once we pay attention to such detail, judgements can be made that are more convincingly valid. Inevitably, this leads to a resolution of the problem of inter-rater reliability.

What both analyses suggest is that continuing and detailed attention needs to be paid to the quality of the qualitative data, and the ways in which judgements are made about its content. This means that, despite the employment of two very different approaches, our analysis stayed on a consistent path.

First, unlike some qualitative researchers, we took seriously the criteria of reliability and validity. Secondly, both methods we used seek to build a consensus among a research team through identifying and resolving hard cases. Inter-rater agreement focuses on interpretations of given transcripts, while conversation analysis treats the establishment of an agreed transcript as a crucial first task for a research team.

Conclusion

Towards the beginning of this chapter, I showed how we often make problematic assumptions about the differences between qualitative and quantitative work. As Table 1.1 showed, it is often claimed that qualitative work is 'soft', 'subjective' and speculative', while quantitative research is 'hard', 'objective' and 'hypothesis-testing'. Yet the two qualitative studies reviewed undoubtedly seek to be 'objective' and 'hard', while, in some respects, the work on medical interviews involved hypothesis-testing. These two studies do more than show how qualitative research can be 'objective' by means of careful transcription. They also offer an alternative way forward which, by their common focus on what participants are doing, allows us to question the assumption that the open-ended interview is the 'gold standard' of all qualitative research.

The last thing I want to do, however, is to impose conversation analysis as the only acceptable method of doing qualitative research. As already noted, everything will depend upon the research problem being tackled. Moreover, thoughtful researchers will often want to use a combination of methods. Thus I am not trying to argue that there is only one analytically sound or rigorous method in qualitative research. As later chapters show, using

observation, interviews, and textual as well as conversation analysis, qualitative methods may be employed to pursue diverse theoretical ends. So the
multiple logics of qualitative research emerge from their relationships with
the general purposes of research projects. In this way, my discussion has
sought to counter the tendency to divide research methods into mutually
exclusive epistemological camps.

However, this benevolent neutrality towards the varying logics of qualitative research co-exists with an appeal to two very strong principles. First,
researchers always need to address the analytical issues that may lie concealed behind apparently straightforward issues of method. Secondly,
qualitative research's concern for an 'in-depth' focus on people's activities (or
representations of those activities) is no warrant for sloppy thinking or anec-
dotal use of 'telling' examples. We owe it to ourselves and our audiences to
generate reliable data and valid observations.

If there is a 'gold standard' for qualitative research, it should only be the
standard for any good research, qualitative or quantitative, social or natural
science. Namely, have the researchers demonstrated successfully why we
should believe them? And does the research problem tackled have theoretical and/or practical significance?

Notes

1 Ironically, the most recent attempt to revive 'positivism' as a term of abuse is to be found
in the attacks by Garfinkel and his followers on what they see as the 'positivist' elements present in conversation analysis (e.g. Lynch and Bogen 1994).

2 As Robert Dingwall (personal communication) has reminded me, it is worth noting that
Cicourel (1964) also provides a chapter devoted to a critique of qualitative research. For
instance, the claims that open-ended interviews offered direct access to 'experience' were
opposed by Cicourel who showed that commonsense reasoning entered into the understandings
of both interviewees and researchers.

3 For a more radical discussion of how the issue of the coding of observations can render
analysis problematic, see Garfinkel (1967).

2

Producing 'Plausible Stories':
Interviewing Student Nurses

Kath M. Melia

At the end of the 1970s, when there was little experience of qualitative research in nursing, I undertook a study of the occupational socialization of student nurses (Melia 1981). The project was in the spirit of Becker et al.'s (1961) study of medical students, drawing on the intellectual legacy of what we have now learned to call the Second Chicago School. Although my research used the ideas that we then called 'symbolic interactionism' and the methodological writings of Glaser and Strauss (1967) on 'grounded theory', it differed from the American work in that there was no participant observation and my data were collected solely by informal interviews. In effect, it was an analysis of student nurses' accounts of their work and training.

At the time, this strategy seemed to be a plausible way of arriving at a picture of the student nurses' world. I saw it as a version of Gold's (1958) observer-as-participant field role: although I had no observational material, I could draw on my own experience and familiarity with the setting to treat the data I gathered as if they were not very different from interview data obtained in the course of participant observation. I analysed the interview transcripts in much the same way as if they had been field notes. As Platt (1983) shows, this is not so far from some of the early practice of qualitative research in inter-war Chicago as it might sound: many of these classic studies owed more to interviews and case reports than tradition allows.

In writing this chapter, I have come to reflect again on the question of the adequacy of interview data for the task of explaining the student nurses' world. I answered the question in the late 1970s, rightly or wrongly, by an appeal to the definition of grounded theory offered by Glaser and Strauss (1967: 3) – 'a strategy for handling data in research, providing modes of conceptualization for describing and explaining' – and to the fact that constant comparison allows for drawing on literature and theorizing in the area under study as well as the more obvious comparison of data with data, and data with emerging conceptual categories. In the late 1990s, we might be more sceptical about the adequacy of the informal interview in this kind of research enterprise. There is a climate of methodological angst about the nature of data and the possibilities for analysis. Qualitative analysis texts have become increasingly concerned with the epistemological bases of the methods we adopt, and the range of methods available has expanded well beyond participant observation and the interview to include conversation analysis, narrative and discourse analysis and phenomenology. These developments demand a re-evaluation of the informal interview as a means of gathering data. However, I still think that the analytical procedures associated with grounded theory – constant comparative method and theoretical sensitivity – can take us beyond the interview data themselves to a more conceptual level.

An important problem for such a justification, though, is that the originators of grounded theory, Glaser and Strauss, have recently disagreed between themselves about the nature of the research strategy they promoted in the 1960s. In this chapter, then, I shall review their argument and try to establish where followers of grounded theory might now have been left by it. In conclusion, I propose a pragmatic approach to qualitative methods, which takes account of philosophical and epistemological debates but does not become so preoccupied with them that any form of research can be vetoed on some ground or other.

Method and methodology

Although it has become fashionable to use the word 'methodology' when it is actually 'method' that is being discussed, the distinction between the two – the 'study of method' and the 'research procedures actually employed' – is a useful one, if only to save the researcher from climbing philosophical heights from which to fall when it comes to the discussion and analysis of data. Much of the current agonizing reflects the challenge of postmodernism and its questions about how we can know anything about the world and what – in that knowing – constitutes data and explanation. At its simplest, postmodernism holds that there are no grand theories, overall explanations or generalized ways of explaining experience and that social life can be better understood as a series of discourses where none is privileged. This position has become entangled with the epistemological justifications that can be put forward for qualitative analysis. If discussions in nursing and health care are anything of a guide to the methods debates in qualitative research, there is cause for some concern. Postmodernism seems to have become something of an excuse for taking what might otherwise be thought of as a rather loose approach to methods.

Atkinson (1995b: 120) has commented on the proliferation of methods texts in qualitative research and the apparent need for some authors to produce taxonomies and neat categories of methods. In his words:

> one may applaud the general intention of clarifying and classifying the array of complementary and contrasting approaches – however it is essentially a text book treatment. As such it can all too easily oversimplify and, ultimately, distort the true picture. This is, moreover, a recurrent problem with many, if not most, listings of qualitative research types. All too often they pull together types and categories that are in different orders of generality.

He goes on to observe that all authors argue for a classification, each produces his or her own list and they are all different. Atkinson's (1995b: 121)
main complaint, which I would echo, is that the lists:

> draw together issues and approaches of very different levels of generality. Some
> represent theoretical schools or traditions that have some affinities with qualita-
> tive research (symbolic interactionism, ethnomethodology, phenomenology); some
> are labels for general approaches to research (ethnography) or strategies of
> research design and analysis (grounded theory); yet others are of extreme gener-
> ality and have no claim to be research methods at all (constructionism,
> deconstructionism, feminism, critical theory).

Atkinson (1995b: 123) concludes that 'the goals of research will not be
served by a slavish adherence to the historical accidents and arbitrary boundaries that separate methodological traditions and particular research
methods.' We should not, he says, 'turn the pedagogical half truths of textbook knowledge into prescriptions for research practice'.

Attempts to bring methodological perspectives into some order need not
have the unfortunate consequences that Atkinson outlines. Denzin (1989b:
7), for instance, makes a heroic attempt to pull a good deal together under
the term *interpretive interactionism*. With this title he is, in his own words,
trying:

> to make the world of problematic lived experience of ordinary people directly
> available to the reader. The interactionist interprets these worlds. The research
> methods of this approach include open-ended, creative interviewing; document
> analysis; semiotics; life-history; life-story; personal experience and self-story con-
> struction; participant observation; and thick description.

According to Denzin, the term 'interpretive interactionism' signifies an
attempt to join traditional symbolic interactionist thought with participant
observation and ethnography; semiotics and fieldwork; postmodern ethnographic research; naturalistic studies; creative interviewing; the case-study
method; hermeneutic phenomenology; cultural studies and feminist critiques
of positivism. This seems to be an impossible task, but it puts interactionist
thought centre stage while allowing space for current methods debates. If
symbolic interactionism has been overrun by postmodernists, Denzin's com-
pass and his caution may offer us a way through this fad. Writing with
Lincoln at the end of their edited collection on qualitative research, he notes
that 'what is passé today may be in vogue a decade from now. Just as the
postmodern, for example reacts to the modern, some day there may well be
a neomodern phase that extols Malinowski and the Chicago school and
finds the current post-structural, postmodern moment abhorrent' (Denzin
and Lincoln 1994: 575).

Interestingly, in the introduction to *Interpretive Interactionism*, Denzin
states that an aim of the book is to continue C. Wright Mills's project of the
'sociological imagination', to allow the examination of private troubles of
individuals to be connected to public issues and public responses. However,
we might also remember another passage from Mills (1959: 215) where he
discusses intellectual craft:

To the individual social scientist who feels himself a part of the classic tradition, social science is the practice of a craft. A man at work on problems of substance, he is among those who are quickly made impatient and weary by elaborate discussions of method-and-theory-in-general; so much of which interrupts his proper studies.

Mills continues by saying it is much better 'to have one account by a working student about how he is going about his work than a dozen "codifications of procedure" by specialists who as often as not have never done much work of consequence'.

It is clearly oversimplifying the case to argue that philosophy and method should be kept apart. It is, however, helpful if what researchers 'do' – method, and the methodological justification for that doing, epistemology – are treated as rather separate entities, if only to avoid the epistemological justification being mistaken for the method itself. Most philosophies can be taken to an ultimate conclusion where research becomes impossible. If the world is only discourse and narrative without structure or context, how can we make sense of, for instance, interview data?

Interviews as text: interviews as data

The basic challenge that all methodological discussion must face is the question: 'how does all this help in the analysis of data and the production of explanation?' What is the connection between the resultant explanation of the data and the epistemological starting point described by the analyst? How close is the methodological rhetoric to the method of doing of the research? If we had not been told in a methodological preamble, would we know that what follows is postmodern, discourse analysis, grounded theory or whatever? The link between what a researcher does and the philosophical position set out to justify the method is often problematic.

In the light of current debates, returning to the work on the student nurses' world has been a curious experience. The growing interest in the analysis of text, and the reluctance to allow interview data to be analysed beyond the textual level, challenges those of us who relied on interviews to produce qualitative data that would shed some light on a substantive topic. The data for the study comprised 40 tape-recorded interviews with student nurses. The interviews were fully transcribed and the transcripts treated as raw data. I used the approach described by Glaser and Strauss (1967) in *The Discovery of Grounded Theory*. Arguably, Glaser and Strauss were the most influential writers in the qualitative methods field in the 1970s and, through the work of Strauss and Corbin (1987), into the 1980s. As qualitative methods have spread, this pre-eminence has, perhaps, faded a little with the rise of ethnomethodology, phenomenology and discourse analysis. However, despite the incongruity, grounded theory is often still yoked to these other positions.

In the late 1970s, when I was working on the student nurse study, grounded theory was assumed to rest on the general tenets of Blumer's version of symbolic interactionism derived from the work of G.H. Mead. Coupled with some awareness of Berger and Luckmann's (1966) version of Schutz and the early work of Garfinkel (1967), these formed the epistemological underpinnings of the project. I started with the premise that life – that of the student nurse in this case – can be understood by asking questions about it so that the person experiencing that life can convey his or her understanding of it by his or her own descriptions and insights. The researcher can then, taking an interactionist approach, seek to communicate the view of the informant and to place it within a more general, second-order framework. This involves allowing the inclusion of interpretation which goes beyond the raw data, drawing upon cognate work and thinking to see the specific case as an instance of a more general social process or institution. This generalization provides an additional dimension to the informant's specific account, which, in turn, also exemplifies or modifies the general account.

The analysis of nursing as a profession was one example. Drawing on previous studies of work, occupations and organizations, the students' accounts were crafted into a discussion of nursing as an occupation and the problems posed for many of its members by the professionalizing aspirations of an influential segment. This took issue with the self-serving accounts that had been written by that segment, while enlarging our general understanding of the differentiation that may occur within professions.

Analysing interviews presents a critical methodological challenge. Are the data to be regarded as straight accounts of the interviewees' experiences or stories about that experience told as an exercise in self-presentation by the interviewee? Here lurks the temptation to abandon the enterprise on the grounds that it is impossible to determine the status of the data. However, if we allow all possible objections to cause us to doubt the status and utility of the data, the chances are that we would not undertake research at all. Notwithstanding the philosophical debates from Wittgenstein to the postmoderns, if we are going to tell a story, we have to be less epistemologically squeamish and get on with it.

Grounding analysis

A greater worry for me is the way in which the originators of grounded theory have fallen out about what it really is. In Glaser's (1992) book, *Emergence vs Forcing: Basics of Grounded Theory Analysis*, he reproduces a letter to Strauss: 'I request that you pull the book [*Basics of Qualitative Research*]. It distorts and misconceives grounded theory, while engaging in a gross neglect of 90% of its important ideas.' He continues, in equally strong terms, with: 'You wrote a whole different method so why call it "grounded theory"? It indicates that you never have grasped what we did, nor studied it to try to carefully extend it' (Glaser 1992: 2).[1] If there is room for dispute between the founders, it is not surprising that qualitative methods debates become so complicated. Glaser and Strauss now clearly have different views about the essential nature of the analytical strategy which they co-originated: indeed, if we were to accept Glaser's version, they may have had different understandings from the outset![2]

Working in the UK means that one is reliant upon the books and papers produced by the originators of grounded theory. Much of the work claiming to adopt this approach, whatever it is, emanates from California (cf. Chenitz and Swanson 1986) and many of the researchers involved are, or have been, students of Strauss. Those using grounded theory tend to cite Glaser and Strauss (1967), possibly Glaser (1978) and then skip to Strauss and Corbin (1990). Glaser's major contribution to the method in *Theoretical Sensitivity* (1978) is well known in the UK. However, my unsystematic enquiries suggest that few are aware of Glaser's latest work and that there is an increasing tendency to rely on Strauss and Corbin (1990) as the main source. Grounded theory seems to be becoming synonymous with the use of the Strauss and Corbin text. At worst, this can amount to little more than a nod in the general direction of grounded theory and then a progression to a generalized qualitative analysis.

The original version of grounded theory stressed the idea that theory emerged from, and was grounded in, data. Careful analysis of data items using the constant comparative method would lead to the emergence of conceptual categories that would describe and explain the phenomenon under study. Several explanatory or conceptual categories would be integrated around a core category and so the theory would emerge. The idea was to follow up conceptually fruitful avenues and allow emergent concepts to dictate the direction and nature of the data collection. Glaser and Strauss described this as a process of 'theoretical sensitivity', whereby data collection and analysis went on side by side until a core category emerged and was 'saturated'.

Glaser, however, is now questioning the extent to which concepts emerge or data are forced into them. He ultimately comes to the view that: 'Anselm's methodology is one of full conceptual description and mine is grounded theory. They are very different, the first focusing on forcing and the second on emergence. The first keeping all the problems of forcing data, the second giving them up in favour of emergence, discovery, and inductive theory generation' (Glaser 1992: 122). In Glaser's view, Strauss is not advancing theory, but producing something he calls *full conceptual description*. This seems to be more formulaic in style than the original version of grounded theory, with a greater use of certain prior concepts which are expected to recur in different settings.

Strauss's (1987) and Strauss and Corbin's (1990) more recent writings have certainly had a procedural emphasis which Glaser (1992: 5) sees as betraying their original vision:

> what is written in Strauss' book is out of the blue, a present piece with no historical reference on the idea level, and an almost new method borrowing an older name – Grounded Theory – and funny thing, it produces simply what qualitative researchers had been doing for sixty years or more: forced, full conceptual description.

In full conceptual description, Glaser asserts, there is a preconceived and verificational approach to qualitative data analysis. In his own expressive terms he says:

> If you torture the data enough it will give up! This is the underlying approach in the forcing preconceptions of full conceptual description. The data is not allowed to speak for itself, as in grounded theory, and to be heard from infrequently it has to scream. Forcing by preconception constantly derails it from relevance. (Glaser 1992: 123)

It is certainly notable that one of the main ideas in both *The Discovery of Grounded Theory* (1967) and *Theoretical Sensitivity* (1978), namely that of 'saturation' – the compilation of data until a conceptual category becomes credible – does not figure in Strauss and Corbin (1990). This was an important element of my use of interview data: the student nurses repeated some very clear story lines again and again. The category which turned out to be the core – 'fitting in' – was well saturated. Almost every student had a tale to tell where the moral was that the student goal was to become a registered nurse and that they would do just about whatever it took in college and on the ward to achieve that aim.

While *Basics of Qualitative Research* (Strauss and Corbin 1990) has been of some help in teaching and laying out some of the ideas discussed in great detail in Strauss's 1987 book, I have a nagging doubt that the procedures are getting in the way: the technical tail is beginning to wag the theoretical dog. On the matter of procedures, it also has to be said that, on first reading, *Theoretical Sensitivity* (Glaser 1978), and its 18 coding families, took some getting used to and produced some of the same feelings of overload experienced on reading Glaser's latest work. The saving grace then, and now with *Emergence vs Forcing*, is the simplicity of the central idea of the constant comparative method. Glaser (1992: 43) argues that Strauss's methods are now unnecessarily laborious and tedious:

> Strauss's method of labelling and then grouping is totally unnecessary, laborious and is a waste of time. Using constant comparison method gets the analyst to the desired conceptual power, quickly, with ease and joy. Categories emerge upon comparison and properties emerge upon more comparison. And that is all there is to it.

Who could resist that?

It has been argued that grounded theory is not that different from long-accepted good practice in sociology. Bechhofer (1974: 77–78), while applauding Glaser and Strauss's call for the generation of theory, wrote in a discussion of theoretical sampling that: 'the search for contrasting empirical situations is suggested by good experimental practices, and the search for conceptually related, but empirically different situations is very much good scientific practice.' If this is the case, and I have some sympathy with Bechhofer's position, it may not matter so much if there are the two versions of grounded theory in circulation. Indeed, if what Glaser and Strauss were doing was what many good sociologists had done for years, perhaps, as

Bechhofer has suggested in a recent personal communication, it is not too surprising that subsequent attempts to make grounded theory appear to be more and more special have led to a split between the two. In the 1967 *Discovery* book, both authors stressed the point that researchers should feel free to develop the method. That this freedom has in the fullness of time included themselves is a matter of record.

This is echoed by Strauss and Corbin (1994: 283) in their recent contribution to a major qualitative methods tome (Denzin and Lincoln 1994), which is, in effect, their reply to Glaser:

> Recently an astute sociologist asked us to say something about the outer limits of research that we would or could continue to call 'grounded theory'. The features of this methodology that we consider so central that their abandonment would signify a great departure are the grounding of theory upon data through data-theory interplay, the making of constant comparisons, the asking of theoretical oriented questions, theoretical coding, and the development of theory. Yet, no inventor has permanent possession of the invention – certainly not even of its name – and furthermore we would not wish to do so. No doubt we will always prefer the later versions of grounded theory that are closest to or elaborate on our own, but a child once launched is very much subject to a combination of its origins and the evolving contingencies of life. Can it be otherwise with a methodology?

Whether or not the current debate would have influenced the way in which I analysed my interviews is a moot point. The account was grounded in the data supplied by the students, yet moved to an analytical level beyond the raw data themselves. The point at issue seems to be more whether the data jumped or were pushed – emergence *v.* forcing – rather than whether informal interviews are up to the job.

I am not sure how Glaser would describe my work (Melia 1987). The 1967 book contains some near mystical passages, but I suspect that that was its charm and ultimately the reason for its success. Strauss's continued interest in writing on qualitative methods can simply be seen as part of the trend noted by Atkinson. Again, we have to ask whether it is the methods text itself that is a problem for qualitative research: if researchers were less hung up on debating methods might we do rather better in getting the story out? Methods texts and epistemological discussions are interesting, but do they lead to any difference in the product? The debate between the fathers of grounded theory gives some substance to the arguments about justification of methods. If the results of Strauss's work provide useful insights and explanations while his methods discussions have become more and more laboured – certainly in Glaser's view and at times in mine – does it matter? Are we, perhaps, looking at two different issues: one being the way in which methods are written up in the increasingly self-conscious 'methods text' genre; the other being the research itself. It is tempting to ask whether, if Glaser had undertaken the substantive work that Strauss published, the results would actually have been very different.

Where does this leave us with the interview?

The starting point for me in this chapter was the student nurse interviews (Melia 1987), and the question remains that of the legitimacy of using them to move to a discussion of the organization of nursing practice and the nursing profession more generally. The original justification lay in grounded theory and an accepted practice in the analysis of qualitative data. More recent phenomenological discussions, with their talk of 'lived worlds' and meanings lying in wait to be uncovered, prompt me to wonder if telling my plausible story was rather naïve or maybe not such a bad idea after all.

Informal interview data are yielded by a series of questions and general lines of enquiry embedded in a seemingly natural conversation with the interviewee. The data can be seen, then, as an account of the interviewee's opinions and views, arrived at as a result of the interaction with the researcher. The effect of this interaction cannot be denied, whether on the pragmatic ground that the interviewee's talk is produced by the interviewer's questions or on the theoretical ground that symbolic interactionism rests on the assumption of the intersubjective construction of social reality. We can view the interview as a presentation of self by the interviewee with the data as a representation that has no further credibility. Or we can see the interview as a means of gaining insight into a world beyond the story that the interviewee tells, a means of getting a handle on a more complex set of ideas than the ones that the interviewee is ostensibly talking about. This is not to say that the interviewer moves into the territory of the paranormal and can somehow see through the data to things otherwise concealed. However, it does mean that a researcher with an interest in, and open mind about, a particular topic can, with practised care, take an analysis beyond its face value. In the case of the student nurses, this moved on from their accounts to become a discussion of nursing as a segmented occupational group with different approaches to the question of profession: a move from interviews about the student nurses' worldview of nursing to a discussion of nursing as a profession. If we were to take a seriously postmodern view, I suppose that we would never know the answer to these bigger questions.

Is the interview an account, a story about a world described or does it provide an index of a world beyond the story? Moreover, does the nature of the analytical route taken through the data – be it discourse analysis, narrative, constant comparative method or full conceptual description – produce an answer to this question of the status of the interview data? Will the answers be different? And, if so, why so and how so? It may be counter-productive to get further and further into a philosophically interesting mire which keeps us from the plausible story. If the world in which we exist manages to get along with its business by means of, for the most part, a commonsense, if cautious, approach to daily experiences, this might be the best, possibly the only, strategy open to the social scientist hoping to understand that world. Ultimately, it becomes perverse to say that life cannot be understood by the same means that it is lived. Data are what we see, hear or read: no more but certainly no less. Even a phenomenologist cannot transcend these material conditions. The challenge is to convert these sense data into an explanation of the situation, an explanation which Becker (1958) points out, in his classic piece on 'inference and proof', has to convince others. Or, as Strong (1979: 250) put it, 'the best we can hope for in this world, even if we study practical reasoning, is a plausible story.'

There is a tendency to treat methods as belief systems and to light upon one, see all its attractions and adopt its rhetoric. As with any new faith, the proselytizing stage is probably the most unhelpful as it usually takes the form of rubbishing other belief systems. In the 1970s, a generalized attack on positivism was employed to legitimize qualitative methods, which, at least in a philosophical sense, still rest themselves on a positivist foundation. As the methods debates have become more philosophical, or at least epistemological, they have become less useful for the doing of research. Whatever high-flown rhetoric is adopted about uncovered meanings and understandings of discourse and narratives, what is required for a discussion of empirical work is some means of translating data from the field – interviews, observations, documents – into an explanation of the topic in hand which can be conveyed to others and understood by others. All the social processes and epistemological considerations that went into problematizing the data gathering and interpretation exist in the understanding of the research output.

This chapter has raised questions about the limits of the interview in light of the recent methods debates, in particular the Glaser and Strauss dispute. The epistemological and philosophical distinctions associated with different approaches to data collection and analysis may have more relevance for methods texts than they do for research practices. If we can collect data with which to tell a plausible story, perhaps we should settle for that. Phenomenology and postmodernism have challenged interactionism, but if the upshot is methodological paralysis it may be better to take a more anarchic, or at least pragmatic, approach to methods and do what is plausible. Mouzelis (1995: 54) has deplored what he terms a 'strategy of dedifferentiation' where there is a 'free and indiscriminate mixture of concepts and ideas derived from philosophy, literature, sociology, psychoanalysis and elsewhere'. He calls for a means of relating one discipline to another, allowing insights from one discipline to be usefully incorporated into another. 'It is precisely this free for all strategy of dedifferentiation, and the abolition of distinctions and boundaries, that has led to the present incredible situation where anything goes, and where complex macro phenomena are reductively explained in terms of signs, texts, the unconscious or what have you' (Mouzelis 1995: 54). He goes on to say:

> It is not surprising that postmodern theorising is marked by a relativism that tries to persuade us that any theoretical construction, however bizarre or crude, is just as true or false as any other. It is also not surprising that postmodernist theory tends to adopt a style where lack of depth and of substantive analysis is concealed by a quasi poetical language glorying in the obscure, the ambivalent, in plays on words and similar gimmicks. (1995: 54–55)

With all that in mind, going off to interview people and coming back to tell Strong's 'plausible story' probably is, as he said, 'the best we can hope for'.

Notes

1 The harsh words are tempered by the signature, 'your pal Barney': indeed, a rather angry book is peppered throughout with friendly comments on the value of Anselm Strauss's work as a qualitative sociologist.

2 Stern (1994: 212) says that: 'students of Glaser and Strauss in the 1960s and 1970s knew that the two had quite different modus operandi, but Glaser only found out when Strauss and Corbin's *Basics of Qualitative Research* came out in 1990.'

3

Techniques of Validation in Qualitative Research: a Critical Commentary

Michael Bloor

In 1903 Blondlot, the French physicist and member of the Academy of Sciences, reported the sensational discovery of a phenomenon that he called N-rays, with properties analogous to, but distinct from, X-rays. His report of his experiments led other scientists to seek to generate the N-rays in their laboratories, but their attempts were wholly unsuccessful. The failure to reproduce Blondlot's findings eventually led one distinguished physicist, R.W. Wood, to visit Blondlot at his laboratory and to observe him at work. Eventually, it was agreed that the N-rays did not exist, they were mere epiphenomena derived from faulty observation, faulty experimental technique, and inadequate laboratory measurement instruments and equipment.

This story (told at greater length in D. Bloor's *Knowledge and Social Imagery*, 1976) is on a theme commonly found within the history and philosophy of science. Findings in the natural sciences are validated or verified by their *replication* by a second independent investigator. Research reports to the scientific community must carry enough information on the successful experiment to allow the identical circumstances to be repeated independently by other members of the scientific community, so that the same results can be observed. Unless findings in the natural sciences can be replicated, they have no validity.

In sociology, by contrast, validation cannot occur through subsequent replication, since identical social circumstances cannot be re-created outside the laboratory. Social life contains elements which are generalizable across settings (thus providing for the possibility of the social sciences) and other elements that are particular to given settings (thus forever limiting the predictive power of the social sciences). To the journalist, for example, there may be arresting parallels between the increase in heroin consumption in some of the ex-coalfield communities of South Wales in the mid-1990s and the earlier explosion in heroin use in some UK cities like Glasgow in the early 1980s: the disappearance of employment opportunities for young males, the ready availability of cheap heroin, and so on. But careful observation suggests a number of differences as well as parallels between the 1990s and 1980s epidemics (the use of heroin in the 1990s within a poly-drug culture, with opiates available alongside a wide range of other drugs, such as ecstasy and amphetamines; the recent growth of drug treatment services; and so on), all of which makes the 1990s epidemic an inadequate testing ground for analyses of the 1980s epidemic. History, contrary to popular opinion, never repeats itself.

Instead of the replication of findings across settings, sociologists (and anthropologists) have developed two main techniques which may be considered as alternative methods of validation. The first of these is 'triangulation' (Denzin 1989a) whereby findings may be judged valid when different and contrasting methods of data collection yield identical findings on the same research subjects: a case of replication within the same setting, rather than replication across settings. The second technique, or rather array of related techniques, judges findings to be valid by demonstrating a correspondence between the analyst's findings and the understandings of members of the collectivity being analysed. The objective of this chapter will be to comment critically on these sociological validation techniques. Referring to three different empirical studies that I conducted, I will argue that all these techniques yield data that are *relevant* to issues of validity in that they provide an occasion and a spur for the re-examination of findings. Nevertheless, it will be seen that they are merely relevant to, rather than constitutive of, validation: all data are shaped by the circumstances of their production, and different data produced by different research procedures cannot be treated as equivalent for the purpose of corroboration.

Triangulation: replicating chalk with cheese?

The term 'triangulation', like Glaser and Strauss's (1967) term 'grounded theory', has become somewhat overloaded with meanings and abused by uncritical usage. Denzin, who took the term from Webb (1966), referred to four basic types of triangulation with a range of sub-types, but most commentators have concentrated their attention on the sub-type Denzin calls 'between-method triangulation . . . the combination of two or more different research strategies in the study of the same empirical units' (Denzin 1989a: 302). Validity is claimed because replication of the findings by different methods minimizes the possibility that the findings may be the result of particular measurement biases.

There is much to commend in Denzin's approach, and a commitment to methodological pluralism is clearly one mark of the careful investigator. Denzin, the symbolic interactionist, although quoting Webb on triangulation as a test of validity, himself usually (but not universally) steers clear of terms like 'validation' or 'replication'. But statements such as 'Archival analysis . . . may additionally be used to validate respondents' reports during the interviewing period' (Denzin 1989a: 303) have provided some warrant for subsequent sociologists to interpret triangulation as a test of validity. There is sufficient ambiguity in Denzin's analysis to allow the popular view that has grown up which treats triangulation as a validation exercise.

The difficulties in treating triangulation as a validation exercise are several. One such difficulty is a matter of logic and needs no empirical illustration. If it is accepted that there are horses for courses and that, for any given topic, there will be one best method of investigation, then triangulation may be said to involve juxtaposing findings gathered by the best available method with findings generated by an inferior method. There seems no difficulty in this, at first sight, when both sets of findings agree. But a problem arises when the two sets of findings are at odds: should the findings from the best available method be set aside on the basis of evidence generated by an inferior method? Logically, there seems little justification for this, but the exercise cannot be a test of validity only when the findings are corroborated and not when the findings are confounded.

The above seems a serious objection, but in practice it will rarely be encountered because findings collected by different methods will rarely be of such a character that they can be readily compared so as to pronounce them to be matched or mis-matched. All research findings are shaped by the circumstances of their production, so findings collected by different methods will differ in their form and specificity to a degree that will make their direct comparison problematic.

An illustration will make the point with more clarity. In the course of an investigation of death certification practices in a Scottish city (Bloor 1991, 1994), I conducted in-depth interviews with a sample of local clinicians whose responsibilities embraced frequent certifications of deaths (general practitioners with responsibilities for old people's homes, junior hospital doctors working on geriatric or psychogeriatric wards, forensic pathologists, police surgeons, and the like). At the conclusion of the interviews, I asked the respondents if they would, at their leisure, read a series of detailed case summaries that I had prepared and fill out dummy death certificates based on those dummy cases. One of the major objectives of the research was to investigate whether there were systematic differences between individuals in their death certification practices, such that these differences might contribute to local differences in specific-cause mortality rates.

In principle, there was an opportunity here to corroborate respondents' descriptions of their certification practices at interview with their responses to the dummy cases. In practice, there was a strong tendency for the clinicians to describe their certification behaviour during the interviews in terms which were much more general than the specific combinations of symptoms and circumstances found in the case summaries. These differences in the specificity of the two sets of data are such that the analyst is seeking to compare chalk with cheese. For example, here is an extract from the transcript of an interview with a general practitioner who was frequently responsible for certifying deaths occurring in his local old people's home:

MB: Uh-huh. Yes. Would some of these cases be dementing patients?
GP: Some. Oh yes, I mean they weren't all 100 per cent alert, rational people [...] But it may not necessarily have appeared on the certificate [...]

MB: If it did appear on your certificate, would it be in Section I or Section II?

GP: I think probably it would've been Section II [...]. I think probably it would be a question of keeping the certification as simple as possible and the things which really had little relevance to the terminal condition, let's put it that way, perhaps not mentioned on the certificate.

MB: Yes. So perhaps you wouldn't use Section II very much?

GP: Not very often.

Two of the six dummy cases given to the respondent for certification embraced descriptions of symptoms consistent with dementia or Alzheimer's disease. In one case, the GP made no mention of the symptoms on the dummy certificate; in the other case, the GP entered 'Alzheimer's syndrome' in Section II of the certificate. (Section II is for the recording of 'other significant conditions contributing to death but not relating to the disease or condition causing it'.) Here is the dummy case in question (derived from an earlier study of death certification by Gau and Diehl 1982) and the certificate:

Case 5

An 86-year-old man has required an indwelling Foley catheter for three years because of urinary incontinence. He is frequently confused during the day and has no recollection of recent events. He requires assistance in dressing and feeding. Two days ago he became unresponsive and was admitted to your ward. He appeared to be hyper-ventilating; although his urine was cloudy, he had no fever and examination of the chest and heart were normal. You prescribed amoxycillin for a presumed urinary tract infection, but despite this the patient became hypotensive and died early this morning.

Cause of death

Section I: renal failure due to urinary tract infection

Section II: Alzheimer syndrome

It can be seen that the information gleaned in the interview and the results of the dummy certification exercise are superficially consistent. But this consistency may well be an artefact of, on the one hand, the general terminology ('probably', 'not very often') used by the respondent in the interview, and, on the other hand, the very limited representation of the possible range of dementing symptoms and the possible combinations with other symptoms found in the much more specific dummy case. Relatedly, any apparent discrepancy between practice reported at interview and practice found on the dummy certificates could be explained by these differences of specificity: a dummy certificate that seemed to conflict with a reported general rule could be explained by the fact that general rules are always defeasible, always subject to qualification in the light of specific circumstances.

Of course, the interviewer may be alive to this tendency of interviewees to over-generalize and the interviewer may seek consciously to compensate by exploring the contingent and qualified applications of general rules of conduct. But such explorations can only be partial, because no interviewee would tolerate interviews long enough to explore all relevant and specific facets of his or her routine practices. In the interview reported above, it will be readily appreciated that the discussion of certification practice in respect of symptoms of dementia was already quite extensive in an interview that was meant to range over the whole of the respondent's certification practice. By the same token, the study of detailed dummy case summaries and the completion of dummy certificates is a time-consuming activity and few interviewees will tolerate the completion of more than a dozen or so. In fact, respondents were asked to complete only six in this study. Since it would take possibly a dozen different case summaries to explore adequately a clinician's certification practice in relation to even a single constellation of symptoms (be it dementia or cancer), it can be seen that systematic corroboration of findings by these two different methods is not possible, due to sheer exigencies of time. As Denzin and others have stated, methodological pluralism allows new light to be shed on topics and allows different facets of problems to be explored, so the mix of different methods has an interactive impact. However, this mix of methods does not allow validity tests on findings.

Member validation: *C'est magnifique, mais ce n'est pas l'accord*

'Member validation' is a term used to denote an array of techniques that purport to validate findings by demonstrating a correspondence between the researcher's analysis and collectivity members' descriptions of their social worlds. Critical discussions of these techniques can be found in Emerson (1981). Without being exhaustive, we can note that such techniques may include the following: first, the validation of the researcher's taxonomies by the attempted prediction of members' descriptions in the field (see, for example, Frake 1961); secondly, the validation of the researcher's analysis by the demonstrated ability of the researcher to 'pass' as a member (see, for example, Goodenough's 1964 brief but elegant overview); and, thirdly, the validation of the researcher's analysis by asking collectivity members to judge the adequacy of the researcher's analysis, taking results back to the field and asking 'if the members recognize, understand and accept one's description' (Douglas 1976: 131). It is with exercises of the latter type that I shall be concerned here.

A philosophical justification for member validation exercises can be found in the work of the phenomenologist Alfred Schutz, who pointed out the several continuities between the 'commonsense thinking' of community members and the 'scientific thinking' of the social scientist. All scientific thinking has its roots in commonsense thinking (if it did not, then it would be dismissed out of hand as non-sense), and collectivity members may be required periodically to provide accounts of their behaviour that may be similar in purpose to scientific accounts. Schutz's 'postulate of adequacy' famously required that scientific propositions be understandable to members themselves (Schutz 1967). Giddens (1976) has castigated Schutz's postulate as an unreasonable requirement for social scientific thinking, without denying the linkages between such thinking and common sense. Member validation may be acknowledged to be an unreasonable *requirement*, while simultaneously being seen as effective *corroboration* of a scientific proposition.

But corroboration too is problematic. The same considerations that cast doubt on the veracity of initial findings will also apply to an exercise to validate those findings: just as the initial findings are shaped by the circumstances of their production, problematized by the frailties of methodologies, so also the results of the validation exercise will be shaped by the data-gathering process itself, by the methods used to elicit members' reactions to the initial findings. Member validation is not immaculately produced. This point can be empirically demonstrated by reference to two different exercises where I undertook to feed research results back to research subjects and where I monitored their reactions.

One exercise was undertaken in the context of an observational study of variations in medical decision-making, where I attempted to differentiate the decision rules and search procedures used by different ENT (Ear, Nose and Throat) surgeons when assessing children in out-patient clinics for possible adeno-tonsillectomy (see M. Bloor 1976). In this exercise I wrote a detailed report for each surgeon of what I believed his or her assessment practices to be and then requested the opportunity to go through each surgeon's reactions to the report in a taped interview.

The second exercise was undertaken in the context of a series of linked studies of therapeutic communities (Bloor et al. 1988). In the second exercise, although some interviews were conducted, many collectivity members fed back their reactions to my draft research reports in 'focus groups' (Morgan 1988), audio-recorded group discussions with the focused task of responding to my pre-circulated report. A focus group format was preferred both on economy grounds and on the grounds of circumventing 'interviewer effects', the witting or unwitting shaping of interviewee responses by the interviewer. The topics of the draft reports varied from therapeutic community to therapeutic community. In one community study, the report centred on the relationship of the informal patient culture to the formal group treatment programme. This topic was explored by two focus groups, one group of patients (all of them ex-patients by the time the analysis was completed and the draft report was written) and one group of staff members; one ex-patient was interviewed separately (see below). In another community study, the report centred on contrasts in staff practices between two halfway-house communities for disturbed adolescents. This topic was explored by a focus group for the staff members of one house and individual interviews and correspondence with the staff of the second house (who had dispersed soon after the completion of fieldwork). In a fourth community, providing 'foster family' care for adolescents who were disturbed and/or had learning difficulties, individual interviews were conducted with both continuing and ex-staff members.

Turning to the results of the member validation exercises, members' responses, on occasion, can be extremely gratifying. Thus, from one of the surgeons:

> Surgeon A: It reads very well. I thought it was fine.
>
> MB: So you felt it quite accurately reflected your . . .?
>
> Surgeon A: Oh yes. I thought it reflected very well. I thought it read well and it was as good a summary as I could have given myself. It was perfectly alright.
>
> MB: What about any omissions? You think there's anything significant omitted from it?
>
> Surgeon A: I don't think so. It covers it very well. Obviously in such a diffuse subject you can't get every detail in, but I would have thought it was very fair. It read well: I would be perfectly satisfied to initial that as being okay.

And from a participant in the halfway-house focus group:

> You were certainly close enough for me to burst out laughing a lot of the time reading it – incidents that you must have been involved in too. Certainly, you got across the essence of certain things that were happening, things that I remember but never actually put into words before. It was very clearly put down [...] I don't think you've got the wrong end of the stick about anything. I don't think there's anything that's been misrepresented.

One member described reading the report as like catching sight of himself in the mirror, while another reported that when he read the report he was sometimes embarrassed by the events it recalled, an effect that he ascribed to the honesty of the research description. Some members said that they used the report to give new and enhanced meaning to previously imperfectly understood events and others found within the report handy terminologies and descriptions that they adopted for their own. As in Giddens's (1976) analysis of the 'double hermeneutic', sociological descriptions may come actually to constitute the reality they purport to describe:

> Nigel: This term 'reality confrontation' – I think that's the essence [of staff practice], a very central part of it. To have that named, that was the most important thing.
>
> Una: Yeah, we went round [after we'd read the report] congratulating ourselves for doing 'reality confrontation'.

Moreover, where member assent was withheld or only conditionally granted, there existed the means to explore the disagreement and modify the analysis. The following very detailed comments from Surgeon B led to a re-analysis of his cases, and some modifications in the report, when it became evident that the particular limited constellations of symptoms he was describing had not occurred in the out-patient clinic sample of cases that I had observed him to assess:

Well, I read it through previously, as you know, and I read it through again before you came this morning. It's very interesting, it's very good, and it's very carefully done. There are one or two points, you know, I'd be a bit doubtful about. It's very good really. I think it's an excellent thing.

Here we are: paragraph 8, page 5. It says: 'It may be that otitis media is cumulatively but not separately important as an indication for tonsillectomy.' Yes, I quite agree this is so. I would certainly agree with that. I wouldn't say 'may be', I think it *is* so.

[...] Okay, there's one over the page, paragraph 12. You said: 'Thus secretory otitis was not, of itself, an indication for adenoidectomy unless there was consequent conductive hearing loss.' I wouldn't agree with that. I think it may well be, even if the hearing was normal [...].

But these morale-boosting encomiums and careful corrections are only half the picture. By no means all the surgeons had read their reports with the attention and precision of this surgeon. Members were required to study a document line by line and to deliberate on its relationship to their own beliefs and practices; the requirement is an unusual one outside of academic circles and demands more commitment and effort than some members were prepared for. One staff member in the 'foster family' community confessed that he simply skipped through the report to read the field note extracts in which he played a part. In other members, paradoxically, too great a commitment might be encountered, eroding the possibility of judgement. Thus, for two members of one staff focus group, my report was defective because it failed to make any reference to the psycho-dynamic concepts on which they based their daily practice:

> it seemed to be naïve, that was my feeling [...] I felt a lot of the . . . I think, well-understood concepts that I base the way I work on weren't being acknowledged (yes, yes) . . . Can I . . .? Can I say that my comment on naïvety is on the basis of what I conceive of as what I'm doing . . . I'm not saying the paper's naïve. The concepts that I hold, it seems, we didn't share.

Emerson and Pollner (1988) recount how their attempts to feed back their findings on the workings of mobile Psychiatric Emergency Teams (PET) were bedevilled by fears of cut-backs being imposed on the service, so that committed PET workers were unwilling to countenance any research findings that might be construed as critical of the service and be used as ammunition for service cuts. As Emerson and Pollner (1988) point out, a member validation exercise is never context-free: it is situated within the world of collectivity members and is expressive of that world. Furthermore, the contexts in which members view researchers' findings are subject to constant change. In one therapeutic community, some staff members were at pains to stress that practice had changed appreciably since the fieldwork was undertaken.

> Enid: I saw a lot of stuff clearer and I saw a lot of stuff that was out-of-date . . .
>   It made me happy but it also made me realize we'd moved on.
> Nigel: It was nice to read it as a measure of where we are now.

Relatedly, the staff member who had previously described my report as naïve happened to be the friend of a friend. Intrigued to see if his views had changed over time, some two years later I arranged to meet over a drink to talk over old times. Indeed, his views had shifted in the intervening two years. He no longer felt that the study was defective in its failure to attend to a psycho-dynamic perspective: there was a distinct psycho-dynamic perspective on the matter, but he now believed that to try to incorporate that perspective would have entailed a different study. He felt that the article I had written (Bloor 1981), based on the draft report, should be required reading for new staff entering the community. Members' responses to researchers' accounts are provisional and subject to change. But it is by no means always the case that distance lends enchantment to the member's eye: one surgeon who had pronounced himself well satisfied with my report of his assessment practices was anything but enchanted when he later read my comparative account of different surgeons' practices: he wrote a highly critical letter to my then research director.

Still more confusingly, not only is member endorsement provisional and subject to change, it is also perfectly possible for members to endorse a researcher's account in terms which the researcher would find unacceptable. The member may read into the account meanings of which the researcher is unaware. Or aspects of the research which the researcher feels to be of relatively minor importance may be dragged centre-stage by the member, while the researcher's supposed central topic is disregarded. For example, one ex-patient paid little attention to my supposed central argument about the latently conflicting nature of prescriptions for patient behaviour. Instead, she kept returning to what for me had been a minor issue and what for her was of central importance: namely, the role of the patient culture in rewarding patients for their progress in group therapy. Uncomfortably, I found my analysis being endorsed for the wrong reasons.

Clearly, members' purposes at hand are not the researcher's. Members' accounts of their social worlds will differ from researchers' accounts because those purposes at hand will differ. In the same way, members may read a researcher's account with different purposes from those wished upon them by the researcher. It is therefore unsurprising if members should find within the researcher's account topics and interpretations which the researcher had discounted or was unaware of. In the staff focus groups, the participants' expertise in interpretation naturally led them, on occasion, into using my report as a vehicle for interpreting my feelings about their communities and themselves:

> Oliver: Can I ask you a very awkward question? How did you come out of the day hospital feeling about therapeutic communities and the day hospital staff?
>
> MB: How do I feel about the staff here? I felt, um, you know, that . . .
>
> Oliver: When someone asks you that, you shouldn't answer it [laughter]. I'll tell you why I asked you: I felt it was a bit cynical at times. That was all. That was just reading it as an outsider.

And from the other staff focus group:

> Una: When I was reading it I couldn't help thinking that the way you were writing it was in some ways slightly more critical of the 'Beeches' [the other halfway house] approach than of 'Ashley' [Una's halfway house]. Reading it, I was thinking: 'Yes, Mick's thinking the same as I'm thinking here.'

Of course, there is an irony here. While the tendency of members to interpret rather than judge sociological accounts seems an unhelpful complication in member validation exercises, the indexical nature of members' responses, as Emerson and Pollner (1988) have shown, requires an interpretative effort on the part of researchers to interpret the sense of those responses. One possible frame of interpretation is the social situation in which the response is produced: all encounters between researchers and researched are species of social relationships governed by conventions of politeness and etiquette; in the case of ethnographic research, the relationship in question may well embrace fondness and mutual regard. Fieldwork methods and fieldwork relations will shape the nature and content of members' responses. In the exchange below, the surgeon, with exemplary courtesy, struggles to maintain a harmonious exchange despite a seemingly serious dispute about an important aspect of his daily work:

> Surgeon C: . . . But I would be very surprised at this. And very reluctant to talk people into an operation.
>
> MB: Yes. There were . . . I got the impression that it wasn't so much cases where the patient manifested reluctance, but where they denied a history of sore throats say, but the symptomatology was of what they would call recurrent colds or something of that nature.
>
> Surgeon C: Um. Fair enough, okay.
>
> MB: Well, I'm, I'm, er . . .
>
> Surgeon C: [laughter] Well, I don't know. But seeing it in cold print like that . . . I, I say: 'Did I, in the absence of a history of sore throats, say that the tonsils have got to come out?' Must have done, must have done, obviously.
>
> MB: But that's, that's the sort of . . .
>
> Surgeon C: . . . That's an interesting point . . .
>
> MB: But it's your impressions of that report, whether you feel it corresponds to your own impressions of your practice that I'm looking for. So . . .
>
> Surgeon C: Yeah. I would have thought I would say 'Oh well there's nothing really of any trouble – you can run along dear.' But if you have observed this, then this is of value . . . I know what you mean: there's often, sometimes . . . they say 'Oh he's not had any trouble with his throat.' And yet they've arrived on your doorstep. So they must have something wrong (um), their own doctor [general practitioner] must . . . (um). Never mind, okay, leave it.
>
> MB: Well . . .
>
> Surgeon C: . . . Does that? . . . No, leave it, this is quite valuable to us, I mean. Because, if you . . . (well) this is your . . . this synthesis . . .

In my report on his assessment practice, I had stated that he was prepared to operate on children whose parents denied any history of sore throats, provided there was examination evidence of tonsillar infection. This clearly failed to correspond to his own experience, but the surgeon courteously struggled to repair any conversational breach or dispute by a variety of means: trying to move us on to fresh topics, generously conceding primacy to my observations over his experience, and offering an interpretation that would reconcile the two viewpoints (that a child's parents might deny an indicative history, but the fact of the child having been referred to his out-patient clinic suggested that the referring general practitioner thought there was an indicative history). A member validation exercise is not a scientific test but a social event, constrained in this case by the social dictates of polite conversation and shaped by the biographies and circumstances of the discussants.

It was an awareness of the impact of the interview format on the valida-tion exercise (and, in particular, an awareness of my own role as interviewer) that led me to adopt a focus group format in the later therapeutic commun-ities study. But focus groups too are social events (even if the researcher is less socially prominent). In the ex-patient focus group the oldest of the ex-patients adopted a chair-like role. In similar fashion, a consultant psychiatrist adopted a chair-like role in one of the staff focus groups. Thus, immediately following his colleagues' remarks on my naïvety for neglecting psycho-dynamic interpretations, the consultant exercised a moderating influence:

> This is a tricky one. I think it deserves some thought because you after all, as you state very clearly in your introduction, came in as a participant observer. And I think that role is a difficult one to hold. Err. And how far do you go one way or the other? I think it's a courageous thing to do really, because, err, it's like being in the middle of the road – you get run down by both sides of the traffic [laughter]. . . .

Focus groups are free of interviewer biases but they are more subject than interviews to participation biases. The group of ex-patients were willing to take part in a focus group because they and I had become close to each other in the course of my fieldwork and their treatment: they were committed to me on a personal basis and committed to making retrospective sense of their treatment experience. But I was aware that not all ex-patients would view the therapeutic community from the same standpoint and so I made an effort to find and speak to some ex-patients whose treatment experience had been less positive and (unlike my focus group participants) had left the therapeutic community abruptly and prematurely. One such ex-patient (whom I inter-viewed) made a most valuable remark. The group therapy programme operated on a five-day week basis, but I only attended for three days per week (varying the actual days of my attendance). The interviewee remi-nisced, to my surprise, that on the days that I attended the patients had seemed a much more cohesive group; when I was absent the patients had seemed more cliquish and divided. He was inclined to attribute this to my alleged 'sunny' manner, but I immediately divined a more painful explana-tion: it seemed to me that, as an assiduous student of the patient culture, I had always sought to talk to the whole spectrum of patients in the community, regardless of cliques or favour; in so doing, it seemed that I taken an important bridging role in shaping the very patient culture that I had sought to study.

Of course, this important (if mortifying) information was not part of the member validation exercise: it simply arose in the course of the exercise. It was by no means the only important information gleaned as an incidental aspect of the member validation exercise. Indeed, much of the material on members' responses, which seems problematic if viewed from the stand-point of a verification exercise, can be viewed instead as further important data, an occasion for extending and elaborating the researcher's analysis. Members' responses to researchers' accounts are not a test of those accounts, but rather they are additional material for analysis all the more valuable for being topically related to earlier data but produced by different methods and under different auspices.

And, finally, feeding back findings to one's research subjects can have other incidental advantages besides the generation of additional research data. It can be an opportunity for researchers to offer thanks and recompense to research subjects (some may feel that etiquette demands this kind of personal feedback wherever such feedback is practical). It can be an opportunity for researcher and researched to deliberate on the policy and service implications of the research. And it can also ease access negotiations where research subjects know that they will have prior sight of the researcher's findings. Member validation is a many-splendoured thing, but it is not validation.

Conclusion

As Emerson and Pollner (1988) have suggested in respect of member validation, there are pendulum swings of fashion in qualitative research methods. Classical sociology took it as axiomatic that collectivity members could not know their social worlds as well as researchers. Subsequently, it was argued that the voice of the member could be the absolute and final arbiter of the researcher's account. More recently, the pendulum has swung back with analysis of the numerous difficulties in member validation exercises. Triangulation is another technique subject to the vagaries of fashion. Currently, it has become almost routine practice for sociological research grant applicants in the UK to bolster their claims to methodological rigour by referring to their planned triangulation of methods. These claims may be overblown where they imply that findings may be validated through triangulation.

It has been my argument that neither triangulation nor member validation can be regarded as a test of research findings. A series of particular difficul-ties with each technique have been outlined and examples given (difficulties in response to non-corroboration, problems of test adequacy in cases of corroboration, problems of comparability, and so forth). All these particular difficulties have their roots in one general unwarranted assumption; namely, that techniques of validation can be treated as unproblematically generated, whereas in practice (and as illustrated) all validating techniques are social products, constituted through particular and variable methodological processes. The very methodological frailties that lead sociologists to search for validating evidence are also present in the generation of that validating evidence. This has two consequences: first, it means that findings and validating evidence (be it triangulation or members' responses) may not be directly comparable since the different circumstances of their production have generated differences between them of specificity and of topical focus; and, secondly, it means that the truth value of any corroboration or non-corroboration found will be unclear because this may be a mere artefact of methodological inadequacies.

However, the conclusion that there can be no tests of validity should in no way weaken the case for practising either triangulation or gathering members' responses to findings. Neither technique can validate findings, but both techniques can be said to be *relevant* to the issue of validity, in so far as both techniques may yield new data that throw fresh light on the investigation and provide a spur for deeper and richer analyses. Triangulation and member validation both allow the researcher to reconsider his or her initial analyses from a novel standpoint: it is not just that additional data are available for study, but also that these additional data may alter the researcher's perception of the initial data. Since one important aspect of this reconsideration is an enhanced awareness of possible methodological biases, it can be seen that these so-called validation techniques may be potent agents for reflexive awareness, for an enhanced understanding of how research findings are constituted in the creative process of the research, rather than being pre-existent and simply awaiting discovery. Validation techniques are not tests, but opportunities for reflexive elaboration (Emerson 1981).

Of course, this reading of the analytical process might be thought unsatisfactory in that it is both progressive and indeterminate, in that elaboration may proceed indefinitely with no final authoritative analysis being achievable. In effect, the analytic process becomes what Cicourel calls 'indefinite triangulation':

> I use the expression 'indefinite triangulation' to suggest that every procedure that seems to 'lock in' evidence, thus to claim a level of adequacy, can itself be subjected to the same sort of analysis that will in turn produce yet another indefinite arrangement of new particulars, or a rearrangement of previously established particulars in 'authoritative', 'final', 'formal' accounts. The indefinite triangulation notion attempts to make visible the practicality and inherent reflexivity of everyday accounts. The elaboration of circumstances and particulars of an occasion can be subjected to an indefinite re-elaboration of the 'same' or 'new' circumstances and particulars. (Cicourel 1973: 124)

However, the necessary residual indeterminacy of sociological analyses poses no problems for the phenomenologist, since it merely mirrors the necessary residual indeterminacy of all commonsense thinking, to which the constructs of social science are indissolubly linked. Just as a member's commonsense thinking about the social world has only that degree of clarity and specificity required for the member's current purpose at hand, so the degree of elaborateness of the researcher's analysis will depend on the researcher's current purpose at hand. It is the researcher's interests and systems of relevance that will determine the practical limits of his or her analysis (Schutz 1970). Techniques of validation provide valuable additional material for analysis and perform further useful functions (such as easing research access), but they do not set the bounds of the analytic task. Those bounds are set not by any technical test or procedure, but by a mix of relevances stretching from the researcher's own intellectual curiosity and scrupulousness to external constraints such as funding limits, supervisory stipulations and (not least!) publishing deadlines.

Acknowledgements

All the studies reported here were conducted with the support of the Medical Research Council. The work on member validation has been much influenced by my correspondence with Bob Emerson, who provided thoughtful editorial comments on an earlier contribution to this topic (Bloor 1983).

PART II

METHODOLOGICAL ISSUES IN QUALITATIVE RESEARCH

4

Accounts, Interviews and Observations

Robert Dingwall

When I began my career, as a graduate student in 1971, the UK had relatively little tradition of formal training in research methods, apart from fairly elementary statistics. (I suspect that I may be a member of the last generation to use log tables and slide rules!) I am not even particularly sure that I consciously intended to be a qualitative researcher: I simply happened to be offered a scholarship by a research group whose work inclined that way.

To the extent that I received any training, it was through being encouraged to read what my mentors considered to be the great books of the 1960s, many of which happened to have used participant observation. My own PhD was an occupational socialization study in medical sociology (Dingwall 1977). The models were defined for me as *Boys in White* (Becker et al. 1961), *Asylums* (Goffman 1961a) and *The Silent Dialogue* (Olesen and Whittaker 1968). The people around me had various other empirical interests. I see from the thesis bibliography that I also read *The Social Organization of Juvenile Justice* (Cicourel 1968; my own title was a deliberate echo of Cicourel's), *The Racing Game* (Scott 1968) and *Identity and Community in the Gay World* (Warren 1974).

As one of my graduate students reminded me later, I wrote an (unpublished) section of my thesis about the PhD itself as an experience in occupational socialization that could be examined in the same way as my health visitors. Occupational socialization is the organizational production of competence, not the internalization of some fixed set of knowledge and values. Although I only fully realized it later, the focus of the study should have been the staff teaching the health visitor training programme and their methods for recognizing and certifying competence in their students (Dingwall 1986). In the same way, the qualitative researchers who taught me affirmed the priority of observation in a way that made it the heart of the studies that their students undertook. To be recognized by them as a competent qualitative sociologist it was essential to be a competent participant observer.

I have done rather less of this kind of work in recent years. I had attributed this to advancing age and to the contingencies of academic careers. When you have to sit on committees, teach classes, supervise PhD students and worry about trying to take some share of domestic and child-care responsibilities, it is genuinely more difficult to organize your life in ways that can accommodate the unpredictable schedules of the field. Researchers cannot make the field fit their lives, but it is not easy to make your life fit the field. My most recent studies have focused on professionals involved in personal injury litigation and on divorce mediators. The first had the attractions of doing interviews by appointment, wearing a suit and sitting in plush law firm or insurance offices drinking tea from porcelain cups. The second was even better: the mediators did not like the idea of being directly observed but were very happy to tape their work and mail it in. This seemed a brilliant scam: lots of data without having to set foot outside the office! Conversation analysis has a great deal to recommend it to the middle-aged. However, having finally secured a post with tenure in 1990 and begun to train my own PhD students, I was surprised to find one of them comment to me that actually there did not seem to be much participant observation going on anywhere any more.

While I think that this is a slight exaggeration, it does seem to be true that the balance has tipped. The dominant kind of qualitative study appears to be one in which the investigator carries out a bunch of semi-structured interviews which are then taped and transcribed. The results are thrown into a qualitative data management package and a few themes dragged out in ways that seem rather like what we used to call 'data dredging'. This involved loading the results of a survey into the mainframe, correlating everything with everything else and seeing what came out. The problem, of course, is that the laws of probability require that a certain number of correlations will be significant purely as a matter of chance: having found them, we still have to determine whether the result has anything more than a statistical significance. This can be done only in the light of a well-thought out theoretical question and in the context of other investigators' findings. Alternatively, the interview study seems to have become an excuse for introspection, an occasion on which to contemplate the sociological navel, and to find it pierced in contemporary fashion. In effect, the researcher is simply looking for some good quotes to illustrate a previously determined position on some personal or political issue.

Both of these tendencies seem to me regrettable and this chapter is directed to challenging them. It seeks, first, to re-establish the primacy of observation and, secondly, to assert that it can still be used to say something interesting about the world rather than about the observer.

Two (or possibly three) methods of social research

I once heard a distinguished anthropologist say something that I have shamelessly plagiarized ever since. 'There are', he declared, 'only two basic methods of social research. One is called "asking questions" and the other is called "hanging out".' Since anthropologists traditionally study non-literate societies, sociologists might want to add a third method: 'reading the papers'. All human beings have used pretty much the same kinds of methods to find out about the social world around them since our species came down from the trees.

'Hanging out' has experienced less systematic refinement than the others. Although it was recognized as a fairly obvious way to investigate certain categories of people, especially low-life, who might not answer questions truthfully, and tribal peoples, who might not understand the modern game of interviewing and take it seriously, it has remained a rather haphazard business. A number of early social investigators used observation as a means of studying the poor. Walter Wyckoff (1971), for example, who was then an assistant professor in political economy at Princeton, published an account in 1901 of a walking tour of the Midwest in 1891, during which he posed as an itinerant labourer, which was partly designed to investigate the reasons for imperfection in the labour market: why did people prefer to remain unemployed in Chicago rather than move to Iowa where the farmers were desperate for labour? However, his description takes the form of a diary or a traveller's tale, although he was clearly quite systematic in observing the behaviour of other itinerants and the local communities. Beatrice Webb worked as a seamstress as part of a study of sweated labour in the 1880s and wrote up her experiences as an influential piece of social journalism, which led to some of her early public appearances in front of Parliamentary Committees (Webb 1946: 312–345). Although she and her husband, Sidney, used observation a great deal in their studies of local government organization, they produced only a formal account of this method in 1932, when they devoted a chapter of their textbook *Methods of Social Study* to 'Watching the Institution at Work'. They asserted: 'An indispensable part of the study of any social institution, wherever this can be obtained, is deliberate and sustained personal observation of its actual operation' (Webb and Webb 1975: 158).

Participant observation became established as the dominant method for anthropological study of tribal peoples during the 1920s and 1930s as students read Bronislaw Malinowski's accounts of his researches in New Guinea during the First World War and tried to copy what they thought he had done. Actually, Malinowski's own diary shows that observation provided a context for the statistical data that he collected and for the structured questioning of informants, both of which were the methods of his predecessors (Kuper 1973).

> In working out the rules and regularities of native custom, and in obtaining a precise formula for them from the collection of data and native statements, we find that this very precision is foreign to real life, which never adheres rigidly to any rules. It must be *supplemented* by the observation of the manner in which a given custom is carried out, of the behaviour of the natives in obeying the rules so exactly formulated by the ethnographer, of the very exceptions which in sociological phenomena almost always occur. (Malinowksi 1922; my italics)

Pat Barker's reworking of W.H.R. Rivers's notes from his 1911 fieldwork in Melanesia for her (1995) novel, *The Ghost Road*, suggests that, in fact, the movement from questioning to observing was already under way before Malinowski's time. In Rivers's own words:

> A typical piece of intensive work is one in which the worker lives for a year or more among a community of perhaps four or five hundred people and studies every detail of their life and culture; in which he comes to know every member of the community personally; in which he is not content with generalized information, but studies every feature of life and custom in concrete detail and by means of the vernacular language . . . It is only by such work that it is possible to discover the incomplete and even misleading character of much of the vast mass of survey work which forms the existing material of anthropology. (Rivers 1913: 7)

Traditionally, sociologists tell the story of participant observation from the conjunction of Robert Park and W.I. Thomas at the University of Chicago around the end of the First World War. However, modern scholarship has reminded us that the work that they inspired was quite diverse and far from being uniquely observational. Platt (1994, 1996) argues that the dominant Chicago method of the 1920s and 1930s may be better described as one of case studies, with a strong emphasis on the kind of life histories and personal documents collected by case-workers in the course of social work with the marginal groups of the metropolis. Although some observation went on, she suggests that there was a relative indifference to specific questions of method; Park simply encouraged students to go out and find the story:

> one thing more is needful: first-hand observation. Go and sit in the lounges of the luxury hotels and on the doorsteps of the flop-houses, sit on the Gold Coast settees and on the slum shakedowns; sit in the Orchestra Hall and in the Star and Garter Burlesk. In short, gentlemen, go get the seat of your pants dirty in real research. (Bulmer 1984: 97; cf. Carey 1975: 155; Platt 1996: 52)

It must be said that Platt tends to reinforce the stock picture of Park as a journalist who happened to wander into sociology, a picture rather at odds with the range and subtlety of his theoretical writing. Remarks like this seem to have been a Chicago style: Atkinson (1977: 32) recounts the story of Howard Becker, on a visit to the University of Manchester, being asked by a graduate student how to choose a paradigm and being told to stop worrying, 'get in there and see what's going on.' As Platt herself notes, though, Becker was one of the major contributors to the articulation of participant observation as a self-conscious method within sociology during the late 1940s and to systematic published exposition during the 1950s and 1960s. Rather than being created in opposition to positivism and the survey, she suggests, observation was another manifestation of a widely shared attempt to create a more scientific and professional way to do social research. Paul Lazarsfeld, the high priest of the survey, and Everett Hughes, the guru of the post-war Chicago School of occupational ethnographers, shared a vision of a methodologically self-conscious discipline, even if they tried to operationalize this in competing ways.

This puts a rather different slant on my generation's occasional bafflement about observational methods. Platt notes that the first textbook treatment of participant observation was Junker (1960), based on Everett Hughes's graduate methods course at Chicago. Before this, anybody doing an observational study would have had either to be trained at a centre where such work was going on or to have invented an approach for themselves. While there was a flurry of relevant texts in the US over the next decade, the lag in transmission meant that my cohort in the UK were being trained by supervisors who were themselves pretty vague about what participant observation research in sociology might look like. The main exceptions were those supervised by anthropologists who had already inspired some work on British field sites through the community studies tradition (see Frankenberg 1966). However, these were not necessarily relevant models for the kind of organizational studies that our American exemplars had carried out, although Chicago ethnography had closer ties with anthropology than many of the later sociological accounts acknowledge: both Malinowski and A.R. Radcliffe-Brown were regular visitors in the 1930s and the intellectual influence of Robert Redfield, Park's son-in-law, and Lloyd Warner on developments after the Second World War was arguably as great as that of Everett Hughes.

In recent years, observation has suffered from the absence of powerful external sponsors. The pressures on the resources available to graduate students and rising expectations about their training requirements have encouraged the – cheaper and quicker – use of interview methods, which have themselves found an external constituency. The informal interview has become a routine tool of commercial research as well as of social science. Interviews, like surveys, seem to represent transferable skills, with an obvious market value. While the world of commerce can worry about its own standards, however, the world of social science professes a concern for the integrity of its conclusions which sits uncomfortably with the neglect of observational research. Other qualitative methods generate problems of validity and reliability which are so fundamental that the neglect of observation, and its proxies in direct audio- and video-recording, fatally undermines many of the conclusions that are alleged to have been drawn.

Accounting and social life

Scientific revolutions are preceded by the accumulation of small anomalies that ultimately pull down the paradigm that has framed them. Given this, it may be difficult to single out the snowflake whose movement ultimately caused the avalanche. The basic anomaly was present from the earliest formulations of interactionist sociology and the notion that humans were fundamentally reflexive beings. During the 1920s and 1930s, G.H. Mead and Alfred Schutz, in slightly different ways, reflecting their different intellectual contexts, restated two propositions that had first been advanced by the Stoics two thousand years before: that our understanding of our actions was derived from others' responses and that our action-projects were designed in the light of the expected responses of those others. These theorists had a limited influence until after the Second World War but their impact was eventually revolutionary. It was felt first in the doing of sociology, in the post-war Chicago studies of work and organizations, with their abandonment of the formal analysis of scientific management for more fluid images of negotiation, uncertainty and conflict and in Erving Goffman's development of strategic models of human action.

The line of argument that eventually emerged in the 1960s at the intersection between symbolic interactionism and ethnomethodology went something like this. Social order is constituted through interaction by a dance of expectations. I produce my actions in the expectation that you will understand them in a particular way. Your understanding reflects your expectations of what would be a proper action for me in these particular circumstances which, in turn, becomes the basis of your response which, itself, reflects your expectations of how I will respond. And so on. At any point, there may be a disjuncture between actions, responses and expectations which requires that the parties engage in some sort of repair work. The whole process is underpinned by what Goffman (1983) came to call 'Felicity's Condition', that we act in such a way as not to disconfirm the assumption of our sanity by those around us. In effect, we are obliged to participate in the everydayness of everyday life or be regarded as incompetent, deranged, disordered and generally unfit to be around right-thinking people.

Once interaction came to be analysed as a matter of impression management in support of personal goals and structured by the expectations of others, however, it could only be a matter of time before the analysis was applied to the tools of sociology. The key text was Aaron Cicourel's *Method and Measurement in Sociology*, published in 1964. Cicourel's book is usually cited for its attack on quantitative social science. It is often forgotten, though, that Cicourel also discussed the practice of participant observation (or field research as he tends to call it) and of interviewing. The chapter on interviewing is remarkable for the clarity with which it lays out the problem. If the interview is a social encounter, then, logically, it must be analysed in the same way as any other social encounter. The products of an interview are the outcome of a socially situated activity where the responses are passed through the role-playing and impression management of both the interviewer and the respondent. This is not the technical problem that survey researchers assume, which might be resolved by better interviewer training, more elaborate scripts or whatever. The interview is an artefact, a joint accomplishment of interviewer and respondent. As such, its relationship to any 'real' experience is not merely unknown but in some sense unknowable.

The implications for the research interview are quite dramatic. The research interview is, above all, an occasion for the elicitation of *accounts*. The term 'account' needs some explanation because it has been employed in two slightly different but related ways. It was first used in an ethnomethodological context by Harold Garfinkel (1967) as he laid out his manifesto in *Studies in Ethnomethodology*. While Cicourel had been clearer about his

criticisms of conventional sociological methods than about his proposed
alternative, Garfinkel formulated an alternative programme. In true Kuhnian
style, Garfinkel asserted that what he thought should be done was incommensurable with the paradigm of traditional sociology. Its object of study
would be 'the activities whereby members produce and manage settings or
organized everyday affairs [which] are identical with members' procedures
for making those settings "account-able"' (Garfinkel 1967: 1). What the
world *is* is the way we call it into existence through talk. But this is not just
any talk. It is talk that shapes a world that others will recognize and for
which they will hold us responsible. 'Accounting' is how we build a stable
order in social encounters and in society.

However, the idea gained a wider currency in the more restricted sense
given to it by Scott and Lyman (1968). They focused on the way people
responded to questions about the normality or the rationality of their behaviour. How did we deal with challenges which imply that our behaviour has
not been in accord with the expectations of the observer? How do we
account for ourselves? Scott and Lyman argued that 'accounts' fell into two
categories which they called *justifications* and *excuses*. This work has had a
wide impact on the sociology of deviance (see Scott and Lyman 1970). John
Eekelaar, Topsy Murray and I used it, for example, to examine how parents
accused of maltreating their children tried to explain their actions in court
hearings to consider the removal of their children or some other compulsory
measure by child protection services (Dingwall et al. 1983). Parents tried to
justify their actions by denying that they exceeded the boundaries of reasonable behaviour, by questioning the right of child protection workers to
judge them, especially if the worker were not a parent, by telling 'sad tales'
about their own upbringing or by appealing to higher virtues, as in the case
of religious zealots who claimed a biblical justification for physical punish-
ment. They tried to excuse their behaviour by pointing to some impairment
of their capacity (by drugs, alcohol or mental disorder), to some biological
drive (particularly in the case of sexual abusers), or by pointing to characteristics of the victim (especially if the child were handicapped in some way).

Scott and Lyman (1968: 61) acknowledged that the production of
accounts was a socially constrained process:

> We want to know how the actors take bits and pieces of words and appearances
> and put them together to produce a perceivedly normal (or abnormal) state of
> affairs. This kind of inquiry crucially involves a study of background expectations.
> On the basis of such investigations, the analyst should be able to provide a set of
> instructions on 'how to give an account' that would be taken by other actors as
> 'normal'. These instructions would specify how different categories of statuses
> affect the honoring of an account and what categories of statuses can use what
> kinds of accounts.

In our study of child protection, we looked at the differential response of
the courts to the various categories of justification or excuse. Basically, it was
only the tellers of 'sad tales' or those with some principled libertarian objection to the agencies' judgements on their standards of child care who had any

prospect of persuading the court to rule in their favour and then only if they could demonstrate what Emerson has called their 'absolute rectitude' (Emerson 1969: 167).

This restriction on the sense of accounting has troubled a number of more ethnomethodologically inclined writers. Atkinson and Drew (1979: 138–141), for instance, show that accounts may be offered without specific charges being made: they use the example of the rejection of invitations where this, dispreferred, action seems to be routinely accompanied by some explanation without that explanation actually being asked for. They note also that people do not necessarily give reasons in such contexts but rather describe situations in such a way as to imply reasons. In analysing the response of a police witness to the Scarman Inquiry into civil disorder in Northern Ireland in 1969, for instance, they note that the witness's inaction is provided for as much through a description of the scene – the petrol bombing of a newsagent's shop where the witness notes that the window was already broken and the premises alight – as through the stated reason that is provided subsequently, 'we were under gunfire at the time'. The witness expects that the tribunal will appreciate that there is no point in him taking the risk of entering a building which is already damaged and burning and from which anyone injured is already likely to have left or to have been evacuated. A possible sequence of questions has been projected and answered. They also note that the difference between justification and excuse is abstract rather than practical. Witnesses use both in connection with the same events and weave around to find whichever is most persuasive in the local context. Similar points have been made by Buttney (1987: 1), who notes the way in which human action 'is all too susceptible to error, unfulfilled goals and unintended consequences'. Accounts are the way in which the fabric of order is restored at the points where it comes under stress.

Interviews as accounts

An interview is a point at which order is deliberately put under stress. It is a situation in which respondents are required to demonstrate their competence in the role in which the interview casts them. At one level, this is the role of respondent: hence some of the difficulties that Isobel Bowler describes in Chapter 5 in dealing with people who do not have a concept of the interview. Her respondents are not members of what Silverman (1997) has called 'the Interview Society', where the self is established as an object of narration. Her Pakistani women do not share her concept of the propriety of talking about themselves and their personal experiences of maternity care. Adequate performance of the role of respondent rests on the essential feature of interviews that people are put on notice to talk about *something*. A key feature of the framing of interviews is that the interviewer defines what the parties are going to talk about and what will count as relevant. The interview is a turn-taking system that requires that the interviewer proposes topics and that the respondent seeks to produce locally acceptable answers. This is true even of so-called unstructured interviews. The sequence may be flexible; the question wording may be flexible; it may be dressed up like a conversation between friends. But an interview is not a conversation. It is a deliberately created opportunity to talk about something that the interviewer is interested in and that may or may not be of interest to the respondent. If the interviewer refuses to propose topics, the respondent is obliged to guess what might be relevant until the interviewer gives some indication that he or she is happy with the line being taken.

An interview is never an occasion for a respondent to tell whatever story comes into his or her head. Try it sometime. Sit someone down in front of a tape recorder and ask him/her to talk about his/her life. You will almost invariably find that the response is, 'What shall I talk about?' The initial talk is punctuated by uncertainty, checks on relevance, requests for confirmation of the direction and so on. What you have done is to carry out a breaching experiment. As Garfinkel (1967) showed, such fundamental challenges to the interaction order can be quite devastating in their impact, although they also provoke quite remarkable displays of ingenuity by those involved as they try to make sense of what is happening. The classic example of this process is McHugh's (1968) discussion of an experiment where people were told that they would receive counselling from a counsellor hidden behind a screen who would only answer 'Yes' or 'No' to their questions. The experimenter's confederate selected the answers at random but the recordings of the recipients show that they treated even radically contradictory responses as indicators of some stable underlying order. The random answers were treated as answers-to-their-questions.

Whether of interest or not, the respondent is still concerned to bring the occasion off in a way that demonstrates his or her competence as a member of whatever community is invoked by the interview topic. This is an inescapable constraint on face-to-face interaction. The consequence is that the data produced by interviews are social constructs, created by the self-presentation of the respondent and whatever interactional cues have been given off by the interviewer about the acceptability or otherwise of the accounts being presented. Once again, it must be emphasized that this is a critique of *all* interviews. It subsumes the standard critiques of the forced-choice survey interview for boxing up experience in ways that do violence to the respondent's meanings: indeed, there may be some reason to suppose that the more rigorous training of interviewers on such studies to minimize their reactions to any response may make the results somewhat less arte-factual than in informal interviews where the interviewer takes an active role in dialogue with the respondent. At least with a formal and heavily structured interview, we have a good idea what the interviewer effects *are*! It also cuts across the so-called public and private distinctions: all experience is expressed through the social medium of language and there is no prior medium. Public accounts and private accounts satisfy the requirements of competence on different occasions. The private account is not the product of a more intimate understanding between interviewer and respondent. Private experience can be expressed only through a social medium in a social setting where the expression will immediately be evaluated for its fit to the range of versions of the self that are sanctioned in that environment. Thus feminist researchers elicit feminist accounts; Black researchers elicit Black accounts; and sociological researchers elicit . . . what?

Interview data cannot offer us literal descriptions of the respondents' reality. This is not to say that no use can be made of them, although a detailed consideration of this lies outside the scope of the present chapter. However, work like that of Baruch (1981), Moore (1974) and Voysey (1975) illustrates how interviews can be analysed for what they can say about the kind of accounts that are treated as legitimate in a particular setting. As Baruch (1981) and Voysey (1975) note, what parents with a handicapped child say in an interview does not tell us what it is like to live in such a family. Ultimately, that experience is unknowable. What they do tell us quite a lot about is the work of doing being a normal family. The everyday lives of these families are natural breaching experiments which reveal the order that would otherwise be taken for granted. The ways in which they seek to restore that order tell us both about its moral force and about the kinds of accounts that are honoured in our society. Moore's (1974) progressive clergymen have a line on the marginalization of the church that nevertheless allows them to demonstrate that they are reasonable men doing a sensible job rather than, say, naïve victims of a delusion who are propping up a bankrupt and irrelevant institution. It may also be that some aspects of the respondent's reality can be glimpsed through the accounts: the selection of details, the choice of 'facts' in the narrative, perhaps. In real life we recognize that the accounts we receive every day contain some mix of the real and the representation and there seems no good reason why the accounts we receive as sociologists should be essentially different. My point is merely that interview data are fraught with problems because of the activity of the interviewer in producing them. At the same time, data are never *merely* accounts or versions, such that any reading is as good as any other. I shall return to this point.

Observation and its virtues

While observation does not entirely avoid some of these difficulties, it does potentially strike out interviewer variation as a first-order problem. Where interviewers *construct* data, observers *find* it. The case must not be overstated: clearly observers also select from the universe of sensations to which they are exposed in any given setting and may exercise some impact on that setting. Nevertheless, the fundamental virtue of observation, whether direct or via the proxies of audio- or video-recording, is that it enables us to document members accounting to each other in natural settings. It is the difference between the experiment on the laboratory animal and the animal in the wild. This gives a quite different purchase on the production of social

order. No longer is it a matter of members trying to make themselves app\
rational to us: now it is a question of how they appear rational to each oth\
How do they make the world a reasonably ordered, stable and reliable ex\
perience? Alternatively, in some settings, how do they deliberately set out to
destabilize it, whether by means of dope or postmodernism? The observer is
a part of the audience but no longer the most important part. He or she will
be here today and gone tomorrow, while the other actors are potentially far
more consequential. In recording their dealings with each other, we come
closer to understanding the production of everyday life in a much wider
range of environments. Interviews tell us about the construction of mundane
reality in the interview. They are documents of the researcher–researched
relationship. Observation is a document of the transactions between members themselves.

If our objective is to understand the foundations of social order, the constitution of society, the organization of settings or any of the classic questions
of sociology, observation must be the method of preference. If our intention
is to change the world, the same is true. As Harvey Sacks frequently
observed, there can be many great events in the world that have remarkably
little impact on the order of everyday life (Sacks 1992: II, 215–221).
Conversely, the obduracy of everyday life can be a massive obstacle to
desired change. Consider, for example, the struggle between agricultural
and industrial time in the transition to capitalism (Thompson 1967) or the
catastrophic failures of technical systems that are ill matched to the working
practices of human operators. Chernobyl, perhaps, where the operators
sought to liven up a dull shift by experimenting with the safety devices? Or,
at a more mundane level, the hitches in the IBM systems used for the Atlanta
Olympics. A company spokesman was reported as admitting: 'Probably the
biggest lesson we learned was that technology in itself is not the solution –
in this case a lot of the work has to be done by human beings' (*The Guardian
Online*, 8 August 1996).

Observation shows us everyday life being brought into being. It does not,
of course, show us what is real. It does not tell us what is going on inside the
heads of the people who are making the world real for each other. But, since
we are not a telepathic species, this is not just our problem. Members have
the same difficulties as sociologists in making sense of what is going on,
deciding what is real and what is fantasy, deciding what is true and what is
false, deciding what is sincerity and what is deceit. But they have solved these
problems, for all practical purposes, partly by creating a shared set of interactional practices, knowledge, presuppositions or whatever, and partly by
creating a set of social institutions that legitimate closure. Professions and
their associated workplaces can, for example, be seen as devices for managing uncertainty: medicine orders the variety of human anatomy and
physiology; engineering orders the elemental forces of nature; law produces
determinacy in the face of ambiguity and dispute. These are not real controls
but they allow others to get on with their lives with a working assumption
of boundedness and stability. Observation tells us about the set of solutions

that have been produced, how people solidify and stabilize their social environment and how, on occasion, they play with it and test it.

Of course, some settings are harder to penetrate than others. Interviews may be a way to glimpse something of what goes on within these boundaries. However, the analysis of interview data must always be reconcilable with what is known about everyday life from observation. We may not be able to observe Cabinet discussions of national security issues: when we interview ministers about them, we must keep in mind what we know of group processes and committee work. A Cabinet meeting is one of a class of occasions, some of which are very accessible, rather than something *sui generis*. If we hear something inconsistent with this, then it is a prompt to ask why our informant is putting a particular spin on to his or her story. There are, of course, some public settings that adopt the interview format: the journalist's interview or the chat show, for example. Sometimes we may have a deliberate reason for eliciting an on-the-record account. In the child protection study, we interviewed agency directors particularly in order to get an 'official version' of the agency. How did the organization represent itself to the public? This gave us some important clues to the tensions within an inter-agency system, where agencies were caught between their separate charters and missions (see Chapter 10) and the unavoidability of cooperation and interdependence. How could members both assert their differences and build trust in each other? The point is that we knew we were creating a particular kind of account, which is well rehearsed by agency directors who frequently have to explain their actions to journalists, politicians, lawyers and the like, but we also understood the context in which it had to be read. It was not a process of triangulation but a recognition that these were different pieces of the jigsaw, that members might have the problem of reconciling what had to be said at one time and place with what was said or done at another. This is not the classic observer's irony: 'Look these people say one thing and do something different.' It is an acknowledgement that different settings and interactions exact different self-presentations but that, from time to time, these differences cannot be kept apart and must be managed.

What is it all worth?

In a previous paper (Dingwall 1992), I discussed some of the problems of validity in qualitative research and proposed three tests that a reader might apply: can she distinguish clearly between data and analysis? Can she see how the study has looked for contradictory or negative evidence and set out to test statements proposed on theoretical grounds or reported from previous studies? Can she see how it reflects the interactive character of social life and deals even-handedly with the people being studied? These tests are designed to screen out those writings which simply explore the emotional or intuitive response of the investigator, which fail to contribute to a cumulative science of society or which are exposé journalism masquerading as scholarship.

I want to return to these issues and conclude the present chapter by restating the case against certain readings of the social constructionist argument.

Dingwall (1992) formed part of an emerging critique of the Romantic movement in ethnography (see, for example, Hammersley 1992a,b; Silverman 1989; Strong and Dingwall 1989). That movement rests on a set of assumptions about the nature of the sociological project that are fundamentally untenable. Three of them are important here. The first may be called the assumption of *authenticity*, the idea that it is possible to locate a real self. This is the mistake that qualitative interview studies frequently make: the idea that greater informality gets the interviewer nearer some ultimate truth about the respondent which is obscured by the pre-coding and structuring of more formal methods. As we have seen, the fact that language is a social medium and the interview is a social situation means that the self presented to the interviewer is an artefact of the encounter. The same, of course, is true of observation of members interacting with each other: their self-presentations, their accounts of the self, are also artefacts.

To the extent that this has been accepted by some Romantics, however, they have drifted towards the second assumption, namely that of *plasticity*. If there is no 'real self', then perhaps there is no 'real world': we can make ourselves and our worlds any way we choose. This is sometimes identified with the 'postmodern turn' in ethnography. It takes much of its inspiration from Michel Foucault's later work, where he came to see us as prisoners in Max Weber's iron cage, where the only chance of freedom and authenticity came through play, irony and transformation. It finds a metaphor in the argot of the Internet, where the speed and impersonality of communication allows us to be anybody we choose in any part of cyberspace that we happen to occupy. I can join a usegroup as a 17-year-old Mormon virgin and be that person for as long as I can sustain the role. Undoubtedly, the Internet offers many interesting issues for social science, although I am reminded of Sacks's discussion of the resilience of interactional forms with the development of the telephone. The technology creates new possibilities but these tend to be framed through existing social forms.

> There's a funny kind of thing, in which each new object becomes the occasion for seeing again what we can see anywhere; seeing people's nastinesses or goodnesses and all the rest, when they do this initially technical job of talking over the phone. This technical apparatus is, then, being made at home with the rest of our world. And that's a thing that's routinely being done, and it's the source for the failures of technocratic dreams that if we only introduced some fantastic new communication machine the world will be transformed. Where what happens is that the object is made at home in the world that has whatever organization it already has. (Sacks 1992: II, 548–549)

In Schutz's terminology, the Internet may offer a new province of meaning, alongside dreams, fantasy, science or whatever. However, it is not the primary reality. We can order food on the Internet; we need physically to consume it. We may play at sex on the Internet; reproduction requires materiality, whether in a physical act or in a laboratory. When our Internet

ection goes down because our hard disks have crashed, we need a
an being with a screwdriver to fix it. The fundamental conditions of our
yday existence, which are, in turn, the prerequisites and the motives for
social organization, can be satisfied only in a material world. Cyberspace
may be a new kind of time-out: it does not displace everyday life.

Within the everyday life-world, the possibilities are not indefinite. Our talk
is organized to produce order and determinacy. That is what language is
about – sharing, coordinating, restricting private meaning in the accomplishment of sociality. We expect and are expected to produce the
simulacrum of a 'real self'. Indeed, to deny this may be to disconfirm
'Felicity's Condition'. Inconsistency is an accountable matter. And the plaus-
ibility of the account is the audience's decision not the speaker's. The sum of
this argument is that we cannot make the world any way we choose. We are
always constrained by the material conditions of our biological existence and
by the responses of those around us.

Which brings us to the third assumption, which I have called *integrity*.
Romantics do not need to worry whose side they are on – they know they are
right. Since there are no constraints on the self, on the construction of the
world or whatever, then we may characterize it in any way we please.
Silverman (1997) has noted his aversion to the results in terms of second-rate
poetry, drama and home videos and called for a return to the spirit of
Wittgenstein's plea for clarity and rigour of expression. It is the difference
between trying to convey a feeling, for which the creative arts may well be an
appropriate vehicle, and a fact, for which the formality of science is not mere
rhetoric but a well-honed tool. The intersubjective construction of reality
through accounting is a social fact. It is there; it is observable; it is reportable.
There is nothing occult about the processes involved in its analysis. It has the
relentless logic of forensic science. But only the corrupt scientist becomes
more concerned with proving guilt than with the truth of his or her analysis.
The result of that corruption is the sort of miscarriage of justice that our
Romantic would unhesitatingly condemn at the same time as reproducing it
in his or her own work. The only protection in the end is the discipline of science, of a concern for evidence, for standards of procedure, for objectivity in
the face of interests. The real world of scientific practice may fall short; this
does not negate the importance of the ideals as standards of judgement.
Unfortunately, this sometimes means that we do not produce politically
acceptable conclusions. But what is the value of a scholarly enterprise that is
more concerned with being 'right on' than with being right?

Observation is the most fundamental discipline for the sociologist. In an
interview study, we can pick and choose the messages that we hear and that
we elicit. In observation, we have no choice but to listen to what the world
is telling us.

Acknowledgements

I am most grateful to Pam Watson for her detailed and critical response to an earlier draft of this chapter, and to Gale Miller for his encouragement and patience through the distractions affecting a (now thankfully ex) department chair.

5

Problems with Interviewing: Experiences with Service Providers and Clients

Isobel Bowler

This chapter describes a failure to obtain data through ethnographic inter-viewing. To be specific, it concerns a failure to obtain consent for formal field interviews as part of an ethnographic study of inequalities in health in Britain (Bowler 1990). The study focused on women of South Asian descent (mainly Pakistani) in a British city and their experience of maternity services. Although data on these women were collected through participant observa-tion, the study failed to obtain interview data from them.

The main method of data collection was participant observation of the delivery of health care in both the maternity hospital and the community, with the focus on women themselves. Originally the intention was to seek women's and midwives' perspectives through ethnographic interviewing. Interviewing midwives presented few problems. However, the plan to inter-view women ran into difficulties. The main findings of the study have been reported elsewhere (Bowler 1993, 1994, 1995). This chapter describes the fieldwork and methods used and analyses the failure to obtain data from interviews with South Asian women. The chapter proposes that interviewing may be a problematic method for obtaining the views of some groups, since it is a cooperative activity and relies upon a shared notion of the process of research.

Methods

There were two parts to the study. The main fieldwork was carried out in the maternity department of a teaching hospital. The primary method of data collection was participant observation which was carried out in all clinical areas of the hospital. Data were also obtained from depth interviews with 25 midwives. These interviews were ethnographic: that is without a formal schedule but with a series of topics to be discussed, many of which were gen-erated through the analysis of observational data. The interviews were arranged in advance but in the field, and lasted up to an hour. Data also came out of spontaneous discussions with midwives and women which occurred during observation. These were sometimes triggered by events or because there was a lull in activity (for example, when travelling in a car with a midwife doing community visits). These discussions were exploratory and the questions were opportunistic and unstructured. Following Fontana and Frey (1994), I term these 'natural field interviews'. It was originally intended that formal interviews would take place with the women who were the clients of the midwives. However, I failed to obtain access for this part of the study.

Interviewing midwives

Midwives were selected for formal interview through contacts made during observation, and the sample was drawn to get a range of ages, experience and seniority. All the interviews were ethnographic and reflexive, drawing on themes generated through the analysis of observational data. In addition, respondents introduced their own themes which were included in subsequent interviews. The interview began with open-ended questions about the mid-wife's work experience. Topics raised included other hospitals they had worked in, other areas within the present hospital, what the midwives liked about the job, what they did not like, the division of work between midwives and doctors, the different types of mothers and so on. I was then able to develop any new topics that arose and introduce themes generated in the observational data. Among other subjects, I told the midwives that I was interested in South Asian women and asked for their views and experiences with this group.

In all interview situations accounts are given and received by the inter-viewer, and the type of account received will depend on the ability of the interviewer to give an honoured account of her role (Scott and Lyman 1968). As I spent more time with midwives, I gained a greater knowledge of their understanding and expectations of research and reflected this in my account of the research. I also acquired the terminology which made me and my account more acceptable. Midwives, although frequently short of time, were happy to talk, often at length. Interviewing midwives was therefore straight-forward.

Natural and formal field interviews with midwives yielded data which have been analysed in conjunction with observational data. For example, the study identified (negative) stereotyping of South Asian women through the midwives' accounts and through observation of interactions between the two groups. The observation also showed that the assumptions about women based on the midwives' stereotyped views had an important effect on the care they gave to the women (Bowler 1993, 1995). There was also evi-dence that the midwives' perception and performance of 'midwifery' and the midwife role can have a detrimental effect on care delivery for all women (Bowler 1994).

As part of the study, natural interviews also occurred with women: for example, as I sat with them during the early stages of labour. However, these interviews were limited by language (many did not speak much English and I did not speak much Urdu). It was important therefore to obtain agreement for formal field interviews from South Asian women and to use an interpreter. This was where the study ran into difficulty.

Problems of research

Since completing this study, I have discovered examples of other studies of black users of the health service that have had trouble obtaining access to data through interview or questionnaire (see McIver 1994). All the recent examples I found were from needs assessment studies from the field of health services research. There are some earlier examples from ethnographic monographs in which anthropologists express their frustration and failure to extract information from the people they are studying (for example, Evans-Pritchard's 1940 account of the uncooperative Nuer who were 'expert at sabotaging an inquiry'). The lack of recent published academic research reporting such difficulties may be attributed to an unwillingness to highlight such events, and to publication bias which is known to favour positive results.

Postal questionnaire studies have been particularly unsuccessful. Researchers attempting to carry out a postal survey on behalf of Wycombe Health Authority achieved a response rate of 73 per cent overall but commented on the total lack of interest on the part of ethnic minorities, despite requesting the help of the local community liaison officer (Barr and Rogers 1989). Citing this and other examples of study failure, McIver (1994) recommends the use of structured interview studies, although she points out that 'access to potential respondents' needs to be carefully planned. Researchers using a focus group method to determine health and social care needs of minority ethnic people in South Glamorgan found that 'recruitment of participants was extremely difficult' (Shah et al. 1993). Another local study in Birmingham successfully recruited respondents through linkworkers (advocates employed to mediate between health professionals and ethnic minority people, particularly South Asian women). The authors comment that what seems to be important in encouraging people to participate in a research project is the patient and careful building up of relationships with a variety of individuals in different networks who then act as intermediaries (Jowell et al. 1990).

The processes of research are not always well understood by potential informants. A recent large national survey of health and lifestyles among England's black and minority ethnic communities ran into several difficulties (Health Education Authority 1994). The groups concerned were Pakistanis, Bangladeshis, Indian Sikhs, East African Asians, African-Caribbeans and Black Africans who make up the largest minority ethnic populations in England. The research was carried out by a market research organization (MORI) and the interviewers, many matched for ethnic group and bilingual in an appropriate language, found that gaining permission to interview was more difficult, and the interview more time-consuming, than was usual in general population surveys.

> Many respondents had no idea what population surveys or social research was . . . Interviewers had to provide far more introductory information for respondents about themselves and the organisation they worked for, what the HEA [Health Education Authority] was and the purpose of the survey, countering suggestions that they were from the Department of Social Security, the council, to do with the poll tax, etc. than they would expect to do in the course of their usual survey work, and this was a time consuming process. (Health Education Authority 1994: 12)

The interviewers also found that respondents wanted information from them.

> When terms were used that people did not understand . . . they often wanted the interviewer to explain what the term meant and give some information about it – examples of this would be 'well-woman clinic' and 'cervical smear test'. The interviewer therefore had to be prepared either to give an explanation (*interviewers are trained not to give any unauthorised information to assist a respondent in answering a question*) or to spend much time explaining why they could not give an explanation without, of course, giving offence. (Health Education Authority 1994: 12–13; my emphasis)

The Health Education Authority/MORI study was intended to establish attitudes to a range of health and lifestyle issues, including smoking, alcohol, sexual behaviour, exercise and fitness, stress and psycho-social health. It also explored barriers to achieving and maintaining a healthy lifestyle which may exist in terms of culture, lifestyle, religion, language and perceptions of health and disease. The survey comprised a structured interview and (for reasons of sensitivity) a self-completion questionnaire on sexual behaviour.

Difficulties in obtaining information may be related to the topic of the study. In my own study, it is possible that experiences of pregnancy and childbirth are sensitive subjects which women may have been unwilling to discuss. During the pilot stage of the HEA/MORI study the researchers had to abandon the self-completion section of the survey because of the high level of refusal by South Asian respondents. The researchers note that there were significant problems both with respondents being unable to read the questionnaire and with those who could read it having strong objections to its coverage. The questionnaire was most acceptable to young people, those educated in the UK and with good literacy skills in English. The pilot interviewers reported that in one tight-knit community word spread rapidly about the content of the self-completion questionnaire after they had spent one day interviewing there, so that on subsequent days they found a much higher rate of refusal. In addition, the researchers found other difficulties in obtaining information from respondents, partly to do with lack of privacy for the interview. Obtaining information on sensitive subjects, such as alcohol consumption and smoking, was difficult when it was not possible to conduct a confidential interview with a respondent.

It was impossible to get a private interview with the respondent in some house-holds . . . Interviewers found themselves having to ask questions on potentially sensitive or embarrassing issues when members of the respondent's family were present in the same room. Family members often wanted to become involved in the interview, husbands wanting to respond on behalf of wives, and vice versa, and also parents on behalf of children. The interviewers reported that some Asian women respondents, especially older ones, would not answer questions on gynae-cological matters, and the circumstances were not conducive to any discussions of problems with relationships or family members. (Health Education Authority 1994: 13)

The researchers had anticipated problems with the research; indeed, they expected to encounter difficulty with the sexual health module of the survey. However, they experienced a conflict between their assumptions and the expectations of those they were interviewing. A key example of this is the way in which Asian respondents saw the interview as something to involve the whole household, rather than as a private one-to-one event. This reflects differing notions of self, and the interrelationship between individuals in a family (how the character of one reflects upon the others), that are particu-larly important in some Asian families (a theme explored in detail in Shaw 1988). In addition, the difficulties interviewers had in applying the interview protocol (highlighted in italics on p. 69) demonstrate how the two groups were not working from the same set of assumptions about research.

In general, those who have been brought up and educated in Western society will have an understanding of research, and take it for granted that their views may be sought on a range of issues. People are familiar with sur-veys, either through participation or by reading results. Being asked for and expressing preferences and opinions is a part of everyday life. This was not the case in the HEA/MORI Health and Lifestyle study, nor in my own. In fact, it is surprising that so many informants will participate in highly sensi-tive interviews about their behaviour, experience and difficulties. Interviews are particularly problematic where there is a difference in expectations and experience between interviewee and interviewer. Unlike participant obser-vation, the interview depends upon the active participation of the research subject, who needs to share the general objectives of the researcher and to provide information or articulate views and opinions.

Research may be carried out for many reasons. Often, however, there is an underlying assumption that the research may 'make things better', and per-haps this is what motivates people to participate. Explicitly or implicitly, respondents perceive a stake in the outcome of the research, not necessarily for themselves but for others like them, or society as a whole. Some respon-dents may just like talking about themselves and their experiences. It is possible that participants in the HEA/MORI study, and the South Asian women in my study, did not share this 'commonsense' view of the purpose of research, were not used to talking about themselves in the way demanded by the interview process, and saw no purpose in participating in the studies.

third agreed. However, she was out when I called at a pre-arranged time and later claimed that she had not agreed to meet me. After that, word must have got round that I was asking these questions, and that women were not discussing it with me. None of the women I had contact with wanted to discuss these topics with me, and I had to abandon the attempt to collect data on their perspectives.

Discussion

The attempt to interview women had failed. Why was this? In planning this part of the fieldwork I drew on the experiences of other researchers, in particular the fieldwork experiences of Alison Shaw and Caroline Currer (see Currer 1983; Shaw 1988) and the written work of Cornwell (1984), Donovan (1986) and Homans (1980). I based my methods on those used by these researchers. In her ethnography on aspects of migration in a Pakistani community in Britain, Shaw describes what is essentially a snowball sampling technique (Shaw 1988). She obtained her introductions to the majority of those interviewed through a woman she met at the house of her Urdu teacher. Currer carried out a qualitative study, using an interview method, of attitudes to mental health among Pathan women in Bradford (Currer 1983), and received many accounts on sensitive subjects from these women. Apart from Currer's work, Hilary Homans's unpublished thesis on the experiences of women in pregnancy (Homans 1980) has good data on childbirth from South Asian informants. She based her thesis on a small number of depth interviews carried out through interpreters with women recruited from antenatal clinics. With the benefit of hindsight, this might well have been a more successful strategy than the failed attempt at a community-based approach.

Two other relevant pieces of work are Donovan's (1986) study of health, illness and health care in the lives of black people in London, and Cornwell's (1984) account of health and illness among white working-class people in East London. Both these authors adopted a case-study approach in their investigations of the experiences and attitudes of the groups under study.

Fontana and Frey (1994) summarize the key components necessary for successful fieldwork as follows: accessing the setting; understanding the language and culture of the respondents; presentation of self; locating an informant; establishing rapport. I analyse the study under these headings.

Accessing the setting and presentation of self

I successfully 'got in' to the group of South Asian women living in the city through becoming a volunteer teacher in the community. This then became my role in that setting. In some ways this was a good role: as described above, women were very keen to welcome me into their homes. However, in retrospect, there were difficulties. Explaining that I was carrying out a study as well as being a teacher was certainly hard. I am not sure that I ever satisfactorily explained my interest, or why I wanted to ask them questions.

Some health services researchers may think that it is unethical to access potential informants in this way. However, in ethnographic research, where settings for research have ranged from nude beaches (Douglas and Rasmussen 1977) and massage parlours (Warren and Rasmussen 1977) to studies of street gangs (Whyte 1981), dope smoking (Becker 1953) and neo-Nazis (Fielding 1982), researchers have adopted any role (sometimes covertly) that will 'get them in'. The ethics of ethnography are discussed in detail in Dingwall (1980a). Since the fieldwork was carried out (in 1988), the rules on gaining medical ethics committee approval for research with a medical component, even non-clinical research, have become much tighter. It is questionable, however, whether a medical ethics committee, whose main area of expertise is clinical trials and studies, would be able to give an informed view about the ethics of ethnographic fieldwork. A departmental ethics committee, made up of academic peers, would have been appropriate, although it did not exist. Instead, the research proposal was agreed by the supervisor of the work, the department in which I was based, and the funding body.

Locating a key informant

Early in the study I identified a key informant: a university-educated woman who was my Urdu teacher. Unfortunately, although she was helpful in explaining Muslim customs and culture, she was from a different social group from most of the women in the study (who were predominantly from rural areas and had received little formal education). Although married, she did not have children, which also made it more difficult for her to interpret and explain some of the issues around pregnancy and childbirth. I also suspected, but was unable to verify, that she also was an outsider in the community.

Establishing rapport

Currer (1983) points out that the relationship between respondent and interviewer is as important, if not more so, than the purpose of the research. It is certainly true that some individuals make better interviewers than others. However, my success in obtaining data from midwives suggests that I had the basic skills to interview successfully. It has been argued that the key to achieving a successful interview is to use 'feminist research methods', where the interviewer is prepared to invest his or her own personal identity in the relationship which leads to a relationship between interviewee and interviewer that is non-hierarchical (Oakley 1981). There are several problems with this: first, by the very nature of collecting data about another person the relationship becomes hierarchical. There are also differences between people – of class, education, race and culture – which cannot always be matched (even if this were deemed desirable) and which introduce elements of hierarchy.

Rhodes (1994) has argued, from her experience of a study of black foster parents, that interviewers who are of a different race from a respondent will collect different data than same race interviewers. She does not suggest that racial matching should always occur, but that, when interpreting data, it is necessary to be aware that interviews, in common with other encounters, are structured by racial and ethnic differences. My ethnicity may have been a barrier to success, although being an educated researcher may have been more of a barrier than being white. There are examples of white women researchers carrying out successful research among black women (for example, the studies of Shaw, Homans and Currer already mentioned). Conversely, there were problems experienced by the matched interviewers in the HEA/MORI study described in detail above.

Had I followed Homans's (1980) methodology, and recruited women through the hospital setting, I might have been more successful. Women could have been recruited in the medical study and then followed up at home. As I had been with women in labour this may well have overcome the problem of discussing a sensitive issue. Nevertheless, I consider that there are some fundamental (although not necessarily insurmountable) difficulties in using interviews to explore the perspectives of black and minority ethnic women. These stem from the fact that the notion of research and its method-ologies and philosophies are structured by culture: that is, that the concept of research has arisen from Western culture and thought.

Conclusion

This study has shown that there can be difficulties in obtaining consent for research on sensitive subjects such as pregnancy and childbirth. In particular, it suggests that formal interviews, where participation has to be actively agreed, whether structured or ethnographic, may not be an appropriate method for obtaining the views of ethnic minority people, particularly those who have not been brought up or educated in the West.

The writing of Edwin Ardener is helpful here. Almost a decade before the upsurge of publications on 'feminist methods' (see, for example, Roberts 1981), Ardener was engaged in a debate with other social anthropologists about the absence of women's accounts in ethnographic monographs. In his essay 'Belief and the problem of women' published in 1972 and the 1975 postscript (both reprinted in Ardener 1989), he describes the 'muting' of women in ethnography. 'Ethnographers report that women cannot be reached so easily as men: they giggle when young, snort when old, reject the question, laugh at the topic and the like' (Ardener 1989: 73). Although women are present in observational data,

> Women rarely speak in social anthropology except in any but that male sense . . . of merely uttering or giving tongue. It is the very inarticulateness of women that is the technical part of the problem they present . . . The brave failure (with rare exceptions) of even women anthropologists to surmount it really convincingly . . . suggests an obvious conclusion. Those trained in ethnography evidently have a bias towards the kinds of model that men are ready to provide (or to concur in)

rather than towards any that women might provide. If men appear 'articulate' compared with women, it is a case of like speaking to like. (Ardener 1989: 73–74)

Ardener suggests that Western models of the world, and ways of analysing and explaining them, are essentially 'male' and that women in his example are 'muted'. He elaborates:

We may speak of 'muted groups' and 'articulate groups' as being along [a] dimension. There are many kinds of muted groups. We would then go on to ask 'what is it that makes a group muted?' We then become aware that it is muted simply because it does not form part of the dominant communicative system of the society expressed as it must be through the dominant ideology. (Ardener 1989: 130)

My own experience reflects Ardener's thesis. The women in my study were muted although present in the observation. Interviews, in particular, use the dominant communicative system. The ways of constructing the world that we take for granted, and the methods of exploring those constructs by asking for views and opinions from respondents, are not neutral but part of a particular social and cultural orientation. Data collection needs to be highly sensitive to differences, not just in the way questions are asked or topics raised, but also in the choice of method itself. Methods are needed that recognize the involvement of an individual with his or her extended family or community, and which allow perspectives to be uncovered gradually. Group interviews, perhaps based on naturally occurring groups, and participant observation may be more successful than one-to-one depth interviews. There is a continuing need to develop culturally sensitive approaches.

Acknowledgement

The research discussed in this chapter was funded through a studentship award from the Economic and Social Research Council.

6

Contextualizing Texts: Studying Organizational Texts

Gale Miller

This chapter discusses how texts may be analysed as aspects of life in contemporary Western institutions. It focuses on public and private institutions that provide services to the public, such as hospitals, schools, nursing homes, police departments, courts, clinics and social welfare agencies. Texts are pervasive in these human service and social control institutions. They include the manuals that institutional officials consult in doing their work, case files that describe the officials' decisions and actions, statistical reports that evaluate the success of institutional programmes, the literature provided to members of the public about the purposes and operation of institutions, bodily images used by physicians in diagnosing disease, and video-recordings that institutional officials use to instruct others about their procedures and practices.

I argue that qualitative researchers are uniquely positioned to study these texts by analysing the practical social contexts of everyday life within which they are constructed and used. Texts are one aspect of the sense-making activities through which we construct, sustain, contest and change our senses of social reality. They are socially constructed realities that warrant study in their own right, and in the manner of Cicourel and Kitsuse's (1963), Garfinkel's (1967), Kitsuse and Cicourel's (1963), Sudnow's (1965, 1967) and Zimmerman's (1969) early, ground-breaking studies in this area. While concerned with different institutions and texts, each of these studies displays how qualitative research can advance sociological understanding of the workings of contemporary institutions by combining an empirical focus with an analytical attitude.

I develop these themes in this chapter by focusing on how institutional texts are inextricably linked to the social contexts in which they are produced. I treat the contexts as interpretive domains (Miller and Holstein 1995, 1996) which structure, but do not determine, how institutional texts are assembled and interpreted. The domains consist of the 'local knowledge' (Garfinkel 1967; Geertz 1983; Gubrium 1989) that setting members use in making sense of their experiences. I begin by considering some general issues associated with institutional texts and their contexts, and then discuss how various qualitative methods might be used to study them.

Contextualizing institutional texts

In her seminal analysis of textually mediated realities, Smith (1984) analyses institutional texts as crystallizations of moments in time and space. Texts become crystallized when we treat them as authoritative representations of stable, objective realities. Texts might be said to 'encourage' such treatment because they are made up of written words, numbers and visual images that objectify the events, objects or issues that they purport to represent. The words, numbers and images 'freeze' the ongoing events of life, making it possible for us to return to them from time to time in order to 'verify' our remembrances of, and others' claims about, them. When we treat them in these ways, we transform institutional texts into authoritative and decontextualized institutional realities to which we and/or others might be held accountable.

To be sure, different kinds of institutional texts crystallize time and space in different ways. Statistical reports, for example, are unlikely to include extensive discussions of statisticians' interpretive practices in constructing their statistics. The processes through which statistical realities are created are likely to be seen as irrelevant and/or uninteresting to both those who assemble and read these reports. Video- and audio-recordings of social interactions, on the other hand, provide viewers and listeners with more information about reality-creating processes, but aspects of context are still left out. The recordings do not, for example, capture the full range of activities that surround the recorded interactions, including how they are related to other features of institutional settings that are not discussed in the recorded interactions. Indeed, the significance of these contextual factors is suggested by institutional officials' practice of explaining (providing contexts for) recordings prior to playing them for others.

We crystallize institutional texts by glossing over the various contingencies and other contextual factors associated with the texts' production and use in concrete institutional settings. For example, we crystallize institutional texts when we ask 'what does this number, report or image mean for the issues at hand', and not 'how did it come to be in the first place?' Indeed, even if we ask the latter question, our answer is, at best, an educated guess since we weren't present to observe the construction of the text, and often have limited knowledge about the setting in which it was created. We have, in other words, no sense of what Smith (1984) calls the 'local histories' of the texts.

Qualitative research and analysis can counter these tendencies to crystallize institutional texts by locating them within the institutional settings in which they are constructed, interpreted and used. Such research emphasizes the spatial, temporal and practical contingencies associated with the texts. These contingencies might be analysed as aspects of the texts' local histories, although they implicate many aspects of institutional actors' local knowledge about institutional texts and settings. For example, the local knowledge that institutional actors draw upon may also include understandings of how the texts under construction might be interpreted and used in other settings (Raffel 1979).

Emerson (1991) and Emerson and Paley (1992) analyse these aspects of institutional actors' local knowledge as decision-making horizons that consist of the various contextual factors that decision-makers may take into account in organizing and responding to practical issues. They further analyse the horizons as involving retrospective and prospective aspects. The former involve the institutional actors' knowledge about 'where, why, and how a case has come to its present point' (Emerson and Paley 1992: 235–236), and the latter involve their assessments of the probable future (or downstream) consequences of available courses of action. Institutional actors, then, construct and interpret institutional texts by assessing, and taking account of, a variety of local considerations about the present, past and future in making decisions and constructing texts.

Indeed, their temporal and related considerations sometimes result in complicated circumstances that are not easily explainable to those who are unfamiliar with the settings in which decisions and texts are made. Krueger (1978), for example, describes a circumstance in which a prosecuting attorney was told by his superiors to get at least one felony conviction against members of a student group who were arrested for a disturbance at the local university. The prosecutor did so by 'overfiling' charges against the students: in one case, charging a student whom the police said had threatened them with a broken soda bottle with assault with a deadly weapon.

The charge was 'overfiled' because, within the context of the prosecutor's office, these circumstances were usually treated as unlikely to result in a felony conviction in court, a risk that the prosecutor was willing to take in light of the expressed desires of his superiors. The charges were reduced, however, when another prosecutor happened upon the complaint form and, assuming that the charges were being made by an inexperienced prosecutor, changed them to express typical practices in the office. The second prosecutor's actions were sensible and warranted given his local knowledge about the circumstances that the staff usually treated as necessary to sustain a charge of assault with a deadly weapon. Viewed from this standpoint, the charges and circumstances did not fit, and were likely to result in the acquittal of the defendant, the assumed undesired downstream consequence of 'overfiling' charges. Of course, what the second prosecutor was not taking into account was the unique, local circumstances associated with the first prosecutor's decision to 'overfile', an omission that was later corrected when the complaint against the student was rewritten to charge him with assault with a deadly weapon.

This incident illustrates another important aspect of the relationship between institutional texts and contexts. That is, while the interpretive resources provided by institutional settings do not determine the meanings assigned to aspects of everyday life by setting members, the settings might be described as 'encouraging', 'privileging' or 'preferring' some interpretations over others. One way in which institutional settings privilege some meanings is by providing members with categories and procedures for classifying events, issues and people, such as those provided on the standardized forms that institutional actors are often required to maintain. As Sanders (1977) notes in regard to police detectives, these forms organize the detectives' orientations to, and perceptions of, possible crime scenes by asking them to take account of predetermined issues and questions.

But institutional settings involve more than standardized forms and categories. Institutional actors must decide which of the available categories apply to the circumstances at hand, and this decision may involve taking account of a variety of contextual factors, including institutional actors' local knowledge about how the matters at hand are usually handled. In Krueger's (1978) study, for example, the second prosecutor's decision to reduce the charges against the student displayed a typical (thus preferred) interpretation of the circumstances described in the complaint. The extent to which it was preferred is perhaps best understood when we consider the micropolitical significance of the second prosecutor's actions which involved overriding a colleague's decision without prior consultation with the colleague. Indeed, the second prosecutor might be said to have acted on the authority of local knowledge and typical practice in changing the complaint form.

It is important to emphasize, however, that while institutional settings may be said to provide their members with resources for constructing meanings, they do not determine the meanings constructed under their auspices. Rather, meanings are constructed and sometimes contested within the particular interpretive domains and decision-making horizons of each situation. Thus, it is possible for institutional actors to construct and justify meanings that might be called 'dis-preferred'. It should also be noted that the textual and other meanings constructed by institutional actors may vary across different institutional settings as they deal with different practical issues and interests.

Consider, for example, Miller's (1991) study of everyday life in a work incentive program (WIN) which was intended to help persons receiving public financial assistance find jobs and become economically independent. In dealing with clients, the staff cited statistics about the high number of WIN clients who found jobs each month (client-hires), stating that the statistics proved that clients who really wanted jobs could find them and that the WIN staff were experts at helping clients find jobs. Indeed, when clients complained that they could not find jobs because none were available, staff members responded by asking 'where do the numbers come from, then, if people aren't getting jobs?'

The staff's practical interests in these statistics were different, however, when high-level WIN officials visited the office to negotiate higher future performance goals for the local staff, including new client-hire goals. Local staff oriented to these meetings as contests in which they tried to keep the new performance goals as low as possible. One part of their negotiating strategy involved casting statistics on past client-hire rates as irrelevant to the issues at hand. They did so by arguing that the statistics did not reflect the fact that staff members were already working at maximum capacity. Indeed, they argued that raising the staff's performance expectations would result in a decline in staff morale which would actually reduce their effectiveness in helping clients get jobs. Local staff members also discounted the statistics by emphasizing that projected changes in WIN and the area economy would make it impossible for them to continue to perform at current levels.

While WIN staff members' differing orientations to the same statistics in these settings might be interpreted as signs of hypocrisy or disingenuousness, Miller (1991) analyses them as aspects of the differing, micropolitical organization of the settings. The latter view contextualizes the staff members' actions by treating them as embedded in, and responsive to, their institutional contexts. The practical significance of the statistics, then, changed because staff members' practical interests, social positions, use of available interpretive resources and accountability to others were different in these very different interpretive domains.

Observing texts and contexts

An intriguing aspect of institutional texts is their relationship to the institutional practices and worlds on which they report. Indeed, they are often constructed within the very settings about which they report. Observational methods are especially appropriate for studying text construction and use in institutional settings, then, because they immerse researchers in the settings in which the texts are constructed and used. The immersion not only makes it possible for the researchers to see and analyse the interrelations between institutional texts and contexts, but also to appreciate the practical and sociological significance of the interrelations.

Consider, for example, Gubrium and Buckholdt's (1979) study of how nursing-home staff evaluated the effectiveness of a bowel-training programme. The evaluation consisted of counting when and how patients had bowel movements. The programme was assessed as effective for those patients who increased their use of the toilet or bed pan, and ineffective for those who persisted in soiling their beds. At first glance, this evaluation procedure is a simple and straightforward counting operation. Its complexities became apparent, however, when one of the researchers observed an exchange between a nurse and nurse's aide about the circumstances surrounding a patient's (Helen's) soiled bed. The nurse initially reacted to the soiled bed as a sign that the bowel-training programme was not helping Helen, but the aide offered an alternative understanding that justified not counting the episode as either successful or unsuccessful. The aide explained that Helen

> knows damn well what she's doin'. She just shit everywhere because I was busy helping Stella [another patient] down the hall and you know how she hates Stella. Well . . . she [Helen] just had to wait a little longer until I could finish. She didn't like that, of course. So she got mad and just BMed all over the place.

This incident is instructive for at least four reasons. First, it displays the usefulness of qualitative (particularly observational) research for studying institutional texts as mundane aspects of ongoing institutional life. A review of the nursing-home's records would provide no evidence of this incident or of the interpretive work done by the nurse's aide in helping to construct the records. Rather, the records would provide us with a set of numbers about Helen's and other patients' responses to the bowel-training programme. The numbers might be augmented with narratives that assessed the meaning of the numbers for patients and staff, but it is very unlikely that the assessments would consider the practical contexts in which the counting took place. For example, the narratives are unlikely to discuss how the nurse's aides who did the counting controlled for 'cheating' by patients which is, in effect, the rationale used by the aide in not counting Helen's soiling of her bed.

The incident also illustrates the staff's orientation to the bowel-training programme as a practical activity concerned with producing information that they might use in serving and managing their patients. In this and other institutional contexts, assessing patients' motives is relevant because patients can negatively affect institutional projects for many reasons that, from the staff's standpoint, are unrelated to the effectiveness of the programmes being evaluated. The aide's decision not to count Helen's soiling of her bed, then, was reasonable and responsible under the circumstances. Indeed, through her account of the incident, the aide displays her accountability to these – local – standards of reasonableness and responsibility.

Thirdly, the aide's actions illustrate how text production in institutions is micropolitically organized. Her decision not to count the bed-soiling incident (but to count other times when Helen moved her bowels) was related to her local knowledge about the purposes of the programme and Helen's relationship with Stella. As the aide states, her own behaviour was implicated in the politics of the bed-soiling incident because Helen was reacting to the aide's helping Stella. Helen's actions might even be understood as a 'power play' intended to punish the nurse's aide for temporarily favouring Stella over Helen. Thus, the micropolitics of text production and use in institutional settings may involve assessments of setting members' motives as politically oriented and meaningful.

Finally, this study illustrates how immersion in institutional settings may provide researchers with opportunities to observe how texts are routinely produced as institutional actors go about their typical activities. Of course, these opportunities are unlikely to be meaningful to the observers unless they have developed a sensitivity to the local and sociological significance of institutional actors' construction of texts. One aspect of this sensitivity is developing an appreciation of the variety of ways in which institutional actors may assemble and use the interpretive resources available in settings to construct differing decision-making horizons and to assign different, but still contextually defensible, meanings to texts.

As the following example taken from Roth's (1963) observational studies of tuberculosis sanatoriums suggests, what is often explained as changing one's mind might also be understood as the reassembling of available interpretive resources to construct new decision-making horizons and textual meanings. The interaction occurred in a meeting about the future treatment of patients, and much of it focused on the interpretation of the patients' X-rays and other medical texts.

> When a medical resident presented a patient as having been in the hospital for two years, a consultant promptly announced: 'That's a long time; I think we should try to get her out of here.' One of the nurses pointed out that the resident had made a slight mistake on the matter of length of hospitalization. The patient had been first admitted about two years ago, but had been discharged after about a year, had spent half a year on the outside, and had then been readmitted. Her second admission had involved slightly less than a six months' stay in the hospital. The consultant replied: 'I'd hate to let her go too soon this time.' This doctor then argued in favor of holding the patient for at least another conference three months later. All this time the physician was looking at exactly the same set of X-rays and was considering the same information concerning bacteriological tests and other diagnostic procedures. (Roth 1963: 28)

Perhaps the most obvious conclusion to be drawn from this incident is that the meanings of institutional texts are always potentially unstable, because they are always open to reinterpretation based on new information or changes in institutional actors' orientations to them. While the X-ray images of the patient's chest and numbers on the bacteriological tests did not change, their practical relevance for the issue at hand changed dramatically as the above interaction proceeded. The meaning of the texts, then, is to be found in observing and analysing how they are interpreted and used in institutional contexts.

This incident also illustrates the usefulness of analysing institutional settings as interpretive domains that provide their members with resources for making sense of practical issues, but do not determine how the members will assemble and use them in any particular situation. Roth (1963) states that staff often voiced concern about the length of patients' stays in the sanatoriums in these meetings, and certainly temporal concerns were implicated in their assessments of the above patient's circumstances. But it is also important to notice that two different concerns for time were available in this interpretive domain, as a problem of keeping the patient in the sanatorium too long and of not keeping her long enough. The first was used to justify releasing the patient as soon as possible, and the second to justify not making the same mistake again.

The practical work of the staff participating in this meeting, then, might be understood as using these and other interpretive resources provided by the setting to assemble a decision-making horizon within which to interpret the patient's circumstances (including her medical texts) and formulate a professionally defensible response to them. The actual construction of particular decision-making horizons is situationally variable and, as we have seen, potentially subject to later reconsideration and change. Thus, institutional settings may be analysed as preferring or privileging some meanings over others, but the practical assignment of meanings to texts is an interpretive, and often an interactional, accomplishment of setting members.

A third implication that may be drawn from Roth's (1963) studies involves the micropolitical significance of institutional texts within decision-making settings. The X-ray images and other medical texts were only one of several interpretive resources available to sanatorium staff in negotiating and deciding patients' future treatments. While relevant to the deliberations, sanatorium staff in the above interaction accorded less significance to these texts than to other practical considerations, particularly to temporal issues. Other institutional settings, however, involve different orientations to the significance of textual versus non-textual depictions of social reality. Micropolitically sensitive observations of everyday institutional life, then, must also consider the relationship between the textual and non-textual interpretive resources provided by settings.

A recent example of this type of analysis is Anspach's (1987, 1993) studies of prognostic meetings in two hospital-based neonatal units. The meetings involved physicians who had little direct contact with the infants under discussion, and nurses who had direct, daily contact with them. One part of the prognostic meetings involved considering various medical texts which Anspach analyses as technological cues, and which both the physicians and nurses treated as relevant to their deliberations. They disagreed, however, on the nurses' direct experiences with the infants on the ward: what Anspach calls social cues about the infants' levels of well-being. The nurses sometimes argued that social cues should be considered along with technological cues, whereas the physicians usually argued for an exclusive reliance on technological cues in assessing infants' physical condition and future possibilities.[1]

A major issue of conflict between the physicians and nurses, then, involved their orientations to these different – but simultaneously available – sources of knowledge. Anspach analyses how these conflicts were usually resolved by treating technological cues as more reliable than the social cues reported by the nurses. This tendency might be understood by considering the social positions of physicians and nurses in these settings: the physicians occupied a more central decision-making role than the nurses. It is also related to the nurses' orientation to technological cues as always relevant to the meetings. That is, their arguments acknowledged the preference for technological cues in this setting (interpretive domain), even as they asked for other factors to be considered.

Anspach's insights into the micropolitical organization of these settings and interactions were unlikely to be reported in the infants' case records, however. Rather, the records were likely to report that the physicians' and nurses' deliberations involved serious consideration of all relevant sources of information about the infants. Indeed, these claims might be made about meetings in which technological cues were treated as the only authoritative source of information about the infants, and in the less common meetings in which social cues were given priority. The issue here is not that the physicians and/or nurses were likely to make false statements in the infants' records, but that institutional texts constructed to explain past decisions inevitably glossed over the openness and complexity of the decision-making process. Once a decision has been made, much of the decision-making process becomes irrelevant to the task at hand which involves constructing texts that others are likely to find reasonable and defensible.

Hence the importance of observational methods and constructionist strategies in collecting and analysing data about institutional texts. These approaches provide researchers with the opportunities and analytical resources for appreciating the practical and sociological significance of the mundane aspects of decision-making in institutional settings, and how texts may be implicated in the processes.

Reconstructing local histories

Qualitative researchers usually study institutional settings that are ongoing and may have lengthy histories of their own. Researchers tap into the settings at particular times in their development, and often after many of the institutional texts that they analyse have been constructed. While these researchers may observe first-hand how the texts are subsequently used and interpreted by institutional actors, they may also wish to consider the circumstances associated with the initial production of the texts. As we have already seen, however, trying to discern these circumstances from a conventional reading of the texts, or by asking institutional actors about the circumstances, are strategies fraught with problems.

An alternative strategy involves researcher immersion in similar and related settings to those in which the texts were initially produced, and the development of an analytical stance that allows the researcher to 'see' the kinds of practical and sociologically significant factors that are likely to have been associated with the construction of the texts at issue. The researchers' involvement in the setting, and perspective on it, will provide him or her with a sense of the interpretive domain in which the texts were originally constructed, including a sense of the decision-making horizons associated with their construction. The informed observer, then, may use this knowledge to reconstruct and analyse the relationship between the institutional texts and their contexts to inform readers better about the practical, micropolitical significance of the texts within the institutional world under study.

An important example of how observational research may be used to this end is Loseke's (1992) acclaimed study of everyday life in a shelter for battered women. Much of the study analyses entries routinely made by shelter workers in the shelter's logbook. The entries were intended for other shelter workers only. The shelter staff treated the entries as accurate and objective descriptions of many of the major events of their work days, and used them to keep other shelter workers informed about their activities and problems that might affect others in the shelter. In allowing Loseke to examine the logbook, the workers stated that it 'was the best information available about this place. To them, the log showed what shelter work was *really* like' (Loseke 1992: 168–169).

One of the shelter workers' major responsibilities involved assessing the claims made by women seeking admission to the shelter. The workers explained that the assessments were necessary because of the limited resources of the shelter, and because the severity of petitioning women's circumstances varied. The variation was significant for the shelter workers because, as Loseke shows, the workers reserved admission for those women whom they assessed as 'truly' battered. While this category shifted as the shelter's resources became more or less available, the workers generally assessed women who were without alternative (financial and social) resources, and whose behaviour could not be construed as contributing to their battering (such as alcoholism) as the most appropriate candidates for admission.

While she did not observe the writing of most of the logbook entries or the circumstances that they described, Loseke draws on her local knowledge of the shelter (gleaned from interviews with shelter staff, observations of everyday life in the shelter, and involvement as a shelter worker) to analyse how shelter workers attended to these concerns in making the logbook entries. Specifically, Loseke analyses how the workers used the entries to explain and justify decisions to grant some women's requests for admission to the shelter, and reject others. Consider, for example, the following entry which reports on a worker's decision to deny a petitioner's request. First, notice the brevity of the entry. The worker describes the woman's situation and her decision in two sentences. Also, notice that the entry includes two pieces of information that might be relevant to other shelter workers' questions about the entry and the worker's decision to deny the petitioner's request. That is, the woman had housing (at least for the time being) and the shelter was full at the time of the request.

> Woman called, staying in motel and can't afford it for too much longer. Told her we were full and suggested [another shelter]. (Loseke 1992: 85)

We may contrast this entry with the following one which explains and justifies a worker's decision to grant a petitioner's (Susan's) request for admission to the shelter. Not only is the entry longer and more detailed, but the shelter worker offers several reasons for admitting Susan that are absent from the above entry. Specifically, the worker stresses that Susan badly needs shelter, has four children, is being stalked by her husband, has been battered, is frightened, and needs shelter until she can relocate herself and her children. With the exception of having temporary shelter, we do not know if any of Susan's circumstances were shared with the above petitioner. Finally, notice that this entry states that the shelter worker consulted with another staff member, and they agreed that Susan should be admitted to the shelter.

> Susan called. Needs shelter badly, has four children, husband searching for her. She's been battered and is frightened – requires shelter till she can relocate. Called [another worker] and we think we should pick her up. (Loseke 1992: 85)

Loseke's analysis (and my use of it) should not be construed as suggesting that the shelter workers treated petitioners' requests capriciously. The issue is not whether the workers acted as responsible professionals, but how they used logbook entries to display their professionalism for others who might – downstream – raise questions about their decisions. But these displays of professionalism are not self-evident in the logbook entries which, as we have seen, provide little direct information about the shelter workers' concerns in deciding which of the women's requests should be granted. Understanding the local significance of the entries, including how they anticipated possible downstream issues, requires the type of local knowledge that Loseke gained from her immersion in the setting, even though she did not observe how each entry was constructed.

It should also be noted, however, that Loseke's study is partly exemplary because she does not 'over-analyse' the logbook entries by claiming local knowledge that she does not have. Rather, she develops her textual analysis by first discussing the various practical considerations, concerns and contingencies associated with the shelter workers' typical activities and relationships. These were matters about which Loseke had first-hand knowledge based on her extensive observations of daily life in the shelter. She then discusses how these contextual factors may be seen in the logbook entries. In sum, Loseke's analysis illustrates how a disciplined reconstruction of these institutional texts may be used to enrich observational studies of institutional worlds.

Conversation analysis and institutional texts

Conversation analysis involves fine-grained analysis of the details of talk in social interaction, particularly the mundane, but often complex, ways in which social interactions are organized as turn-taking sequences (Atkinson and Heritage 1984; Boden and Zimmerman 1991; Button and Lee, 1987; Sacks et al. 1974). Conversation analysts study, for example, how interactants signal to others that they are ending their turn at talk or that they wish to talk, select and change the topics of discussion, and display to others that they are properly attentive to, and involved in, the interaction. Analysing these issues involves paying close attention to features of social interaction that are often missed or glossed over by even the most careful observers of institutional settings who have only one opportunity to observe each social interaction. By recording social interactions and making transcripts of them, conversation analysts may observe a single social interaction many times, scrutinizing its sociologically significant features.

In their studies of institutional settings, for example, conversation analysts show how setting members position themselves by taking different roles and responsibilities in their interactions (Drew and Heritage 1992; Heritage n.d.). Usually, institutional officials assume the role of setting organizer by directing the content and flow of the interactions. They may do so by dominating the talk in a setting (as in a speech or lecture), or by asking questions that specify to others the types of information that are relevant to the settings (as in legal interrogations, medical interviews and oral examinations in school). Other setting members, often clients and members of the public, may collaborate in these interactions by responding in ways that might be seen as appropriate. Whether a response is appropriate or not is an interactional matter that is determined by others' immediate responses to it and future developments in the interaction.

A major way in which conversation analysis may contribute to the study of institutional texts is by analysing the often subtle ways in which the texts are interactionally constructed, interpreted and used by members of institutional settings, including clients and members of the public. Social settings are social constructions for conversation analysts, then, because interactants literally co-produce the social conditions that they take into account in organizing their actions in situations. They do so by drawing upon their knowledge (including local knowledge) about the organization of social settings and through talk in social interaction.

Consider, for example, Marlaire's (1990, 1992) and Marlaire and Maynard's (1990) studies of how test-givers are implicated in the testing processes that they guide. The testing practices at issue were intended to measure children's cognitive skills by asking the children to respond to a variety of questions asked by clinicians. The children's answers were reported as numerical scores which might be compared and contrasted with other scores that are assumed to have been produced under the same social circumstances. For example, one type of question asked that the children recognize and elaborate on word-association patterns, such as 'small is to large as happy is to . . . ?' The clinicians recorded whether the children's responses were appropriate or not, thus producing institutional texts that they and others might consult in the future in assessing the children's levels of cognitive development.

Marlaire's (1990, 1992) and Marlaire and Maynard's (1990) analyses show that the tests involved more than questions and answers because the clinicians also responded to the children's answers in a variety of verbal and non-verbal ways. Sometimes, for example, the clinicians responded to children's 'correct' responses by saying 'good' and to 'incorrect' responses with 'okay' or by re-asking the question. As the following exchange shows, the clinicians also sometimes responded to the children's answers by asking them to specify their answers further, suggesting that the answers already given by the children were unclear or incomplete. Indeed, notice that in line 10 the clinician (CL) formulates a 'complete answer' for the child (CH) by asking if his answer is 'Watch TV?' Also, notice lines 4 and 12 where the clinician signals to the child that she has accepted an answer and is moving to a new topic. She does so in line 4 by stating 'Okay', and in line 12 by beginning her turn with 'And uh—oka:ay.'

1   CL: Oka:ay. How bout (0.3) What do you
2   do when you see your HANDS are dirty?
3   CH: You wash 'em.
4   CL: Okay – what do you do when you go to a room that is dark?

5 CH: Watts.
6 CL: What?
7 CH: Watch.
8 CL: Watch?
9 CH: TV
10 CL: Watch TV?
11 CH: Yah.
12 CL: And uh—oka:ay. What do you do when you see your SHOE is untied. (Marlaire
      1990: 251)

While the clinician's management of this interaction might be faulted by some observers, Marlaire (1990) offers a different understanding of this and the other testing sequences that she analyses. Marlaire concludes that test-givers are inevitably implicated in testing situations and relationships, thus reports of test scores should be understood as co-produced by test-givers and test-takers. The issue here is not the bias of the testing procedure or test-givers' incompetence, but the many local contingencies that test-givers take into account in managing testing situations, not the least of which are getting the children to pay serious attention to their questions and clarifying answers that the test-givers find to be ambiguous. Yet, these locally managed contingencies are not discussed in texts that report the outcomes of the testing process. Only decontextualized test scores are reported.

Attending to these contingencies is one of the test-givers' professional responsibilities in testing situations. Indeed, not attending to them might be treated as grounds for accusing test-givers of acting incompetently or in biased ways. In the above exchange, for example, the clinician might have been accused of being professionally lax if she had not asked the child to clarify his answers about 'what do you do when you go to a room that is dark?' Treating test results as co-produced, then, is one way of reminding the readers of institutional texts that the texts have local histories that are unlikely to be evident from a typical reading of their contents, while not impugning the professionalism of test-givers.

In sum, conversation analysis is a distinctive approach to analysing institutional texts. It involves both distinctive data (transcripts of audio- and video-recordings of social interactions) and a unique perspective for analysing the data. Although it is seldom done, research on institutional texts and settings might combine both conversation analytic and observational methods. The combination enriches both types of analysis by simultaneously considering the general contextual factors usually emphasized in observational research and the conversational organization of settings on which conversation analytic studies focus (Miller 1997). Had Roth (1963) or Anspach (1987, 1993) included conversation analytic components in their studies, for example, they could have also analysed how the physicians and nurses used the interactional resources available in evaluation and prognostic meetings to privilege, discount and negotiate the relevance of institutional texts for the issues at hand.

Conclusion

I conclude by discussing how the strategies presented in this chapter might be extended to consider some related issues involving method, focus and analysis. The first issue involves my omission of interviewing methods, perhaps the most frequently used approach to qualitative research. My concerns about this approach are implicit in much of the prior discussion. They involve the ways in which institutional actors descriptively reassemble the circumstances of text construction after the fact, thereby producing highly structured and linear accounts of processes that observers report to be much more open, contingent and fluid. This is not to say that interviewing strategies should always be avoided, but to suggest that, where possible, they should be combined with observational and/or conversation analytic methods. When qualitative researchers exclusively rely on interviews, they should proceed with care and with great sensitivity to the analytical issues discussed here.

The second issue involves the relationship between the texts produced and used within institutions, and the public arenas within which related social issues are debated and public policies are constructed. The issue might be asked as a question about how the micro- and macropolitics of institutional texts are related. At minimum, institutional texts may be implicated in public debates as sources of 'factual' information about the issues in debate or as reports on institutional actors' success in fulfilling the aims of the public policies that they are required to implement. Both orientations to institutional texts involve treating them as decontextualized statements of fact.

Thus, strategic qualitative research which contextualizes institutional texts may contribute to public policy debates by describing the local circumstances associated with the construction of the texts under discussion, including the text constructors' 'propagandistic' (Altheide and Johnson 1980) interests in, and uses of, the texts. Qualitative researchers might also follow Loseke's (1992) lead in analysing how institutional actors' construction, interpretation and use of institutional texts orient to, and manage, differences in the assumptions of public policies and debates, on the one hand, and their practical experience with the problems, on the other.

Qualitative sociologists' primary contribution to these debates is not to discredit institutional texts by casting them as without any value. Rather, it is to provide public officials and other citizens with new understandings of the information found in institutional texts. These understandings focus on the interactional, interpretive and contextual factors involved in the construction of institutionally generated information (Holstein and Staples 1992; Sanders 1977). The information is still informative and useful, but in new ways and for new reasons. At the very least, it tells us a great deal about the cultures and operations of contemporary institutions.

The final and related issue involves the ways in which the construction and use of institutional texts are aspects of the 'relations of ruling' (Smith 1990) through which we participate in the management of our lives and opportunities. These relations include a variety of forms of institutional participation (ranging from high-level policy-making to being a 'cooperative' client) and involve the abstract categories and symbols of institutional and other texts as much as face-to-face encounters between institutional superiors and subordinates. Contextualizing studies of institutional texts contribute to sociological understanding of these relations by countering the orientations to texts that objectify and justify relations of ruling, analysing how the relations are micropolitically organized, and displaying the contributions made by diverse institutional actors to the maintenance of such relations. Demystifying institutional texts is one way of demystifying institutional authority.

Acknowledgements

I would like to thank Robert Dingwall and K. Neil Jenkings for their helpful comments on a prior draft of this chapter.

Note

1 Dingwall et al. (1983) offer a complementary analysis of the institutional processing of child abuse and neglect cases in Great Britain. Here, the competing knowledge sources were clinical evidence constructed through clinical tests and social evidence gleaned from investigations of the children's social environments. Unlike the prognostic meetings studied by Anspach (1987, 1993), however, clinical evidence was not privileged in the deliberations about child abuse and neglect.

7

Using Computers in Strategic Qualitative Research

Tom Durkin

Much of this book focuses on strategic decisions made early in research projects. Identifying troubles and puzzles, framing salient questions, choosing methods and sampling frames, interview questions and schedules – these are all crucial issues. I use an American Bar Foundation qualitative project to describe a seemingly more pedestrian process, that of using computerized qualitative data analysis (QDA) programs to help analyse data. These QDAs may seem pedestrian, but they have important benefits for analysing data and crafting representations of the social world.

First, a caveat and a reassurance. QDA programs neither promise nor threaten to think. QDAs cannot theorize, nor do they automatically create complex data codes. What they can do is improve our relationship to data. Used properly, QDAs can help increase reliability and validity (Silverman 1993: 146–155) by reminding us of data and their contexts at all stages of research.

QDA programs can both fit and expand your methodological preferences. They make it much easier to do a more thorough job on important but time-consuming tasks – constructing, refining and relating analytical categories, and coding and retrieving data (Hammersley and Atkinson 1995: 195–198). They keep better track of data. By doing so, QDAs help us develop and test interview questions and schedules, test theories, find patterns of action, preserve actors' rhetoric and actions, analyse our own rhetoric and actions (Holstein and Gubrium 1995), and provide access to recently developed tools like Boolean (using and/or/not) multiple-coded data retrievals. By managing your data, QDAs can enhance team research, case and comparative studies, theory-building and testing, content or policy analyses, or any combination of these tasks.

A major goal of qualitative research is to use data to document how actors construct, and are constructed by, interaction in context. QDAs are helpful whenever data are important. We have all sat through frustrating conference presentations where researchers believed (or worse, proved) that data were irrelevant to their conclusions. QDAs have the ability greatly to improve parts of qualitative research – fortunately, the most tedious parts. QDAs can make research easier and better. QDA programs constantly remind us of data contents and contexts. QDAs contribute an ability to do the same things we now do, but more quickly and completely. They promise an ability to emphasize and analyse data in new ways.

By keeping you close to data, QDA programs make it easier to ground data in context, and to test theory. For Charmaz (1983: 114) these two are inextricably linked in qualitative analysis. She argued that fully attending to data at all stages makes it possible to test relationships between data and descriptions, representations and theories. Pure induction is probably impossible, and pure deduction – where possible – is too often sterile. What Ragin (1994: 47) called 'retroduction' and Richards and Richards (1994: 449) called 'data-theory bootstrapping' stress constant, ongoing testing of theory with data, and data with theory. Emerson (1983: 94) stressed that in qualitative research, analysis occurs at the same time as data collection and coding. The interactive nature of QDA programs make this possible to an unprecedented extent.

Generally, QDA programs quickly and accurately retrieve coded data, enabling researchers continually to refine their work. There are different types of programs designed for different methodologies and coding methods. Simple indexing programs search for key words without any coding required. Most programs are designed to allow coding and retrieval of researcher-defined 'data chunks', or coded segments. Some programs are designed for a particular theoretical approach, like network or comparative case analysis. Some presentation programs are designed for mapping out ideas and data, creating flow charts, and brainstorming. More sophisticated programs allow you to construct theoretical trees, helping explore patterns and relationships between concepts. QDA programs allow us to apply types of analyses (even quantitative!) that until now had been literally inconceivable with text, conversational and interview data.

An analogy makes the benefits more clear. Quantitative programs revolutionized that research by making it possible to crunch more numbers, more accurately, more quickly, and in more ways.[1] Now, fewer research methods students have to memorize formulas or calculate gammas by hand (I was not so lucky, but my students are). Much of the tedious, boring, mistake-prone data manipulation has been removed. This makes it possible to spend more time investigating the meaning of their data.[2]

In a similar way, QDA programs improve our work by removing drudgery in managing qualitative data. Copying, highlighting, cross-referencing, cutting and pasting transcripts and field notes, covering floors with index cards, making multiple copies, sorting and resorting card piles, and finding misplaced cards have never been the highlights of qualitative research. It makes at least as much sense for us to use qualitative programs for tedious tasks as it does for those people down the hall to stop hand-calculating gammas. After all, emphasizing the mundane, average everydayness of life should not require that our own lives become more average every day.

The American Bar Foundation project

The choice to use a QDA is not an easy one, but it is getting much easier. Using a QDA does change how we do research, and potentially how we think about methods (Coffey et al. 1996). It requires choices of computer software and hardware that many of us have never had to make. It requires a little extra effort to keep current with changes in computing. However, these efforts pay off. With the ongoing development of QDAs, it is harder to make an inappropriate software choice. Old habits die hard, however, and decisions to use these tools are often driven by opportunities and resources not always under a researcher's control.

Sometimes researchers are fortunate enough to have both opportunities and resources, and can make these decisions under less pressure. The American Bar Foundation (ABF) was such a place.[3] I joined an ABF research project on comparative law fairly early in the project. Some interviews had been completed, but the parameters of the project were still being discussed. As the project evolved, gaining resources and becoming longitudinal, we had the opportunity to try out different types of QDAs for different purposes.

The ABF project began in 1987, and analyses and data collection are ongoing. Based at the American Bar Foundation in Chicago and Oxford University's Centre for Socio-Legal Studies in England, we explored differences in the United States (US) and United Kingdom (UK) civil justice systems. We focused on the social construction of litigation, how actors in both legal systems constructed institutional, organizational and personal responses to asbestos-related diseases. We interviewed over 235 plaintiff and defence lawyers, doctors, victims, victim activists, judges, insurers and bureaucrats (resulting in over seven megabytes of interview data). There have been several conference papers and articles resulting from the ABF project, ranging from legal and policy analysis, to the social nature of time, including descriptions of medical and legal work, constructions of risk, organization and network theory.

It was a good time to test QDAs as the market was emerging. We experimented with a few QDAs early in the project. They helped shape the research by allowing us to do more, and more varied, analyses. While we had resources, we also had the difficult issues and problems experienced in most qualitative projects. QDAs helped us with many of these strategic issues, and even some of the theoretical ones.

Team research

First, the ABF project was a team effort. As in much qualitative research these days, team members brought different training (law and sociology) and experiences to the project. We often focused on different issues. As we were often in different time zones and interviewing different people, we needed a way to keep current on our data. A QDA allowed us to code and compare the interviews as they were completed, keeping us informed about each researcher's interviews and preliminary findings. QDAs helped us avoid a great peril of qualitative research: focusing on the most recent or exotic interviews to the exclusion of more representative, indicative ones (Hammersley and Atkinson 1995: 198; Silverman 1993: 153). While some individual cases were very telling, especially for analytic induction projects, a QDA helped us discover and focus on patterns in the data.

Identifying social troubles

Our ABF project began when one of the senior researchers was in the UK, working on an unrelated civil law project. He had earlier written on US asbestos litigation, and was surprised by the lack of UK litigation. When he asked about it, he discovered that the litigation existed, but it was organized in a very different way. Unlike in the US, UK asbestos litigation involved very different actors, organizations, standard operating procedures, and networks of relationships (Durkin 1990; Felstiner and Dingwall 1988).

We began by interviewing specialist lawyers, doctors and related experts in both countries. Starting with the social trouble, or puzzle, of very different litigation rates for very similar medico-legal problems, we needed several types of data. In addition to our concern with individual and organizational constructions of legal realities, we began looking for specific pieces of data. We sought actor estimates of the number of claims filed, the number of asbestos disease victims, location and frequency of claim filings, amount of awards, and timing of awards. Early interviews were done (for the most part) separately by the two senior researchers. All interviews were exploratory and open-ended, which yielded rich and complex data.

QDAs also helped in the next stage. We had to identify what we had, and what might be theoretically interesting about the data. When all the preliminary interviews were transcribed, we discovered a number of different directions in which the research could go. The first issues we followed were to investigate estimates of the number, size, and social and medical distribution of legal claims. We began with a very simple QDA that indexed the data by marking (changing) the interview data files. We went through each interview, coding the text with distinctive symbols for each of these issues.

This simple indexing QDA assembled the data on these varied issues. The QDA did a form of automated indexing, identifying the relevant clumps of coded data. Separate data retrievals gave us the interview data related to number of victims, number of claims, locations and timing of claims, and the like. This made it easier to compare interviewees. When we initially called up the marked data, it led us to a number of new social troubles and puzzles. Among the most fascinating were: media-framed asbestos litigation as a legal crisis in the US, but a medical problem in the UK; differences between epidemiological evidence of disease rates, on one hand, and the medical and legal recognition of diseases, on the other; pockets of high or low litigation rates within and between countries, the UK having lower claim rates but higher disease rates; organizations as influential positive and negative gatekeepers to legal systems; and lawyers and doctors having very different types of relationships to each other.

Framing salient issues

Once we identified a few troubles to investigate, we moved on to the next phase, and to a different QDA (Qualpro). Robert Dingwall, the senior researcher more experienced in qualitative research and methodology, took over at this point by constructing a coding system. He used his experience on other research projects to develop a system that encompassed the identified salient issues, and left room for expansion into other topics as the research evolved.

At this point, there was very little difference between regular research and QDA-aided research. We all discussed the structure and contents of the code, making sure coding rules were clear, inclusive and exclusive. We talked about the theoretical approaches that would be most appropriate to describe these realities, and made sure that the appropriate data could be clearly coded. At this point there was no substitute for expertise in qualitative methodology. No QDA replaces the need to craft coding systems carefully, nor would we want one to do so.

What the new QDA provided was many new opportunities to improve the reliability and validity of team research. These more complex QDAs code not by marking up the data directly, but by building a separate code reference file. One benefit is that data are not modified. A more important benefit is that inter-coder reliability checks are easily accomplished within the QDA. While we scored very high on inter-coder reliability, this report would quickly identify coding problems. If coding rules were unclear, or redundant, the QDA would uncover these problems. This is especially useful because it makes the crucially important coding task easier to perform at all stages of research.

This QDA code file system has additional research benefits. Because the codes are in a separate file, each bit of data can be coded in many different ways. There is no danger of cutting up a transcript and thus disturbing its context because the data are always there in the original context and in coded data chunks. There is no need to decide which code is more important because there are few restrictions on the number of codes assigned to each piece of data. Most QDAs now retrieve data chunks and note all overlapping codes. This makes it easier to keep the data in context by emphasizing how the data are embedded in other issues.

Another great benefit of QDAs is that the code files are easy to modify in the light of new findings or ideas. We modified code files with a word-processing program. As our ideas and data grew, it was a simple matter to add or remove codes. When I had created too many codes for the different sub-types of asbestos diseases, I collapsed the codes quickly and easily. This required no copying of transcripts, different colour pens, or cutting and pasting.

Sampling frames

Our sampling decisions were not really enhanced by our QDA, but it did make it easier to keep track of our progress. For strong theoretical reasons, we chose snowball sampling (Babbie 1994: 287). We argued that because asbestos victims, doctors and lawyers were not randomly distributed, and because there were no directories of such specialists, random sampling was not at all appropriate. These actors, especially the professionals, worked within a very small legal niche where the influential actors were all known to each other. For good reasons in both countries, actors were suspicious of people they did not know. We gained access to most through people they knew or trusted. For these reasons, snowball was the most appropriate sampling method.

The QDA did make it easier to keep track of which actors we had spoken to. It was simple enough to compare a list of mentioned names with the interview directory (one of the many reports available on the QDA). We knew we had reached near closure on the influential actors when the snowball sample question ('who else do we need to interview?') yielded only names of people we had already interviewed.

Interview questions

Again, the questions we asked were based on expertise in research methodology. Again, the QDA was not a substitute for well-planned research. Rather, it was a tool enabling us to update the questionnaire as we made new discoveries. We also used it to ask previously interviewed experts (where we had already established a strong rapport) quick questions.

The QDA was important here because we continually updated the questionnaire. Resources continued to flow to the project and we moved towards longitudinal research. The memory power of a QDA allowed us to notice data trends more easily. One trend was the evolution of asbestos litigation. The QDA allowed us to discover trends, for example in the selection of medical experts. As epidemiological research became more important in the UK (to some extent eclipsing pure clinical research), legal battles and tactics changed. Experts came and went, depending on their training. Settlement amounts varied, reflecting these changes. Unions changed law firms, and law firms altered their tactics and clients. Of course, we should have noticed this eventually, but the speed and accuracy of QDA data searches made these theoretically interesting changes much more visible.

Analysis

This is the area where a QDA makes its greatest contribution. A QDA is no substitute for good methodology or theoretical insight. Its contribution is not to think, but to keep data and their contexts close at hand as we think. If coding is done well, data searches yield near instant access to the raw material from which analyses are forged. It is here that QDAs can make research much better. The great concern with representativeness of qualitative data (Hammersley and Atkinson 1995) and thoroughness of analysis (Silverman 1993) are best addressed by assuring the audience that researchers have considered all the available data. It is here that QDAs are 'pushing the envelope' of qualitative research into fascinating new areas. Programs like Anthropac have been designed to discover and probe networks of relationships between concepts and actors. While the output does not look like traditional qualitative research, these programs are faithful to qualitative data while providing innovative and fruitful ways to further it.

Coffey et al. (1996) recently described exciting new possibilities for qualitative research. Because of the depth and character of qualitative data, we researchers have often been criticized for creating idiosyncratic explanations. Coffey and co-workers envision the day where we can trade data sets, using hypertext links to probe connections in each other's data. This is fascinating. Several of our findings, especially about the differing patterns of asbestos claims, pushed us toward organizational and network explanations of legal action. As the prevailing analyses were micro-economic or macro-cultural, the greater efficiency of a QDA would allow us to probe other researcher's data sets. For Coffey et al. (1996), the benefit would not be in multiplying the number of qualitative data sets, but in multiplying the number of theoretical perspectives applied to each data set. Competing explanations could then be compared based on the same data!

Choosing a program

The first (and last) time I spent $100,000 of someone else's money on a computer system, I learned that the best approach is first to identify the software that can do what you want and then to buy the hardware that runs the software. This seemed rational and utility-maximizing. But people do not always act this way. We often choose hardware and software based on habit, training, recommendations and sunk costs (whatever systems a university or agency has decided to purchase and support). There are three general factors that should enter into the choice of a QDA program. Two of these – hardware and software costs – are primarily pragmatic.

The more important strategic issue is to decide what you want to do. How do you manage data–theory interaction? The gist of critical enquiry is, of course, in its strategy: what data do you seek; how do you manage the data; and what can you say with the data? Fortunately, hardware and cost issues are decreasing in importance, allowing researchers to focus on managing the relationship between their data and theories. Also fortunately, it is getting harder to make a bad decision. Not only are the software systems getting better, but the information available about different systems is improving (Weitzman and Miles 1995). Researchers with access to the Internet can search numerous sites with information on QDAs, both from developers and consumers. NUD*IST even maintains a newsgroup, where interested researchers ask each other, and the software developers, questions about research.

Hardware and operating systems

As a participant at an early (1989) qualitative computing conference in Breckenridge Colorado, I learned that a new era of computer-assisted qualitative research was dawning. At that time there were about a dozen QDA programs in development, and most were restricted to a single computer type and its operating system (or platform).

The choice of hardware has often been settled before the research begins. Hardware constraints effectively dictated software choice. Several QDA programs were being developed for Macintosh, the favourite operating system of many qualitative researchers. Many were being developed for DOS, taking advantage of the growth in personal computers. A few others ran only on mainframes, and required expensive supporting software. A couple of programs were written in German, and the translations of instructions were (to put it politely) challenging. Almost all were still under development (a constant condition as software and market demands evolve) and unfortunately not user-friendly.

New users can benefit from three recent trends that make hardware choices less important. First, hardware advances, like the Power Macs and new operating systems, mean that the primary distinction between Macs and PCs is becoming less important. Secondly, programs initially written for one platform have been rewritten for others. A 'Mercedes' of the field, NUD*IST, now runs on mainframes, Mac, Windows, and DOS. Other programs, like Inspiration, come in Mac and Window versions. Thirdly, expansion of the market has contributed to the creation of niche programs. For example, a comparative case-analysis program called QCA constructs 'truth tables' (Ragin 1994). Network programs like SemNet help chart networks of relationships and structural holes. Illustration programs like Inspiration and More help to represent findings graphically. Similar programs are available on mainframes, Macintosh, Windows, and DOS. We are nearing the point where, whatever your hardware tastes, there are QDA programs to fit your methodological needs.

Software costs

Cost has always been an important issue, but it should become less important. Many universities and research agencies have added QDA programs to their software inventories. Increased competition has affected the cost of many programs, especially academic editions. As the number and variety of programs increases, researcher choices get better. The market offers an expanding range of programs at an even wider range of prices. No program does everything, but all programs do something useful. An excellent recent sourcebook, Weitzman and Miles (1995), describes almost all of the QDA programs in great detail.

Strategically, it makes sense to find QDA programs that fit and expand your preferred methods. You do not want to be constrained by the capacities of any program, so you need the programs that do what you do (Richards and Richards 1994: 445). You will probably want access to several different types of QDA program. Most QDA developers offer demo versions of their package, and some can even be downloaded from the Internet. In the long run, such access will allow you to take advantage of new techniques for managing data.

At the same time, you cannot buy every program. Prices for different types of QDA programs fluctuate, and range from free development versions on the World Wide Web to $25 (QCA) to $44 (Qualpro, academic version) to $200 (NUD*IST, academic version) up to $1600 (Metamorph) (Weitzman and Miles 1995: 316–325). Now, your choice depends more on your data than your wallet.

Fortunately, there are data-finessing techniques to make the less sophisticated programs more useful. Many researchers will find that, depending on how they manage data, the most expensive QDA programs are desirable but not necessary for their work (Hammersley and Atkinson 1995: 201). In fact, the learning curve of more expensive and extensive QDAs may detract from the more straightforward projects. The strategic task remains to match your data-management needs with a QDA program's strengths. Pragmatically, what is the best choice for managing the data you have (or plan to collect)? Programs vary from simple search and count programs to ones that bill themselves as theorizing tools.

Many researchers have already invested in particular methods, and have decided what their data should look like. Different QDA programs deal with different methods of manipulating data. Your research question may also identify different types of data for developing your ideas. We used intensive interviews, television documentaries, media content analyses, field notes, pictures, documents, research notes, articles, epidemiological data, impressions, literature reviews, and even those problematic official statistics in describing legal institutions and practices (Dingwall et al. 1990; Durkin 1994; Felstiner and Dingwall 1988).

For most QDA programs, it does not matter where the data set comes from as long as it can be entered as a computer file. New computer technologies for voice transcriptions are advancing rapidly, although they are still expensive. Some programs, like NUD*IST, support coding of videotaped data. Most programs have ways of entering interviews, documents, memos, comments, field notes, and even statistics. Different types of data can be searched individually or in clusters. Pragmatically, what matters most is how complex your chosen methods and data are. This distinction can lead you to different types of QDAs.

Search QDA programs: little or no coding required

All researchers understandably want to analyse their data quickly and easily, with a minimum amount of time invested in learning QDA programs.

Researchers whose methods, data and coding schemes are straightforward will probably want to use these search programs. Search programs are most appropriate when methods require locating or counting terms, searches for particular words or embedded codes, structured questions, small data sets, or homogeneous data.

Search programs have many benefits in the right situation. Unlike other programs, there is little or no coding necessary. Data are ready to be analysed almost immediately. There is a very steep learning curve, as these programs are very intuitive. They bear some resemblance to the 'search' component of advanced word processors. They locate instances of key words or phrases. As with LEXIS (legal research) commands, these programs are able to bring up text in context. These programs also provide frequency and distribution counts, which are especially useful for many types of conversational and textual research.

Search programs are also useful in many areas where straightforward codes are used. Many projects have well-defined parameters. Many researchers know their data so well that coding is relatively simple. For example, linguistic researchers with well-developed coding systems could embed their codes into transcripts, making it simple to find, count and compare codes. Once the data are coded, it is easy to retrieve all relevant data chunks.

Sometimes there is room for structured questions in qualitative research, although these may cause problems (Holstein and Gubrium 1995: 52–59). Sorting data by categories of age, gender, professional role or location is often theoretically important, and can easily be done by many QDA programs. For example, searches (even a Boolean search) can be initiated by requesting the answers to specific questions. A theory about gender and regional differences among divorce lawyers (Sarat and Felstiner 1995) must begin by sorting data by gender and region. In comparing how constructions of legal and professional work differ by type of insurance agency (Dingwall and Durkin 1993), you clearly have to retrieve data by agency type. QDA programs can easily do this.

Search programs are also useful where subjects tend to use the same words to describe meanings or phenomena. Depending on how narrowly defined a research issue is, a search program could find the data without any coding at all. A single researcher with a moderate number of interviews could easily search for keywords like 'family' or 'lawsuit'. However, as in the ABF case, where people in Great Britain, Scotland, and Northern Ireland (to say nothing of the US) use different words and spellings to refer to the same phenomena and the same words for different phenomena, a more complex QDA program is recommended.

Flat coding

Flat coding is the assignment of codes to researcher-defined data chunks. An example would be the one we used in the ABF project, Qualpro. This method is probably the one most familiar to qualitative researchers, where researchers apply specific codes to chunks of data. The obvious difference is that it is done on a computer rather than on pieces of paper. This familiar, active coding effort is required where the data and coding schemes are more complex. Meanings and ideas are more difficult to discern. People will often answer questions indirectly, especially in open-ended interviews. They make connections that we did not anticipate, frame issues differently, use different words to refer to the same phenomena, or the same words to refer to different phenomena.

Fortunately, qualitative researchers are used to complex data. The most common types of qualitative data are not structured answers, but open-ended interviews, field notes, memos, impressions, documents, pictures, and even artefacts. Most 'flat' QDA programs are designed to manage these data by maintaining separate file formats which can be searched singly or in groups.

Flat coding proceeds by establishing, based on the researcher's knowledge of theory and the data, a list of analytical categories or codes. The researcher then reads the data (either on hard copy or the screen) and assigns codes to user-defined data chunks (words, lines, paragraphs, even pages). This is comparable to sorting index cards, but with two major benefits. First, the data remain in context, so that the whole is always as easily accessible as the parts, this reduces the 'decontextualization risk' (Tesch 1991) that threatens research. Secondly, much time is saved as a QDA program's ability to cross-reference data chunks eliminates the need to copy data.

Most programs have intuitive, menu-driven coding systems. These programs differ from relational coding's manipulation of codes (see below) by using relatively static categories. While some early QDA programs sharply restricted coding options, it is now possible to assign multiple codes to each researcher-defined chunk. Data chunks are then retrieved by following (generally) simple instructions.

Again, the computer does not do all the important work – just the most tedious. With a little foresight and computer experience, these flat programs can emulate some valuable features of more advanced programs. Experienced researchers make their greatest contributions at this point by developing adequate coding schemes. With sufficient knowledge and preparation, it is possible to create a somewhat relational coding scheme for flat-coding QDA programs.

These generally lower-cost programs can, with the use of a word processor, allow you to finesse a simple version of a relational coding scheme. As data retrievals generate not only the coded sections but co-occurring codes, researchers can manipulate their coding schemes by carefully reading the output. Some QDA programs were made to be used in conjunction with a word-processing program. As these programs generally do not embed codes in the text files but maintain a separate code file, code categories can be easily edited by anyone with basic word-processing skills.

Relational coding

Relational QDA programs include some of the most sophisticated programs. They do everything the flat-coding programs do, and more. These programs are relational because they allow you to manage data by moving them around as you test and build theories. Most also provide a graphical depiction of your data, making it easier to see relationships hidden in a linear list of codes.

These QDA programs are especially useful at the start of research. Imagine a tree with many branches representing concepts and issues in your data. Relational coding lets you truly manage your database as it is being built. In essence, you watch the data tree grow, and then move branches around to craft a better representation of your data. In our case, the importance of network changes and connections emerged as the data grew. It alerted us to the very limited utility of using popular explanatory concepts such as 'utility maximizing' or 'national culture' in describing social action.

Places where data diverge, converge and overlap are crucial for noting patterns and trends. This information can be used to change interview schedules, samples and goals. Serendipitous findings – as in the surprising irrelevance of religion in explaining Northern Ireland's higher rates of workplace litigation against British companies (Felstiner and Dingwall 1988) – can push you and your theories in new directions.

Network and concept coding

Recent advances in network theory have been accompanied by advances in network software. Whether on the massive but still qualitative scale of Heinz and Laumann (1994), the more modest scale of the ABF project, or mapping family and social relationships in a small community, many researchers have found network terms very useful in explaining how parts of the world work. Events such as the International Sunbelt Network Conference bring together quantitative and qualitative researchers – anthropologists, economists, historians, political scientists, sociologists – who share an interest in charting relationships between actors and events. Crucial explanatory concepts such as symmetric and asymmetric links, elites, hollow cores and structural holes emerge as the data are mapped.

It was reported recently on the NUD*IST newsgroup (a helpful on-line newsgroup dedicated to questions about research using NUD*IST) that the latest version of SemNet is now available, and it is one of the most sophisticated of these programs. Other programs such as Inspiration, C-Map and Learning Tool allow researchers to map and investigate relationships. These programs not only sum up the data, but allow you to find anomalies – links, elites, holes – not apparent when collecting the data.

These programs work by assigning actors or events to nodes, then graphically describing connections between nodes. Generally, boxes indicate the nodes, and lines of varying strength and direction connect some of the boxes. While some researchers develop four-dimensional maps (Laumann and

Knoke 1987) to explain political action, simple maps are also very helpful in clarifying issues. Researchers conversant with the ideas of network theory have adopted these programs to develop richer explanations of social action. Many of the actors we interviewed used network terms, and luck, to explain how they came to act. Finding quotes such as 'had it not been for Dr X' or 'if lawyer Y hadn't stopped by after she visited a co-worker' described the significance of being embedded in different networks.

Comparison programs

One step beyond the goals and methods of many qualitative researchers is the comparative method. Here the distinctions between qualitative and quantitative techniques become fuzzy. Once the data have been collected on a number of individual cases, it is theoretically tempting to explore why some cases are deemed successes, and some failures. Ragin (1994), following his description of this comparative process, developed a QDA (called QCA) program to help researchers find patterns in their data.

This QDA program can be applied to many cases. It is useful in determining what conditions are favourable to a particular outcome. You build a matrix, with a dependent variable (i.e. filing a legal claim, remaining in a public service legal office, the presence of a school tracking program) on the right. The relevant variables are arranged on the left, and scored as either present or absent. In this way, Ragin (1994) showed how important contingent variables (a teachers' union, race, community structure, income) are to the result. Patterns become apparent as more cases are added, helping the researcher to advance an argument and direct further research.

Conclusion

More and more, qualitative as well as standard social research methods texts are paying attention to QDA programs. While the discussions are rarely in great depth, they do endorse such programs for a very important reason: QDA programs are proving their value in research projects. They allow us to do the most important tasks more accurately and thoroughly. In contrast to a mere five years ago, programs have become less expensive and much easier to use. As qualitative research becomes more relevant to policy issues (Dingwall and Durkin 1995; Silverman 1993), it is more important to do it well. Recently, Dingwall and many others in the UK have used QDA-based analyses to question the premises of public policy. In the US, qualitative research has been used to evaluate and redirect public policies on law, crime and the homeless. While a QDA will not salvage a badly conceived project, it will strengthen a well-conceived one.

The opportunities to do research well are expanding, and QDAs are an important part of that expansion. More and more, qualitative researchers rather than programmers are creating these QDA programs. Programs are becoming more theoretically informed. Computers, once a Procrustean bed limiting research activities and frames, are now tools for doing what we really have always wanted to do, only better. As the above classification shows, recent developments in the field allow you to choose programs that fit most methodologies. We now have more chances to do more things with our data. The often difficult work of collecting and coding data now can have a bigger payoff. The most beneficial result is that, unlike some quantitative programs, QDAs allow us to examine our data more deeply and carefully. In essence, QDA programs allow us to go purposefully mining in our data, rather than just fishing in them.

Notes

1 Some might question the benefits of this advance. As one who uses numbers where and when they are helpful for an analysis, I hope to avoid that fight here. Using numerical data is often crucial to supporting researcher representations, especially through triangulation. Further, new statistical techniques are being developed to discover patterns in text and interview data.

2 And as with qualitative research, there is no guarantee that they will get these meanings right, or even provide helpful interpretations. However, by not having to hand-calculate the gamma for a 5 by 5 table, researchers have more time to think more deeply.

3 The ABF provides a wonderful environment for socio-legal research. There are a number of first-rate sociologists, academic lawyers, historians, political scientists, economists, social psychologists and anthropologists who share projects, resources, office space and ideas. There are regular lunchtime sessions where research experiences and findings are shared. Because of the ABF's connections, there are a number of internationally respected academics who visit the ABF while in Chicago, further enriching the mixture of ideas.

8

Dramaturgy and Methodology

Scott A. Hunt and Robert D. Benford

To date, the goal of dramaturgical analysis has been either to understand the processes and techniques of impression management or to reveal the underlying meaning of social interaction. However, systematic rendering of a dramaturgical methodology has not been attempted. This chapter addresses this gap in the literature by outlining a methodology of dramaturgy. We suggest that the theatrical metaphor provides a means to bring together methodological insights from a variety of sources to form a consistent whole. Illustrating our perspective with examples primarily from social movement research, we attempt to show how the theatrical perspective of dramaturgy influences all aspects of an investigation. The purpose of this chapter is to provide a basis for a reflexive understanding of research productions. In so doing, we point out how dramaturgical methods can highlight common research hazards and provide a means to overcome them. We also contend that dramaturgical methodology supplies a useful framework for social scientists to examine their own research critically. While concentrating primarily on participant observation studies, we none the less suggest that a dramaturgical method is useful in understanding and carrying out all research productions.

Dramaturgy is a perspective that uses a theatrical metaphor to understand social interaction. The approach takes *act* to be its central concept (Burke 1945, 1968). From a dramaturgical point of view, humans, in a specific social and temporal context, act to create meaning and demonstrate purpose (Perinbanayagam 1982; cf. Burke 1945). Goffman (1959) referred to such action as 'impression management', suggesting that individuals present themselves to others so as to foster and maintain particular images or fronts. In their performances, individuals construct some images intentionally and provide others inadvertently.

There have been a few laudable efforts that use dramaturgy to explore particular, isolated methodological concerns. For instance, Gusfield (1981) makes several suggestions as to how dramaturgy might provide a means of studying public problems. Hill (1993) used Goffman's (1974) framing language to devise a method of conducting archival research. Snow (1980) and his colleagues (Snow et al. 1981, 1982, 1986) employed dramaturgical concepts to analyse the disengagement process in field research, the construction of research roles, crowd behaviour and 'interviewing by comment'. Drawing

extensively on dramaturgical theory, Berg (1995) offered qualit
researchers guidelines for conducting interviews. Finally, Griffiths (1
devised dramatic role-plays to study how girls make sense of their gendered
experiences as adolescents. Each of these efforts, although quite insightful in
its own right, fails to provide an over-arching methodological approach.
We seek to overcome this shortcoming by pulling together a variety of
research to form a coherent dramaturgical methodology.

To do this, we draw upon our recent dramaturgical analyses of social
movements (Benford and Hunt 1992; Hunt et al. 1994; Zuo and Benford
1995). In those studies, we used dramaturgy to examine how social movement organizations advance their views about 'real' and 'ideal' power
arrangements. Following Goffman (1959) and others (Burke 1968; Lyman
and Scott 1975; Messinger et al. 1962), we suggest that movements construct
and communicate power via four dramatic techniques – scripting, staging,
performing and interpreting. Building on this framework, we show how
social scientists use the same dramatic techniques in research productions.
For heuristic purposes only, the four techniques are presented sequentially,
treated as if they are independent. In practice, they are interdependent,
simultaneous processes. We will consider how each of the dramatic techniques affects and guides research.

Scripting

Scripting refers to the construction of a set of directions that define the
scene, identify actors and sketch expected behaviour. Rather than providing
fixed texts to be followed mechanically, it produces guides for action. Scripts
emerge from the interaction between and among antagonists, protagonists
and a variety of audiences. They guide action and consciousness, often providing behavioural cues to allow for improvisation when unforeseen events
occur. Scripting not only occurs off-stage prior to a performance, but is also
improvised front- and backstage as individuals interact with each other and
their audience.

A substantial part of scripting revolves around four core framing tasks: (a)
a diagnosis of some imputed problem; (b) a prognosis for corrective action;
(c) a rationale for taking particular action; and (d) strategic and tactical
directions (Benford and Hunt 1992; Snow and Benford 1988; Wilson 1973).
The first two deal with the actors or agents of an act. They construct identities and roles, essentially developing *dramatis personae*. The latter two
involve demonstrating meaning or purpose and identifying an 'appropriate'
means or agency by which to act. They guide the dialogue and direction for
performances and actors.

Developing dramatis personae

With respect to social movements, scripts construct dramatis personae or a
'cast of characters' (Zurcher and Snow 1981). This entails the development

of identities and roles for movement participants, including antagonists, victims, protagonists, supporting cast members and audiences.

Regarding ethnographic investigations, the scripting of field researchers' identities and roles is of crucial importance. Snow et al. (1986) suggest that social interaction between a researcher and the members of an observed group, in part, involves the negotiation, reinforcement and alteration of the investigator's roles. Most importantly, scripted roles limit the amount and kind of information gathered. Anderson's identity as a 'buddy-researcher' of the homeless, Benford's position as an 'ardent activist' of the disarmament movement, as well as Snow's roles as 'controlled sceptic' of a proselytizing Buddhist organization and 'credentialed expert' in an examination of homelessness, each had different informational yields. Their distinct identities and roles provided them with varying degrees of access to data from direct experiences, observations, members' narrations and official records.

Securing and maintaining identities that facilitate data collection are problematic for field researchers (Adler and Adler 1987; Lofland and Lofland 1995; Warren 1988). For example, a role fostered by a researcher might not be entirely acceptable to those being studied. Likewise, a researcher might believe that a role conferred upon her is too restrictive or demanding. The management of such scripting tensions often determines whether a project is completed successfully or abandoned completely.

While all fieldwork studies must manage the scripting of a suitable identity, research of strongly partisan groups, such as social movement organizations, political parties, religious communities and the like, presents an additional complexity. Many scholars involved in such groups assert that there simply are no neutrals. Consequently, most partisans, either initially or after the observer has had 'sufficient' time to learn the 'truth', would object to or be suspicious of a researcher claiming to be a neutral, detached social scientist.

To illustrate how the partisan character of movement organizations influences the development of field researchers' roles and identities, we refer to an incident from one of our participant observation studies. When Hunt (1991) enquired about the possibility of studying a peace and justice organization, the group's state coordinator raised the question of neutrality. 'Exactly what would you see yourself doing? . . . I mean in regards to taking part. Would you be here to just watch or would you want to join in and be a part of our activities?' Upon hearing Hunt's reply that he intended to participate in the group's endeavours, the coordinator remarked that the members of the organization would be more likely to allow the research if it were done by someone committed to their cause.

While the above illustrates overt scripting strategies for addressing the problems of neutrality, some have utilized covert tactics (Douglas 1976). In such cases, researchers seek to hide their true identity, thereby adopting a variety of 'passing' techniques (Goffman 1963a). This is done because covert researchers realize that subjects have the power to blow the investigator's cover and thereby terminate or severely alter the study. Finally, both overt and covert researchers attempt to script roles and identities that carefully manage the influence they might come to possess within the group being studied.

Dialogue and direction

While the scripting of dramatis personae identifies a cast of characters, dialogue provides actors' rationales for taking a particular line of action (Benford and Hunt 1992). This involves the construction of a 'universe of discourse' (Mead 1934) and a vocabulary of motives (Mills 1940; Scott and Lyman 1968). Vocabularies of motive supply social movement adherents with answers to questions concerning the severity and urgency of the problem as well as the efficacy and propriety of taking action (Benford 1993). Dialogue and direction also entail general instructions for 'appropriate' performances, suggesting who should do what, when, where and how.

Similar to movement participants, researchers script dialogue and construct vocabularies of motive to justify their particular investigations. This is often done prior to entering the field, but also occurs during and even after a project has been completed. Parallelling those of social movement actors, research vocabularies of motive concern the severity and urgency of the problem as well as the efficacy and propriety of taking action. Vocabularies of motive are quite important in that they often help secure grant money, research assistants, release time from teaching and other resources necessary to stage a study. Additionally, researchers develop vocabularies of motive to justify their work when it is called into question by significant others or even themselves. For those doing ethnographic studies, vocabularies of motive are drawn on to rationalize the many hours spent gathering data, typing field notes and so on.

Rationales for conducting research are given for all empirical work, regardless of methodological and theoretical predispositions. They are clearly evident in the cultural artefact known as the academic journal article. Almost without exception, the research vocabulary of motives appears at the beginning and end of journal articles. Researchers, to legitimize the 'appropriateness' of their work, link their efforts with previous studies, making copious references to existing literature.

Related to propriety is the issue of severity. Social scientists must ask: is the identified problem significant enough to warrant study? In the academic world of knowledge construction, a claim alluding to a gap in understanding is a most severe indictment. Researchers must also address the issue of efficacy. That is, they are compelled to demonstrate that their investigations make a difference by contributing to our stock of knowledge. Efficacy claims are facilitated, to a large extent, in that refereed journal articles are published – at least ostensibly – because they make a notable contribution to the field.

Staging

A second dramatic technique – *staging* – refers to processes of acquiring and administering materials, audiences and performing regions (Benford and Hunt 1992). Social movement staging typically involves the mobilization of money, labour and other tangible resources. But staging also entails the use of 'politically correct' symbols, as well as the engagement and control of 'appropriate' audiences. Without an audience, a performance cannot take place. Moreover, as Goffman (1959) suggests, the content of a performance is usually constructed with a particular audience in mind. Once an audience is obtained, its members must be prevented from getting uninvited glimpses of backstage activities that could compromise the entire performance.

Similar to social movement dramas, research productions face staging problems. Social analysts must concern themselves with procuring money to support themselves and their research as well as securing the labour of research assistants, adequate library facilities, data tapes and so forth. In addition to these material issues, there are staging problems involving costumes and props as well as audience segregation and backstage control.

Costumes and props

A significant matter encountered by field researchers, but seldom mentioned in their formal accounts, is the use of symbols that are acceptable to the group under study. In more dramaturgical terms, this amounts to using 'proper' costumes and props. To illustrate, in Benford's (1987) examination of Texas peace and justice organizations, he discovered that wearing a Dallas Cowboy (football) T-shirt to movement activities was considered inappropriate costuming. Such attire evoked images of local 'good ol' boy' power structures and violent sport which were antithetical to the peace movement's scripted themes of gender equality and non-violent interaction.

Galliher (1980: 303) acknowledges that he, too, has paid particular attention to issues of costuming and props:

> In my research . . . I have been careful to try to present myself as someone as much like my respondents as possible. I have gotten a haircut and shaved my beard and worn a business suit and necktie. While I was in Utah, I wore only white shirts, in keeping with the usual Mormon garb. My success as a researcher was manifest in zero rate of refusal from Mormons and several invitations to dinner, as well as invitations to join their church . . . My tactics in this regard go beyond the usual practice of dressing so as not to distract or annoy respondents.

What this suggests is that costumes and props are powerful in that they can enhance or diminish a researcher's capacity to gather data. While they can establish or strengthen rapport, costumes and props 'go beyond' this customary practice. They are symbols that signify a researcher's potential either to discredit or complement a group's everyday performances. Shirts depicting 'macho' football stars could potentially undermine a peace movement's affective line by suggesting that aggressive male behaviour is laudable.

Conversely, wearing Mormon garb supports the acceptability of that community's emphasis on conservative, conforming social and political arrangements.

Audience segregation and backstage control

The other staging problem considered here revolves around the issues of audience segregation and backstage control. For field researchers, these two concerns involve the management of two distinct and equally significant audiences: the group being observed and the academic community. As the foregoing discussion of scripting research roles and identities implies, members of the group being studied often scrutinize the words and deeds of the investigator. Equally important, as the above consideration of dialogue and direction suggests, is the academic audience that assesses the presentation of research proposals and reports.

These audiences witness different research performances based on two separate 'theatrical frames' (Goffman 1974). Members of the observed audience see the research act as a performance by a participant who happens to be an observer. For the individuals in the group being studied, the participant role expectations of the researcher absolutely overshadow the observer identity. For example, when Benford (1987) off-handedly commented on the status of his research in the presence of several peace activists, some expressed surprise that he was 'still doing that stuff'. Snow's (1980) difficulties with disengaging from observation studies also illustrate this point. His researcher identity was totally overlooked by members of a proselytizing Buddhist organization when Snow attempted to leave the field. Members of the Buddhist group interpreted Snow's disengagement as the defection of a convert, not as the termination of a research project.

Members of the academic audience, on the other hand, view the researcher's activities in the context of a different theatrical frame. They interpret the investigator's activities as a scientific observer who happens to be a participant. An academic audience wants a research performance to inform them about the purpose of the study, its methodology, the act being explained, the context of that act, the actors' motivations and analytical conclusions. For this audience, participant role expectations are often considered superfluous.

The physical segregation of the observed and academic audiences is not particularly problematic, even though some overlap of the two might exist. However, a tension exists in that the two theatrical frames might impinge upon one another. For example, if a member of the observed group enquires about the researcher's findings, the theatrical frame is switched from participant observer to observer participant. In situations where attention remains fixed on the researcher's role as observer, the group being studied might guard or alter their performances in ways that seriously disrupt the study. The classic example of this problem is the infamous Hawthorne effect (Roethlisberger and Dickson 1939).

Tension between the two theatrical frames compels researchers either to pursue their observational activities backstage or to embed them inconspicuously into front-stage performances. This concern over front- and back-stage management of data collection is often discussed in the context of taking field notes. Because the potential for a theatrical frame break exists, experienced field researchers warn novices about taking notes front-stage and suggest that it should be done backstage.

> [the] general rule of thumb is 'Don't jot conspicuously' . . . [it] seems wisest not to flaunt the fact that you are recording . . . You need not increase any existing anxieties by continuously and openly writing down what you see and hear. Rather, jot notes at moments of withdrawal and when shielded. (Lofland and Lofland 1995: 90)

Lofland and Lofland (1995) go on to suggest that note-taking can be performed front-stage in contexts where the recording of words and actions is commonplace. Benford (1987) used just such a strategy to minimize the reactive effects of recording data. At every opportunity, he volunteered to act as scribe for the groups he was studying. Quickly earning a reputation as a reliable stenographer, he was able to take ample notes without being conspicuous. Further, his ability to script an identity as a 'camera bug' allowed him to unobtrusively photograph many of the movement's activities. By providing prints to individuals and representatives of peace and justice groups, he became recognized as the movement's photo historian.

In a similar attempt to embed backstage research behaviour into front-stage activities, Snow et al. (1982) utilize the method of 'interviewing by comment'. They note that the direct question is threatening to many respondents. It is based on the observer participant theatrical frame, putting the researcher front- and centre-stage as investigator and potential menace. Snow et al. (1982) present interviewing by comment as an alternative to the direct question. They argue that certain kinds of comments elicit informative responses without calling unnecessary attention to the researcher's role as observer. In other words, rather obtrusive methods of data collection can be done front-stage if couched in a non-threatening context that reinforces the participant observer theatrical frame.

In sum, both academic and observed group audiences have capacities to interrupt or halt a research performance. If a researcher cannot mobilize necessary resources from an academic audience, a project might not ever move beyond the planning stage. Similarly, if an observed group breaks the theatrical frame of participant observer, actions might become so guarded or altered that they compromise the study. From the point of view of the observed group, a researcher has the capacity to disrupt or foil their everyday performances by conspicuously acting out her role as data-gatherer, thereby displaying an overriding loyalty to and preoccupation with professional goals rather than participant obligations. The researcher must therefore utilize staging as well as performing techniques that can secure material resources and manage the tension between the two theatrical frames.

Performing

A third dramatic technique is *performing*. It makes visible notions about confrontations between protagonists and antagonists. Additionally, performing empowers the actor. By acting, participants undergo a self-transformation, changing from someone acted upon by external powers to an agent actively affecting the scene. Performances depend upon several dramatic techniques. Borrowing from Goffman (1959), we consider how field researchers rely on the techniques of dramaturgical loyalty, discipline and circumspection.

Dramaturgical loyalty

Goffman (1959: 212) states that *dramaturgical loyalty* requires performers to 'act as if they have accepted certain moral obligations'. It includes a commitment to keeping group secrets, checking temptations to exploit front-stage positions, accepting minor roles, presenting sincere performances, avoiding 'over-involvement' and suppressing criticisms of the team so as to foster impressions of solidarity to outsiders. Dramaturgical loyalty, in essence, implies an allegiance and devotion to a group's constructed definitions, frames and norms.

For researchers, the concept of dramaturgical loyalty raises an immediate question: to whom are researchers to be loyal? As previously noted, researchers perform for at least two audiences: an academic community and an observed group. The relationship between an investigator and these audiences is rather unique in that the researcher is often claimed as a team member by both. Consequently, dramaturgical loyalty for researchers has the added complexity of simultaneous and sometimes competing demands being made for allegiance and devotion.

One potential problem associated with dramaturgical loyalty is the perception by the observed group that the researcher is under-involved. Often, the dramaturgical reality from the perspective of the actors is that there are only two sides: supporters and opponents of the group. This represents a dramatic form of the vintage labour-organizing slogan: 'which side are you on?' Researchers who answer this question 'incorrectly' from the observed group's perspective, risk being seen as under-involved. To counter this perception, researchers frequently find it necessary to demonstrate their commitment publicly.

Another potential problem stemming from dramaturgical loyalty is the academic audience's perception that the researcher is over-involved. A widespread belief among academicians is that field researchers who get 'too close' to their subjects, by adopting the worldview of the observed group, place the objectivity and integrity of the study into question. The most extreme case of this perceived over-involvement is discussed in terms of 'going native', the forgoing of research in favour of becoming a member of the formerly observed group. While some have pointed to the limits of objectivism, suggesting that understanding can come only through researchers' direct experience of others' subjective realities, they still warn against the danger of 'going native' (Denzin 1989a; Forrest 1986).

To prevent the over-involvement of 'going native', field researchers are encouraged to pull back from participant roles and to act as social scientists by maintaining close contact with mentors as well as other members of the academic audience, engaging in data analysis, presenting research findings and so on. This amounts to reassuring an academic audience that a person's primary role is that of researcher, thus demonstrating loyalty. Additionally, the performance of such tasks as checking in with colleagues, recording data and analysing field notes gives the researcher's definition of self as social scientist the 'thickness of reality'.

Dramaturgical discipline

In addition to loyalty, successful performances depended upon *dramaturgical discipline*. A disciplined actor maintains self-control when performing, thereby avoiding the unintentional divulgence of secrets, possessing the 'presence of mind' to 'cover up on the spur of the moment for inappropriate behaviour', approaching matters with an 'appropriate' attitude and so forth (Goffman 1959: 216–218).

Dramaturgical discipline is particularly important when studying partisan groups. When observing those with strong ideological commitments, researchers are at times confronted with beliefs and values that run counter to their own. If a researcher chooses to attack the ideological positions of the observed group, she jeopardizes her position in the research setting. With this in mind, a researcher might choose to 'hold her tongue', thereby exercising dramaturgical discipline by suppressing lines that she would freely deliver in other contexts.

Exercising dramaturgical discipline does not mean that researchers should avoid asking respondents difficult or troubling questions. Rather, it implies that researchers should have the 'presence of mind' to pose such questions in a manner that does not dispute the 'appropriateness' of respondents' attitudes, beliefs, values and behaviours.

Dramaturgical circumspection

Research performances also rely on *dramaturgical circumspection*, the ability to make advanced preparations and to fashion impromptu adjustments necessitated by unanticipated conditions (Goffman 1959). Circumspection is a central component of research. Indeed, with such things as research proposals and designs as well as review boards, social scientists have made advanced preparation subject to public scrutiny by institutionalizing circumspection.

The ability to adjust to unforeseen circumstances in a research performance affects all forms of enquiry, even experiments. Johnson's (1976) report on his experience researching a religious crusade provides an insightful illustration. Fearing that the faculty members would not approve of his unconventional thesis proposal to conduct a field experiment on the effects of a Billy Graham revival on individuals' religious views, Johnson spent a considerable amount of time being circumspect, laying out an iron-clad research design, anticipating objections, reading widely in the area of persuasive communication and so on. After his proposed research had been approved, Johnson told the subjects of the experiment that they were to attend an upcoming Billy Graham revival at which they would observe and record various aspects of the event. Johnson then trained his subjects to be field observers.

Fully trained and prepared, the observers were instructed to arrive 30 minutes before the scheduled starting time and to take assigned positions within the coliseum. Long before the time the observers were told to show up, the coliseum was filled. In fact, an overflow crowd of several thousand people gathered outside the coliseum. Johnson's inability, understandable as it may be, to anticipate the early arrival of the crowd, presented the possibility that his research performance would be cancelled. Johnson suspected that the observers, blocked from the research setting, would simply turn away from the filled coliseum and go home. To his surprise, 'virtually all of the observers who had been unable to secure inside seating found, on their own, other locations which they then mapped on the cover of the instrument, identifying their location in the crowd' (Johnson 1976: 238). This exemplifies dramaturgical circumspection on part of the novice observers. They had adjusted their rehearsed performance to accommodate unforeseen factors. In effect, they had carried out a theatrical imperative: the show must go on.

Interpreting

Thus far, we have presented the dramatic techniques of research as though they were separate, time-bound stages. We view these techniques, however, as interdependent. The interconnectedness of the techniques makes them difficult to discuss analytically because there are, for example, scripting processes intertwined with those of staging and performing.

Further blurring the analytical boundaries between the dramatic techniques is their dependence upon interpretative processes. By *interpreting*, we refer to individual and collective efforts to give meaning to symbols, talk, action and the environment to explain what is going on (Blumer 1969; Goffman 1974; Mead 1934). It is an unending process that makes research scripting, staging and performing possible.

In research productions, interpreting – the process of determining what is going on – is sometimes referred to as 'theory construction'. Interpretations are not only essential to all aspects of research production, they are also the central purpose of conducting empirical and theoretical work. Research attempts to affect audiences' interpretations of 'reality'. It identifies 'real' causes and effects, debunks 'false' ideas, supports 'true' hypotheses and so forth.

In addition to the interpreting based on theoretical, epistemological and ontological choices, researchers in the field continually interpret the interaction before them. Of the things heard and seen, researchers must decide what is important, what is not, what is worth recording and what is background noise. Frequently, field interpreting occurs in a *post hoc* fashion. Long after some event or encounter has taken place, sometimes even after the researcher has left the field, data are reinterpreted, sometimes placing new emphasis on material previously designated as superfluous and other times 'realizing' the 'undue' attention paid to 'trivial' information. This continual process of figuring out what is going on and what went on in the field is lost in final research reports. An image most researchers like to foster is that they knew exactly what the 'correct' interpretation of the data was from the beginning. Absent are accounts of the interpreting processes, of the days on end spent shuffling and re-thinking the significance of particular field-note entries, of the hours devoted to massaging data, of the restructuring of papers around the unforeseen correlation between a dependent variable and a variable first designated as a 'control' but later elevated to the status of a 'major effect'.

Part of this process involves interpreting an audience's interpretations of the research production. For ethnographic studies, researchers interpret the actions of some group so as to make sense of what is going on. During a study, a researcher will frequently attempt to interpret how her research performance is being perceived by the observed group as well as by an academic audience. Concerning the imputed perceptions of an observed group, a researcher might believe that her performance is seen as a detached, perhaps insincere, academic exercise. To enhance rapport, the researcher might become more involved, taking a leading role in the group. Later, the same researcher might feel that the group has come to look to her for direction, thereby suggesting that her participation has significantly altered group action and has thus contaminated her research. With regard to the interpretations of an academic audience, researchers are concerned whether their work is perceived as serious, productive, publishable, interesting and valuable.

In short, interpreting is a continuous monitoring process that takes place before, during and after a research performance. As Mead's (1934) work suggests, interpreting is the foundation of all social interaction, including scientific research. Of the dramaturgical techniques outlined above, interpreting is a necessary component for each. As a common element in all the other techniques, interpreting links scripting, staging and performing together to form a coherent research production.

Discussion and conclusion

In this chapter we have used examples from social movement research, as well as other substantive areas to suggest how dramaturgy might provide a reflexive sociological method. It was our intention to make several method-ological contributions. First, our approach presents a conceptual framework for understanding research productions generally and field studies more specifically. Dramaturgical method also illuminates common pitfalls in social scientific work, implying that researchers might be well advised to pay par-ticular attention to the details of impression management as well as the problems of securing resources, audiences and the like. A third contribution is that dramaturgical method furnishes a vantage point for social scientists to examine their own research productions critically. By equating research with drama, we have sought to limit the pretentiousness that seems endemic to most social scientific work. Instead of presenting a window to 'reality', a dra-maturgical method serves as a constant reminder that researchers are in the business of 'reality construction' (Berger and Luckmann 1966).

We have focused our attention selectively on certain key issues, while neglecting several others. One vital area that further discussions of dram-aturgical methods should address is ethics. To say that research is like theatre is not to condone fraudulent analysis, gross manipulation of respondents or other offensive practices. Perceiving research in terms of drama is not to advocate an 'anything goes' policy. Milgram's (1963) experiments, for exam-ple, used dramaturgical techniques effectively, but will remain infamous for their ethical improprieties.

A dramaturgical method, however, does tend to blur ethical lines some-what. For instance, from a dramaturgical perspective, there is no clear-cut distinction between overt and covert research. Nor is there a sharp distinc-tion between impression management and manipulation. A dramaturgical method suggests a continuum, where research is more or less overt and more or less manipulative. This raises some serious ethical questions. At what point is research too manipulative? What kinds of impression-management techniques are inappropriate because they might endanger the physical or psychological well-being of others? When are research 'cons' acceptable and when are they not? While these are crucial questions not addressed in this chapter, we suspect that framing such ethical issues in dramaturgical terms might provide fresh, invigorating answers to old ques-tions (cf. Dingwall 1980a).

Another important concern not discussed here centres around the idea of 'fabrications' (Goffman 1974). It is well known that observed group mem-bers sometimes lie to social scientists. Survey researchers are concerned about respondents lying so as to appear more socially desirable. Margaret Mead (1923) was perhaps hoodwinked in Samoa. Even Tally lied to Elliot Liebow (1967). Concerning fabrications constructed by observed groups, dramaturgy might have an advantage over other methodologies. While other method-ologies tend to assume that actors are basically honest, dramaturgy is much more cynical in this regard. A dramaturgical perspective sees actors engaging in manipulative behaviours designed to manage impressions. Goffman's efforts alone have provided concepts such as 'con', 'dupe' and 'fabrication', thereby alerting researchers to the possibility of being intentionally misled by members of an observed group. Dramaturgy seems to provide sufficient conceptual weaponry to confront fabrications. Indeed, further consideration might show how dramaturgy represents a method for studying the tension between fabrications and the 'reality' they attempt to conceal.

Many issues concerning the utility and limits of dramaturgical methods are still left to be explored. Our efforts here have tried to bring together loosely associated pieces of research by emphasizing what we see as some underlying methodological themes. This type of endeavour leaves us open to the criticism of 'putting old wine into new bottles'. We prefer to think of our efforts as placing bottles of wine from a common vineyard into the same crate, the collection being worth more than the sum value of its parts. We also see work of this kind as satisfying a compelling need. With the emergence of deconstructionism, postmodernism, feminist methods and the like, sociology, a modern science, stands to be severely discredited as a 'legitimate' enterprise. As others have claimed, sociologists need to keep pace by developing more reflexive and critical theories and methods. This chapter represents one voice in a new and expanding discourse.

Acknowledgements

An earlier version of this chapter was presented at the Annual Qualitative Research Conference in Toronto, Canada, 1990. The authors thank Gale Miller and Robert Dingwall for their helpful comments.

PART III

ANALYSING INSTITUTIONS AND ORGANIZATIONS

9

Network Analysis and Qualitative Research: a Method of Contextualization

Emmanuel Lazega

A method of contextualization

Part of sociologists' work is to contextualize individual and collective behaviour (Silverman and Gubrium 1994). Contextualization has both a substantive and a methodological dimension. Substantively, it means identifying specific constraints put on some members' behaviour and specific opportunities offered to them and to others. Methodologically, it is a necessary step for comparative analysis and for appropriate generalization of results.

Network analysis is an efficient way of contextualizing actors' behaviour, based on description and inductive modelling of a specific aspect of this context: the relational pattern, or 'structure', of the social setting in which action is observed. It requires collecting specific data on the relationships and exchanges between all the members, and analysing these data using specific procedures.[1] In fact, it can be seen as a systematic and formalized version of a kind of analysis that sociologists and ethnographers have always done intuitively: collecting information on relationships among members of a social setting, mapping these relationships using visual graphs, clustering members in different sub-sets along different criteria (for instance, similar characteristics, similar political alignments or similar ties to others). Its technical development during the 1970s and 1980s, however, has provided sociology with new concepts and has renewed old theoretical debates. Based on this method, a new form of 'structural' sociology has developed. It uses its own concepts – such as structural equivalence, cohesion, centrality or autonomy – to participate in developing the theory of individual and collective action.[2]

This is especially the case with complete networks; that is, networks in which researchers have information on the presence or absence of a tie between any two members of the setting. As a consequence, organizations have been among the settings most studied by network analysts (besides urban communities, kinship systems and company boards; see Nohria and Eccles 1992, for a review). Although certain general topics are dominant in this production (such as organizational integration; relationships between centrality, autonomy and power; influence of ties on decisions; informal discriminatory mechanisms and invisible competitive advantages), such studies deal with many substantive issues. For instance, they describe the ways in which 'friendship', advice or influence relationships cut across internal hierarchical, functional and office boundaries. They show the ways in which systems filter information reaching their members and the effects they have on the distribution and exchange of resources among them.

As a method of contextualization of behaviour, network analysis can dramatically enhance qualitative research. Conversely, it is impossible to design a network study, or to interpret the results provided by this type of analysis, without having previously performed a careful ethnography of the setting using classical approaches and questions. Used exclusively on its own, network analysis is a purely formal exercise. This chapter is meant to convey the spirit in which such studies are conducted. I first summarize, in a non-technical way, the standard procedures of network analytical approaches. Secondly, I provide an illustration, based on a case study, of the result of two of the main procedures. Thirdly, I look at the way network analysis and symbolic interaction can be combined by the practice of 'multi-level' contextualization. Finally, I summarize the added value provided by this method to qualitative approaches and some precautions to be taken when using it.

Bridging the micro and macro levels

A complete (analytically closed) social network is generally defined as a set of relations of a specific type (for instance, advice, support or control relationships) between a defined set of actors. Network analysis is the name given to a number of procedures for describing and modelling inductively the pattern of relations or 'relational structure' in this set of actors. Therefore, analytically speaking, relationships among actors have priority over their individual attributes. Structural reasoning is usually differentiated from 'categorical', which is based on more standard statistical reasoning. Researchers start with relations and structures, before they bring in characteristics of actors or actors' behaviour, in order to make sense of the structures emerging from the analysis, to explain the emergence of this particular structure, or to explain the observed behaviour as a function of actors' position in it. The main point is that researchers start with data on relations, adding information on attributes and additional behaviour only at a second stage. The main contribution of this method to theory-building is its capacity to contextualize behaviour by describing relational structures in a way that bridges the individual, relational and structural levels of analysis.

Describing the relational structure of a social setting first consists in identifying sub-sets of actors within this system. Such sub-sets can be reconstituted based, for instance, on measurement of the 'cohesion' or density of ties among members: one may say, for instance, that a sub-set of members constitutes a 'clique' when relationships among them are direct or strong. Sub-sets may also be reconstituted based on measurements of members' 'structural equivalence': in that case, actors are clustered together in a sub-set called a 'position' or 'block' because they share a similar relational profile (they have approximately the same type of relationships with the other actors in the setting, and not necessarily because they have strong ties with one another). Thus, structurally equivalent actors are located in the relational structure in an approximately similar way, which means that they may have, for instance, at the time of the fieldwork, the same 'enemies' and the same 'friends', be paralysed by similar constraints or be offered similar opportunities and resources.

Based on this initial description of the relational structure, structural analysis can be said to consist in three types of procedure:

1 Procedures reconstituting the morphology of the setting using partitions and descriptions of relations between sub-sets: network analysis reconstitutes 'cliques', 'blocks', or 'positions', but also relationships between such sub-sets, which is one of its most significant differences from classical sociometry. The latter did not leave the relational levels of analysis to reach the 'structural' one.

2 Procedures for positioning of actors in this structure. Each member of the social system can be located in this structure, for instance, based on his/her membership in a clique or in a position, or with individual scores such as centrality, prestige or autonomy. Such procedures are of particular interest to theoreticians because of their flexibility: they allow a constant back and forth movement from the individual and local level to the structural and global level, without losing sight of the individual (as would standard statistical aggregations of individual attributes).

3 Procedures associating members' position in the structure with their behaviour. The pattern of relations among actors can be considered to be an independent variable (among others) and its influence on members' behaviour disentangled from other effects and measured.

Contextualization works here through an association between members' position in a relational structure and their behaviour. In theory as well as in practice, this association between position and behaviour is never a deterministic one. It only describes trends. For instance, it often happens that some social settings cannot be partitioned in cliques or clearly defined positions, or that a considerable proportion of members have a unique relational profile (that is, which is not very similar to that of any other member of the setting). Therefore, researchers must constantly compare threshold effects, control for results by using different clustering or partitioning methods, mobilize their ethnographic knowledge of the field to choose what they consider to be the most reliable technique, and make sense of the results within such boundaries.

The use of network analysis requires two additional but important preliminary tasks: a justification of the boundaries defined for the social setting under examination, as well as the relationships used to reconstitute the informal structure (Marsden 1990). Concerning boundaries, rigid delimitations of a social setting are always arbitrary, but the flexibility of network analysis offers ways of defining and redefining them in an analytical and exploratory way. Usually, social systems do not have clear boundaries, and this flexibility allows researchers to define temporary boundaries after exploration of the process of boundary definition by the members themselves. Two comments can be made regarding the definition of the relationships involved. First, the pattern of any network of ties – for instance the advice network in the firm – can be considered to be an approximation of the relational structure of this organization. Technically, network analysis can study networks separately; it can also superpose them and reach a transverse overall view of the relational structure. The question of which specific tie produces the pattern which is the closest to the overall informal structure is a substantive one. Secondly, the study of a specific network is not a goal in itself. It is part of the study of behaviour and processes that researchers are trying to contextualize. Without dependent variables, the description of the structure often remains sterile. In that sense, observing a specific network must have a meaning for the behaviour under consideration. The method itself does not establish *a priori* a hierarchy between the relations selected and examined. To give more importance to one type of relation than to another is a choice for which researchers must account prior to fieldwork.

The pattern of relationships that emerges from this analysis represents an important dimension of the structure of the setting. The specificity of this method is that this dimension of the structure has an internal and an external reality. It is internal in that it is built inductively based on the specificities observed among members, often identified and interpreted by them. It becomes external in that it characterizes a collective level on which separate individual members do not have much influence. Here, the distinction between micro and macro levels becomes much more manageable than with 'usual' statistical techniques because this method allows the researcher to travel from one to the other in a very flexible way. When interpreting the pattern at the structural level, it is always possible to go back to the individual level, check who belongs to which position, then reason again at the collective level using that information.

As in classical theory, the conceptual link between structure and behaviour is provided by the notion of *role*. However, in current network analysis this notion has two distinct meanings. The first definition refers to the function of a position (that is, the sub-set of structurally equivalent members). In a network where a specific resource flows, relations between positions usually display a division of labour in the production and exchange of this resource. It is often hypothesized that members of a position who are integrated in the network in a relatively similar way will tend to have similar behaviour in this system of production and exchange. The second definition refers to a combination of relations compounding two or more different networks. Members' behaviour is not necessarily exclusively determined by their relations observed here and now, in one single network, but by their integration in several different networks. For example, one's spouse's boss can be considered to be a role because it articulates two different 'relational worlds'.[3] White et al. (1976) are the first to have tried to partition collections of relations and to conceptualize the notion of role for multi-relational data sets. Roles become here complex and abstract constructs marking the simultaneous effect of several networks (past or present) on behaviour.

Network analysis can thus be conceived of as a method of contextualization and quantitative framing for qualitative approaches to members' behaviour. The description of the relational structure by identification of subsets (cliques or positions), in one or several networks, is a way of identifying inductively collective actors present at a specific moment in a social setting, as well as the relationships or exchanges between them. In turn, the description of these relations, or absence of relations, between blocks identifies a system of interdependences between these collective actors. The analysis thus detects underlying regulatory mechanisms and offers useful indications for a qualitative and strategic perspective.

Seeking advice in a corporate law firm

Substantively, I will draw on a case study (Lazega 1992b, 1995) in the sociology of organizations to illustrate one way in which the bridge between micro (individual and relational) and macro (structural) levels is established. The study is based on fieldwork conducted in a New England corporate law firm (71 lawyers in three offices, comprising 36 partners and 35 associates) in 1991. All the lawyers in the firm were interviewed. In Nelson's (1988) terminology, this firm is a 'traditional' one, as opposed to a more 'bureaucratic' type. It is a relatively decentralized organization, which grew out of a merger, but without formal and acknowledged distinctions between profit centres. It adopted a managing partner structure during the 1980s for more efficient day-to-day management and decision-making, but its managing partners are not 'rainmakers' and do not concentrate strong powers in their hands. Given the informality of the organization, a weak administration provides information, but does not have many formal rules to enforce. Although not departmentalized, the firm breaks down into two general areas of practice: the litigation area (half the lawyers of the firm) and the 'corporate' area (anything other than litigation).

Interdependence among attorneys working together on a file may be strong for a few weeks, and then weak for months. Sharing work and cross-selling among partners is done mostly on an informal basis. Given the classical stratification of such firms, work is supposed to be channelled to associates through specific partners, but this rule is only partly respected. Partners' compensation is based exclusively on a seniority lock-step system without any direct link between contribution and returns. The firm goes to great lengths – when selecting associates to become partners – to take as few risks as possible that they will not 'pull their weight'. As a client-oriented, knowledge-intensive organization, it tries to protect its human capital and social resources, such as its network of clients, through the usual policies of commingling partners' assets (clients, experience, innovations) (Gilson and Mnookin 1985) and the maintenance of an ideology of collegiality. Informal networks of collaboration, advice and 'friendship' (socializing outside) are therefore particularly important to the integration of the firm (Lazega 1992b).

To illustrate contextualization and bridging of levels of analysis, I focus here on the advice network among lawyers. Advice is an important resource in professional, collegial and knowledge-intensive organizations. In a law firm that structures itself so as to protect and develop its human and social capital (Gilson and Mnookin 1985; Nelson 1988; Smigel 1969), such a resource is particularly vital. Given this importance, one could easily believe that flows of advice in the firm are 'free', or at least that they do not encounter structural obstacles which would systematically prevent exchanges of intelligence between any two members. However, even in a context that is saturated with advice, many factors create obstacles for exchanges of ideas. Most importantly, advice-seeking is influenced by the formal and informal structure of the firm. These dimensions of the structure constrain exchanges of ideas among members. In turn, such constraints are managed in different ways by the members of the firm, which creates disadvantages and inequalities among them (Lazega 1995). To follow the flows of advice in the firm, I used the following name-generator which, among many others, was submitted to all the lawyers in the firm:

> Here is the list of all the lawyers in the firm. To whom do you go for basic professional advice, not simply technical advice, for instance when you want to make sure that you are doing things right – for instance handling a case? Would you go through this list, and check the names of those persons.

To give an idea of the task performed by the interviewee, here are some of the statements provided along with the sociometric choices:

> Usually advice involves something of another area of law, one that I am not practising. Among the people who can answer, I choose those with experience and the smartest, those who have proved that they have good ideas. With associates, it is different: I can ask for their reaction, but I have to decide for myself. One thing I have learned is that nobody knows everything. Don't ignore the young people. The most stupid guy can sometimes have a good idea. (a partner)

> It's a mixed bag. If advice includes issues related to firm management, Smith I would ask on ethics type of questions, or on legal conflicts. He's been around longer than most. Jones for anything having to do with the management of the Hartford office, I rely on him for that. Brown for associate staffing type of issues and also general advice too, what he thinks of where the firm is going. Robertson

was basically a managing partner in another firm before he came, I can ask him all sorts of questions on what he would do about this or that. (the current managing partner)

On a particular file, I would go to the partner with whom I work on this file. So the list looks a lot like the co-workers list, although not entirely. There have been times where I got other people's perspective, for instance when other partners with whom I have already worked on similar files have helped me, or when I need to know the implications for the client in other fields. I am a corporate lawyer, and the people I ask are usually in the litigation department. (an associate)

In quantitative terms, answers to the question vary extensively. At both extremes, we have a partner who says that he does not need nor ask anyone for advice, and another partner who declares seeking advice from 30 other colleagues. On average, lawyers have in their network 12 colleagues with whom they can exchange basic work-related ideas. However, such indexes may be misleading. They hide structural effects constraining resource flows, as well as advantages from which some members benefit given their position in the informal structure of the firm. Formal as well as informal dimensions of the structure of the firm have an influence on the choice of advisers. Here, I describe briefly the effect of selected formal dimensions. I then use an analysis of structural equivalence to describe more at length the informal relational structure emerging from this advice network.

It is possible to describe the effect of several dimensions of the formal structure on members' choices of advisers. Members' status (partner versus associate), specialty (litigation versus corporate) and office (Boston, Hartford or Providence) all have significant effects on the choices of advisers. For instance, it is much more frequent for associates to seek advice from partners than the other way around. Exchanges of ideas and intelligence in this firm are indeed affected by status games among members. The same is true of members' office and specialty. In this firm, litigators have a significantly higher probability of choosing advisers among other litigators rather than among corporate lawyers. A similar trend is observed among the latter. Thus the formal structure of the firm weighs heavily on advice-seeking behaviour.[4] This reflects the existence of informal and unspoken rules regarding exchanges of advice in this firm.

However, such rules are not rigid. The figures show many deviations from them. Thus, other, more informal, constraints also contribute in shaping flows of advice. To describe the ways in which they do so, network analytical techniques provide finer tools for uncovering the invisible pattern of advice-seeking which characterizes this specific firm. This pattern is described below, using an analysis of structural equivalence among members (Burt 1982, 1991), which clusters in the same 'position' actors with similar relational profiles in the network examined. Eleven clearly different positions are thus identified. Regardless of the number of individuals in each position, the positions and the relations between them create a complex pattern, or informal structure. Figure 9.1 provides an overview of the relations between these positions.

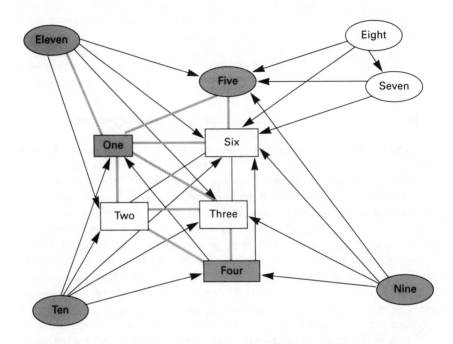

Figure 9.1   *Relations between positions of structurally equivalent actors in the advice network of all lawyers in the firm. Positions represented by a square box are composed mainly of partners; positions represented by a circle are composed mainly of associates. Positions in grey have at least one rival position among the other positions in grey of similar status. Grey lines represent reciprocated advice relationships between positions. A detailed description of these positions and the relationships between them is presented in the Appendix.*

A detailed description of these positions and the relationships among them is available in the Appendix. To summarize, Position One, the 'hard core' of the firm, is composed of Boston partners of all specialties. Position Two clusters the 'atypical ' attorneys (either 'laterals', i.e. lawyers recruited from other law firms, or of non-lucrative corporate specialties) from both main offices. Position Three is that of Hartford core corporate partners. Position Four is that of Hartford core litigation partners. Position Five is that of the 'coordinators', mostly senior women litigation associates in Boston. Position Six clusters the firm's 'universal advisers', all litigators in Boston. Position Seven is composed of a group of Boston litigation associates called 'the boys'. Position Eight is that of the most junior associates in the firm, all Boston litigators and called 'the beginners'. Position Nine clusters Hartford litigation associates. Position Ten is mainly that of lateral corporate associates in the whole firm. Position Eleven is mainly composed of 'atypical' Boston corporate associates. A category of 'residual' actors (i.e. actors whose relational profile is different from that of everyone else) does not appear in this figure. As an example of relations between two positions, notice that members of Position Ten tend not to seek advice from members of Position Eleven; or that members of all positions tend to seek advice from members of Position Six.

The analysis of the directions taken by the flows of advice in the firm provides useful insights into the context in which members of this firm exchange this type of resource. Very generally, this context can be described by an obvious stratification between those who are often sought out for advice and those who are almost never (or very little) consulted. Within each of these two categories, interesting absences of relations can be detected and interpreted as specific characteristics of this context.

The first category includes members of Positions One to Six. It is not surprising to find that blocks of partners (as opposed to associates) occupy a central place in this informal pattern. As shown by Figure 9.1, the five positions of partners (One, Two, Three, Four and Five) form a sub-set towards which requests for advice converge from all positions. For instance, exchanges with Position One are very frequent; all tend to seek its members for advice, and they often reciprocate, except with Position Four (Hartford litigation partners sometimes perceived as rivals). Position Six is the most effective at integrating the firm with regard to the distribution of this resource: its members tend to be sought out for advice by the members of all the other positions, but it only reciprocates to Positions One and Five (and especially not to Two, Three and Four).

The second category includes members of Positions Seven to Eleven. For instance, members of Positions Seven and Eight have access to the rest of the firm through Position Five (the coordinators) or Six (the universal advisers) members. Positions Ten and Eleven members are exceptions to this trend. Their members reach directly the most important partners in the firm. Such trends can be explained by the ethnography of the firm: we know, for instance, that most associates in Positions Ten and Eleven are laterals; they did not 'grow up' in the firm, and may not have interiorized the norms and informal boundaries which inhibit other associates who came up through the ranks. In addition, given their seniority, they may try to intensify their direct ties with partners to get themselves known and increase their chances of becoming a partner.

Absence of relations between positions show asymmetries in the flows of advice across the firm. They describe the context in which advice-seeking occurs in terms of informal stratification (concentration of choices on an 'elite' of advisers and on specific positions in the overall pattern) and polarization (between offices and specialties). In such a context, some members have direct access to advice from important partners, whereas others have to pay a relatively higher price to get access to the same resources. The informal structure thus creates or reflects inequalities among members. Moreover, to seek advice, members also cross the boundaries identified above in the description of the effect of specific dimensions of the formal structure. Such infractions to the rules may be tolerated for some, and less for others.

For instance, concerning the absence of exchanges among associates, notice that members of Positions Seven, Eight, Nine and Eleven exchange advice within their own group, but very little with the members of other positions. This may be explained by the fact that members of each group have to strike a fragile balance between cooperation and competition. They need each other for advice, but they also tend to be rivals in their relationships with partners. This is particularly true for the members of Positions Five, Nine, Ten and Eleven who were supposed, at the time of the fieldwork, to come up for partnership in the next two years. This competition between associates can result in the design of different relational strategies. Position Five members, for instance, may try to reduce the number of situations in which the members of other positions of associates will get a chance to show their capacity to provide advice, for instance by insulating them in compartmentalized domains defined by traditional and formal internal boundaries. Similarly, lateral or 'foreign' (from another office) associates may let themselves be used more often because they are perceived to be easier to exploit or less threatening in terms of loss of status for the advice-seeker.

But the most striking and special aspect of the pattern in Figure 9.1 is the absence of direct reciprocity between certain positions of partners (between Positions One and Four, and between Positions Three/Four and Six). Focusing on the relationships among partners shows again that the One–Six axis is dominant in the control of the flows of advice, but also the absence of reciprocity in these flows, especially among Boston and Hartford litigation partners who compete for the best associates, and for status and prestige within the firm. This asymmetry – which cannot be explained by economic incentives to withhold advice or let other partners down – is even stronger when Figure 9.1 is simplified to retain only reciprocal relations between positions, i.e. true collective exchanges of advice. Polarization between Hartford and Boston is still present, as well as the centrality and power of Position One in terms of advice flows. Members of this position, for instance, obviously prefer to seek advice from associates of Position Five rather than from their own partners in Position Four.

A compartmentalized structure emerges, where some have more or better resources to deal with competition and get access to resources such as advice, whereas others are clearly cornered and dependent. This context of advice-seeking is thus constraining in terms of efficiency, but also in terms of control and internal politics. Although exchange of advice often justifies the existence of such firms, actors' strategies at different levels often orient these flows and structure a 'market' for advice in a specific way.

To summarize, this example started with the effect of dimensions of the formal structure (boundaries imposed by stratification, division of work and differences in office membership) on the flows of advice. A network analytical procedure has described the pattern of advice relationship at the collective and structural level. This pattern represents the relational context in which individual members seek advice from one another. In turn, this contextualization of individual behaviour helps in understanding how members strike a balance between competition and cooperation within the firm in terms of access to, and management of, such resources. It shows in particular how flows of advice are clearly shaped by symbolic games of membership, recognition, inclusions and exclusions, identification and social differentiation. The description of this specific advice-based dimension of the relational structure of the firm allows us to look at the relationship between members' position in the structure, their behaviour in terms of advice-seeking, and their advantages or disadvantages in terms of access to resources. The same approach can help link any relational structure to any behaviour, including assertions, attributions of different meanings to different stimuli (Emerson and Messinger 1977; Lazega 1992a) – provided that they are observed in a systematic way – as well as the type of actions on which interactionist and qualitative studies currently focus.

Network analysis and symbolic interaction

One of the potential uses for this method is to develop the structural dimension of interactionist approaches. It provides rigorous and flexible tools for analysing behaviour at the individual, relational and structural levels simultaneously. Therefore, it is of interest to such approaches when they try to combine both the actor's perspective and the system's perspective in their account of individual and collective action. Compatibility between the two approaches is both methodological and substantive.

Network analysis is an inductive method. This inductive character is precisely what makes it compatible with approaches to social phenomena such as that of symbolic interactionism. From both perspectives, researchers at the beginning of their fieldwork do not have a precise picture of the morphology of their social setting, the number and composition of collective actors in presence, or the configuration of the relationships and exchanges between them. Observers progressively reach this picture of the system and its regulation at the structural level. Although it introduces a quantitative dimension in the analysis, this formalization does not reify the method, nor does it rely on a reified conception of the structure.

As demonstrated by Maines (1977), many symbolic interactionists have taken structures into account, defining the specificity of the contexts in which they were doing research and giving considerable importance to structural constraints when describing actors' behaviour.[5] 'Structuralist' symbolic interactionists – from Hughes (1945, 1958) to Freidson (1976, 1986), Bucher (1970), Benson and Day (1976), Day and Day (1977), Strong and Dingwall (1983), Dingwall and Strong (1985) – developed a less 'subjectivist' framework than theoreticians more attracted to social psychology. Symbolic interactionist work taking social structure into account relies on a less rigid and less stable conception of the structure than does the functionalist tradition (which is why, from the latter perspective, the interactionist definition of the structure often seemed non-existent). But it has not done so in a truly systematic way.

Based on the previous sections, it is possible to argue that network analysis can provide symbolic interaction theory with a systematic contextualization tool. In fact, such a contextualization has *multiple levels*. This multi-level character is best explained by a link between the concepts of structure, identity and the definition of the situation.

Describing relational structures is only a first step in the contextualization of behaviour. It is based on members' local perception of their ties, which are then aggregated and combined into an informal pattern at the global or collective level. But the construction of ties, or choice of exchange partners, does not happen in a vacuum. A second step consists in looking at the effect of formal structural dimensions on the choices of ties. For instance, members of organizations looking for exchange partners often choose others similar to themselves with respect to various characteristics (for example, specialty, status or office membership). As a consequence, an emergent context of behaviour is itself shaped by background formal contexts. From a symbolic interactionist perspective, the latter can be defined as a set of institutional identities formally attributed to some members, with various degrees of authority attached to them.[6] Consequently, formal dimensions of structure can be said to have a double effect on behaviour, directly and indirectly: directly, because formal structure translates into identities and rules to which members can refer when monitoring their behaviour; indirectly, because they do have an influence on the choices of exchange partners, and therefore on the formation of relational and informal patterns.

Understanding contextualization in this way resonates with the symbolic interactionist conception of the link between structure and individual behaviour or 'rationality'; that is, the 'definition of the situation'. This link is based on the concepts of identity and role. Actors use attributes provided by formal and informal structures as sources of identities in their definition of the situation. Contextualization thus has both a theoretical and practical meaning. For theorists of individual and collective action, it means understanding constraints potentially orienting members' behaviour. For actors themselves, it means actually activating specific identities when evaluating the appropriateness of their behaviour (Lazega 1992a).

This multi-level method of contextualization complexifies the study of human behaviour under structural constraints by combining formal and informal dimensions of structure, as well as combining quantitative and formalized approaches with qualitative and ethnographic ones. Network analysis can thus help transform symbolic interaction into a fully fledged theory of collective action capable of expanding its explorations. It solves the main problem that the 'negotiated order theory' (Strauss et al. 1963; Strauss 1978) wanted to solve; that is, going beyond the difference between formal and informal structure. Informal sub-sets emerging from the analysis are different from, but closely intertwined with, the formal morphology of a setting. A comparison between prescribed and emergent structures becomes possible because formal (for instance, the chart) and informal dimensions of the structure can be described in the same terms, both being representable as networks of ties and as sets of identities. In addition, attributes of individual and collective actors can be combined with characteristics of their relations. Here again, this points out that, for both approaches, members themselves contribute in constructing the structures which end up constraining their own behaviour. Network analysis as a method of multi-level contextualization can thus help symbolic interaction follow this process and travel from the actor's perspective to the system's perspective and backwards.

Such a *rapprochement* still raises several conceptual difficulties, to be addressed by theoreticians, or by researchers on a case-by-case basis. First, the existence of ties is inferred from reported or observed interactions, exchanges of resources and common activities. To identify the specific type of interaction or tie of interest in the reconstitution of a network, researchers have to rely on shared meanings specifying such interactions or ties. 'Shared' means that the tie and action have to make sense to all the members of a social setting in a broadly similar way. As put by Fine (1991, 1992; Fine and Kleinman 1983), structure's reality is separate from its interpretation, but must be mediated through perception of conduct options and external forces. Network analysts know that, in order to reconstitute a network, one needs a clear definition of the ties constituting this network. They rely on the idea that networks are exchange networks. Therefore, the definition of meaningful ties (i.e. ties through which resources flow) is left to the researcher and negotiated with respondents prior to the collection of network data. Network analysts, however, have not given priority to this issue: they do not account much for differences in the way members of a social settings define what resource a specific relationship represents; for instance, for the variety of definitions of friendship among the members of an organization. Furthermore, network analysts have not, up to now, paid much attention to redefinitions of relationships. Members are not assumed to be strategic, capable of changing the meaning of their relationship. The link between renegotiation of the meaning of a relationship and the dynamics of relational structures is not systematically addressed.[7]

Secondly, although it is an issue that goes beyond the scope of this chapter, this *rapprochement*, in order to become truly significant in the study of individual and collective action, has to produce theoretical developments as well. Two issues illustrate the need for such developments: the problem of an inductive and deductive theory of structure, and the problem of an integrated theory of role.

First, from the symbolic interactionist perspective, social order is constructed through meaningful, self–other interaction (Blumer 1969) under the 'surveillance' of reference groups, an audience which is not necessarily empirically present, but nevertheless exercising social control, and thus constraining behaviour by judging its appropriateness. In this context, the question of the structure is raised in terms of institutional constraints influencing negotiations of identities or appropriateness judgements (Lazega 1992a; McCall and Simmons 1966). Since most interactions take place in situations that are never completely structured, nor necessarily clearly defined in actors' minds, the latter may not necessarily know which of their identities will be involved in the ongoing interaction, and which behaviour is more appropriate given the choice of such identity. A phase of mutual identification, of identity negotiation and ranking, is necessary for interactions to take place. The link between the structure of the social setting and the interactive processes which take place within them is theorized through this negotiation. This basic theory thus offers an abstract and deductive way of contextualizing behaviour which needs to be articulated with inductive methodologies practised by interactionists and by network analysts. Whether formalized or not, descriptions of relational contexts in which actors' behaviour takes place do not offer a synthesis of both inductive and deductive approaches. Such a development must rest on a theory of social control and the notion of network constraint (White 1992): actors' interactions create relational constraints which in turn end up constraining their interactions in a way that must be interpretable in terms of social control, management of identities and legitimacy. This process is inherent in the interactive construction of social structure, but invisible in the mechanics of network analysis.

Secondly, an example of conceptual proximity between network analysis and symbolic interaction through contextualization at both the individual and collective levels can come from the comparison between the notion of role as used in both perspectives. As seen above, a conceptual link between structure and behaviour in network analysis is provided by the notion of role, which can be understood as the function performed by a position (for instance, a sub-set of structurally equivalent members), or as a combination of relations compounding two or more different networks. This operationalization of the concept of role, like any model, simplifies the description of constraints on behaviour, especially because it is exclusively relational. For critics (Brint 1992; DiMaggio 1992), the role of normative and cultural orientations may be as important in the explanation of actors' behaviour, especially when structural constraints are multiple and sometimes contradictory. In addition, for most general theories of action, such as Nadel's (1957), a role results from normative expectations and relations with associates carrying these expectations and sanctioning deviance. To the extent that behaviour is guided by interiorized norms, it may be difficult to connect a relational basis for all rights and duties; for instance, by finding authority figures which represent them or speak on their behalf. Roles are not only a synthesis of individual and social levels, but also of cultural and relational dimensions. Structural analysis, which focuses on the relational dimension of roles, presupposes norms of values or recognizes them *ex post facto*. But when researchers cannot reconstitute an empirical relational basis for a norm, the latter is not recognizable. In that sense network analysis, on its own, cannot take cultural elements sufficiently into account so as to ground a general theory of collective action. The ways in which the two dimensions of collective action have to be articulated can only be theorized using additional theoretical assumptions, such as those provided by symbolic interactionism.

Conversely, Blumer (1969) and Turner (1962) see roles as sets of informal rules created and re-created through interactions, especially through negotiations between individuals and their associates (Handel 1979; Meltzer et al. 1975). Actors and their interactions construct the roles and rules that govern their behaviour. Individuals participate in defining their own roles, which have many variations, and they usually undergo change (Stryker and Statham 1985). In that sense, two largely descriptive steps are involved in the analysis of roles. One is the description of the extent to which the informal definition of the role (role-making) is closely related to the formal definition (role-taking). The second is the description of the extent to which this redefinition is itself subject to relational constraints. These negotiations re-create and reshape roles, often with dogmatic emphasis on (always temporary forms of) conformity and consensus among homogeneous stakeholders. Such a dogmatic emphasis may also be weakened by network analysis. Individuals' role-related behaviours are determined by expectations of their associates, and such expectations are themselves culturally coded. In order to link institutions and individuals, the structural approach can define roles as sets of norms that are widely endorsed by an actor's associates. But these associates may change. Here again, network analysis can help symbolic interactionists go beyond local negotiations, and reach the broader structural contexts within which these negotiations and changes occur.

Finally, this comparison between the notions of role used in both perspectives raises questions related to the concept of identity. As seen above, network analysis as a method of multi-level contextualization deals with the question of a hierarchy of allegiances and identities. However, it still does so without a consistent theory of identity. Is identity a benefit that actors extract from belonging to a specific position in a relational structure? Is it a key for the construction of ties (access to resources) and for individual rationality and orientation of action within a specific structure (formal and informal)? Do relational structures produce identities (expand the set of identities available to actors when defining the situation) or provide only a sense of appropriateness in using formal attributes (that is, constrain the choices of formal and pre-existing identities)?[8] With which kind of attributes (if any) do informal structures provide actors for orientation or co-orientation of behaviour? For example, are marginal actors less constrained in terms of negotiation of identities than central and highly visible actors?

To answer such questions, it is important to study the way in which formal and informal structures intertwine to constrain behaviour and offer opportunities. Such studies should pay particular attention to dimensions of structure which offer identities that actors can and do use in their definition of the situation and appropriateness judgements. Thus, without further developments (of an approach both inductive and deductive, of a synthesis between a relational and a cultural contextualization of action and exchange, of a structural theory of identity), the two approaches will not be brought together into a flexible framework suitable for a systematic study of individual and collective action.

Conclusion

Network analysis reconstitutes inductively the relational structure of social settings, based on knowledge of ties among members (Burt 1982; Wasserman and Faust 1994; White et al. 1976). Its procedures provide a rigorous method for analysing social phenomena at the individual, relational and structural levels simultaneously. The result is a flexible link between micro and macro levels of analysis, one which does not reify the concept of structure. As a method of multi-level contextualization of behaviour, it has much in common with the work of symbolic interactionists interested in behaviour from participants' and from the system's perspective simultaneously. This connection between network analysis and symbolic interaction needs further theoretical clarification. But researchers doing ethnography can use network data from observation or records and attempt similar analyses. 'Triangulation' of methods can thus enhance rigorous qualitative research that raises new theoretical issues.

It should be stressed that, in spite of being theoretically consistent with symbolic interactionist theory of action, this contextualization is sometimes difficult to achieve. Boundary specification and choice of relations have an effect on the external and internal validity of research. Also, data collection can meet with understandable resistance from members whose relationships, exchanges and power games are exposed. In addition, sociometric interviews are time-consuming for individuals and for organizations, which may encourage researchers to look for indirect ways of observing relationships among members. Thus, only the methodological imagination of researchers can overcome such disadvantages. Within such limitations, this method of multi-level contextualization has a clear potential for contributing to qualitative and ethnographic research, from which it originally stemmed.

Appendix

Detailed presentation of Figure 9.1

All Boston and Providence senior partners, including the managing partner and two more junior partners, of all specialties, occupy Position One (Partners 1, 2, 4, 8, 9, 10, 11, 12, 15, 16, 17, 20, 29, 34). They exchange advice among themselves and seek advice from partners from Positions Two, Three and Six, mixing all specialties and offices, as well as from Boston associates of Positions Five and Eleven. Note that they do not directly seek out Hartford litigation partners, or Hartford litigation associates with little experience or seniority. However, their advice is sought out by the members of the positions they seek out (Two, Three, Five, Six and Eleven), but also by members of positions Four (Hartford litigation partners) and Ten (atypical associates from all offices). This confirms an asymmetry between Boston and Hartford partners within the same specialty. This asymmetry is probably caused by a certain prestige competition between the main litigators of these offices, by the critical mass – in terms of the number of litigators – reached by the Boston office, but also perhaps by a certain 'arrogance' of its members. This is suggested by their prominence scores (Burt

1991). More than half of the most prominent partners in the firm (in the advice net-work) belong to this position. Therefore, I call it the 'hard core' of the firm. Its members are more often sought out and listened to than others.

The second position clusters 'atypical' (non-lucrative specialty and lateral recruit-ment) mainly corporate partners and associates from both offices (3, 7, 19, 25, 45, 46, 50, 60). This does not mean that their advice is not sought out. On the contrary, they exchange advice among themselves and seek out partners from Positions One, Three, Four and Six, mixing specialties and offices. They do not seek out any asso-ciate in the firm, thus playing more status games than members of the previous position. Their advice is sought out by partners from Positions One, Three and Four, but not Six, as well as by atypical associates from both largest offices (Positions Ten and Eleven). It is interesting to remember that lateral associates have to rely almost exclusively on their competence to become a partner, and that they may consequently have a more instrumental attitude in exchanges of advice. They have less time than other associates to make themselves known to partners, and may take advantage of these exchanges to meet them more systematically. They are also members of both offices, and constitute an unexpected bridge between them. They almost never seek out associates from other positions, but are sought out by the latter (especially from Positions Ten and Eleven). Atypical partners and associates thus tend to exchange ideas more often with one another than with more typical colleagues. This particu-lar circuit in the advice flows may explain that this second position cuts systematically across specialty and office boundaries. I call it the position of 'atypical' attorneys.

The third position clusters exclusively Hartford corporate partners (14, 28, 32, 35) who exchange advice among themselves and seek out partners from all the other posi-tions (One, Two, Four and Six), but almost never associates. This is perhaps due to the fact that there are few corporate associates in Hartford, and that direct access to Boston corporate associates may be a delicate matter, unless through Boston partners, which introduces a certain dependence. Their advice is sought out by partners from Positions One, Two and Four (but not Position Six), as well as by associates from Positions Nine, Ten and Eleven, i.e. atypical associates from all offices and Hartford litigation associates. Notice that Boston corporate associates do not seek out these Hartford partners of the same specialty. I call this position the position of the Hartford corporate partners.

The fourth position is composed exclusively of Hartford litigation partners (5, 18, 30, 31) who exchange advice among themselves and seek out partners from all the other positions (Positions One, Two, Three and Six) but again very rarely from asso-ciates. Their advice is sought out in return by the members of Positions Two, Three and Six, but not One, the Boston 'hard-core' litigators. One finds here again the pres-tige competition, the critical mass and independence of Boston, the perception of arrogance described above. Hartford litigation associates (Position Nine) seek them out as well as Boston litigation associates of Position Five (who play a broker role between litigation partners and associates in the whole firm) and Ten. Associates from Positions Seven, Eight and Eleven do not have direct access to these Position Four partners, from whom they are separated by status and office boundaries. I call this position that of Hartford litigation partners.

The fifth position is exclusively composed of women litigators in Boston (27, 38, 39, 43): the most senior woman partner in the firm and the three most senior women associates in the firm. They exchange advice among themselves and seek advice from partners in Positions One, Four and Six, mainly the most prominent partners in the advice network, Boston and Hartford litigation partners. They are very close to the most prominent position in the network and focused exclusively on advice relationships with other litigators; they do not seek out other associates, corporate partners, or atypical partners described above. They do, however, exchange ideas with Hartford litigation partners (Position Four), which may be a sign of independence from Position One partners. Their advice, however, is sought out by members of six positions (One, Six, Seven, Eight, Nine and Eleven). They centralize many requests and even Boston partners (corporate as well as litigation partners) ask for their advice, as do all the litigation associates in the firm. Notice that even Hartford litigation associates (Position Nine) seek them out for advice, which may allow them not to bypass their own Hartford litigation partners and take less risk with their reputation there (they do not have to go for advice to their own direct and local 'bosses'). This position is also clearly a bridge between prominent Position One partners and firm litigation associates who do not have access to them directly (for instance, Positions Seven and Eight). Finally, members of this position have very few advice relationships with the atypical lawyers in the firm and with the corporate side of the firm. They are a pure product of the Boston office, its training and promotion system. I call this position that of the women litigation coordinators.

The sixth position is made of the partners most active in firm administrative committees (managing partners and deputy managing partners excepted), that Nelson (1988) calls *minders*,[9] as well as two of the most senior male associates in the firm (13, 21, 24, 26, 40, 41). All are litigators from Boston. They exchange advice among themselves and seek out Position One partners and Position Five associates, thus confining themselves within their own office. All are among the most prominent lawyers in the firm, and their position is the most central in the whole pattern. Their advice is sought by members of all other positions. They are the most 'universal' and reachable advisers in the firm: they are sought out by lawyers regardless of status, office or specialty. Notice that, although it is very Bostonian, this position is different from Position One precisely because of its high reachability and homogeneity (it is exclusively made up of litigators). I call this position that of the universal advisers.

Position Seven is exclusively made of Boston medium seniority (three or four years with the firm) male litigation associates that other associates call 'the boys' (49, 52, 54, 55, 56, 57, 62, 65 and 68). They exchange advice among themselves and seek out Position Five associates and Position Six partners, all litigators. Note that they do not have direct access to Position One partners, despite being also pure products of the Boston office. Thus, in terms of exchange of ideas and advice, they are relatively isolated from the rest of the firm. They are themselves sought out only by more junior associates (Position Eight).

The most junior associates in the firm (66, 67, 69, 71), recruited six months before the interviews, all Boston litigators, also have a position of their own, Position Eight. They exchange advice among themselves and seek out Position Five, Six and Seven members, mostly more senior associates and the universal advisers (who are partly in charge of associates). They do not dare bother other partners and stick to senior associates of their own office and specialty. Nobody seeks them out in the advice network. This relative isolation is a classic characteristic of first-year associates in law firms. I call them the 'beginners'.

A ninth position is composed exclusively of Hartford litigation medium seniority (three or four years with the firm) associates (51, 58, 59). They exchange advice among themselves and seek out litigation and corporate partners in Hartford (Positions Three and Four), as well as the coordinators and universal advisers in Boston (Positions Five and Six). It is obvious that associates in Hartford have more direct access to partners in their office than their peers in Boston do. This may be due to the smaller size of the Hartford office and to its specific climate. Like the majority of Boston associates, though, they cannot have direct access to partners of the other office, and have to use intermediaries. Seeking them out directly would be perceived as deliberate bypassing (and lack of trust in) partners in their own office. Nobody seeks out their advice. I call this position that of Hartford litigation associates.

Position Ten is made of relatively marginal associates in the firm (44, 47, 61, 70), i.e. corporate laterals or members of the small Providence office (at the time of the fieldwork). They do not exchange advice among themselves and seek out directly partners from Positions One, Two, Three, Four and Six partners, who do not reciprocate. Just like the members of Position Two, they contribute in blurring internal specialty and offices boundaries. No one seeks them out for advice. I call them the 'peripheral associates'.

Finally, Position Eleven is composed of Boston corporate associates (42, 48, 53, 64), also relatively atypical in the firm (one lateral, one 'permanent associate', etc.). They exchange advice among themselves and seek out members of Positions One, Two, Three, Five and Six. The main difference between these associates and the others of similar profile (such as Position Ten associates, for instance) is that partners from Position One, one of the most prominent in the firm, seek out their advice. I call this position that of the Boston atypical corporate associates.

A 'residual' category (Burt, 1991) includes seven members (6, 22, 23, 33, 36, 37, 63) whose relational profile in this advice network is very different from that of any other member in the firm.

Notes

1 For an introduction to network analysis, see, for example, Berkowitz (1982), Wassermann and Faust (1994), and the documentation of software such as UCINET 4 (Borgatti 1991) and STRUCTURE 4.2 (Burt 1991).

2 A 'network' is not understood here as a specific type of collective actor or specific form of coordination of collective action, one which would offer a third option, for instance, between markets and organizations.

3 There is currently no consensus on the notions used here. For differences, see Burt (1982), Wasserman and Faust (1994) and White et al. (1976).

4 For a more detailed description and explanation of these effects, see Lazega (1995) and Lazega and van Duijn (1997).

5 Symbolic interaction theory has long been criticized for its lack of interest in macrosociology in general, in the existence of social institutions, of bureaucracies, power structures and stratifications of any kind. This reputation, however, is undeserved. Fine and Kleinman (1983, see also Fine 1991, 1992), Maines (1977, 1988) and Stryker (1980) show that the interactionist movement is not homogeneous. It takes into account, much more than is generally acknowledged, the structure of social settings as a determinant of behaviour.

6 Statistically, relationships between formal and informal dimensions of structure can be studied by looking at the effect of actors' attributes on their choices of exchange partners (Lazega and van Duijn 1997).

7 This, however, does not mean that quantitative network analysts exclude meanings from their consideration of social structure. There is a risk of uniformization of meanings with the standardization of name-generators. But, intrinsically, the method focuses on a shared and temporary meaning of a relationship. Discovering what relationships mean to participants is done before systematic data collection. This collection will usually have to focus on specific

types of meanings for empirical and analytical convenience, not because the meaning of relationships is not taken into account. Within this constraint, the main purpose of network tools, as they stand today, is to describe structural constraints on members' behaviour and opportunities given their position in the relational structure of a social setting.

8 In effect, we usually know that we have a formal attribute and we use it as an instrument in our judgements of appropriateness or definition of the situation. But we do not necessarily know in the same way that we belong to a specific position in a specific informal structure, and that we are structurally equivalent to (have roughly the same relational profile as) someone else.

9 *Minders* (as opposed to *finders* or *rainmakers*, who find clients, or to *grinders*, who do most of the actual legal work) concentrate their attention on the functioning of the firm as an organization and on long-established clients.

10

The Interactional Study of Organizations: a Critique and Reformulation

Robert Dingwall and P.M. Strong

This chapter is intended as a contribution to the debate about the condition of the 'negotiated order' approach to the study of organizations, which was the topic of an *Urban Life* special issue (October 1982). The chapter reviews the evolution of this approach and related developments in organizational theory and argues that these have failed to resolve the problems of the relationship between social and formal organization in a manner that is either theoretically or methodologically satisfactory. The chapter outlines alternative proposals, drawing broadly on contributions from ethnomethodology and the sociology of language.

The negotiated order approach to the study of organizations can be viewed, at least in part, as a reaction to the model that has dominated the study of organizations since the First World War. This model, based on a particular reading of Weber (1947), has variously been described as 'rational' (Benson 1971), 'goal oriented' (Georgiou 1973) or 'structural–comparative' (Davies 1979). It draws a sharp line between the study of social organization and of formal organization.

> In contrast to the social organization that emerges whenever men are living together, there are organizations that have been deliberately established for a certain purpose . . . Since the distinctive characteristic of these organizations is that they have been formally established for the explicit purpose of achieving certain goals, the term 'formal organizations' is used to designate them. (Blau and Scott 1963: 5)

This classic model of formal organizations stressed their supra-individual character as rational, rule-governed systems for the pursuit of specified goals. Research involved the comparison of structures for their efficiency in achieving intended objectives, neglecting the problem of how such structures were constituted in the first place. This neglect, however, contributed to the rapid accumulation of anomalous findings within this paradigm. Four such anomalies, all relating to the separation of formal from social organization, are relevant to the present discussion:

1 Observations of members' actual behaviour proved difficult to reconcile with the requirements of the theory. As the Hawthorne studies (for

example, Roethlisberger and Dickson, 1939) had already shown, members simply did not act in a consistently rational and rule-governed manner.

2 Investigators were unable to sustain the assumed unity of purpose in formal organizations or even to specify their goals in any meaningful fashion (Gross 1969; Perrow 1961).

3 The assumption that formal rules indicated the existence of organizations independently of members' actions collapsed under two challenges. First, it was shown that rules did not have any necessarily rational basis, but depended on the aims and bargaining power of particular interest groups (Rushing 1964). Secondly, developments in the philosophy of social science (for example, Winch 1958) cast doubt on whether human action could ever sensibly be described as rule-governed (see Albrow 1968).

4 The notion of a clearly identifiable hierarchy and source of power was shown to be untenable (Mechanic 1962). Lower-status personnel could resist or influence the actions of their formal organizational superiors by their control of resources.

During the 1950s and 1960s, various attempts were made to accommodate these findings by splitting organizational life into 'formal' and 'informal' aspects. The latter reintroduced issues of social organization into discussions of unofficial work groups, norms and relationships, but left them with a residual status as a random source of 'noise' in the system (see Benson 1977a: 9–10). Nevertheless, there has been a growing disillusionment with traditional organization theory.[1] Starbuck (1982: 3), for instance, bleakly observes:

> Organization theorists have carried out numerous studies of so-called objective phenomena and their aggregate finding is that almost nothing correlates strongly and consistently with anything else. This null finding fits the hypothesis that organizational structures and technologies are primarily arbitrary, temporary and superficial characteristics.

This discontent is expressed in two separate but parallel developments: the negotiated order approaches of the 1960s and the 'new organization theory' of the 1970s.

Negotiated order

The negotiated order approach to the study of organizations seems likely to be regarded as one of Anselm Strauss's most distinctive contributions to sociology.[2] He summarizes it in terms of six axioms: all social order is negotiated; these negotiations take place in a patterned and systematic fashion; their outcomes are temporally limited; the negotiated order constantly has to be reconstituted as a basis for concerted action; the negotiated order on any day consists of the sum total of the organization's rules, policies and local working understandings or agreements; and, finally, any change arising within or imposed on the order will require renegotiation to occur (Strauss 1978: 5–6).

This approach eliminated the problems caused by the split between social and formal organization by abolishing the very distinction. Formal organizations were merely ecologically bounded social organizations in which actions were united only by territorial or temporal coincidence. A hospital, for instance, was simply 'a professionalized locale, a geographical site where persons drawn from different professions come together to carry out their respective purposes' (Strauss et al. 1963: 150).

No assumptions were made of a separate order of organizational reality, of uniform goals, of rational rules or of institutional hierarchy. Everything was negotiable; the appearance of formality in some social organizations was an epiphenomenon:

> The realm of rules could then be usefully pictured as a tiny island of structured stability around which swirled and beat a vast ocean of negotiation. But we would push the metaphor further and assert what is already implicit in our discussion: that there is *only* vast ocean. (Strauss et al. 1964: 313)[3]

The challenge posed by Strauss was largely ignored by mainstream organization theorists but attracted the attention of a number of writers with Marxist leanings, who saw its potential for the analysis of praxis (for example, Benson 1977a,b; Day and Day 1977). As they pointed out, however, discarding the notion of formal organizational structure made it difficult to deal with issues of constraint and coercion as limiting factors on negotiation settings. Similar points were also made by some interactionists (for example, Lofland 1970; Maines 1977: 243–244). Strauss (1978: 247–258) replied by elaborating two new subsidiary concepts, the 'negotiation context' and the 'structural context'. The former refers to those local properties of a situation that enter directly as conditions in the course of negotiation.[4] The latter involves the overall framework of conditions within which negotiations occur. In this respect, structural context is constituted by conditions such as the state of production technology, the size and differentiation of firms in an industry, and the extent and nature of fixed and variable investment.

Despite the limitations of these concepts of negotiation and structural context,[5] their re-emergence does acknowledge that some account of extra-situational constraints on the negotiation of social organization may sometimes be necessary. These constraints are likely to be reflected in formal devices that, while not governing action in the simplistic way assumed by traditional organization theory, will definitely be experienced as limiting or determinative by members.

Here one can cite the evidence of everyday language. This example is a health visitor (an English public health nurse), employed by a health authority, talking about her relations with other agencies with reference to one particular case:

> I can't see why an organization like Housing can go happily on its own to the detriment of family life leaving Social Services Departments and the Health Service

with the results of its policy. We had been here a year ago and had a meeting about this family and I was asked if the child was at risk and I said that I thought at that time he was at risk and it was agreed that we had to formulate a policy for the family including Housing Department and then Housing agreed to work closely with the Social Services Department but that agreement hasn't been honoured.[6]

Although she is describing past negotiations, notice the way in which she anthropomorphizes the other departments. Housing 'can go on happily' and 'agreed to work closely'. Its actions are governed by 'its policy'. Such characterizations could be multiplied indefinitely.

Yet, in rejecting traditional organization theory's distinction between formal and social organization, negotiated order may well have inverted the original error. Having denied the existence of any distinction, interactionist writers are then forced into awkward accommodations to reincorporate it.

The 'new' organization theory

Recent versions of organization theory, especially that developed by Meyer and Rowan (1977), reformulate its problematic on a phenomenological basis by depicting formal structures as legitimating myths. This approach rests on a reading of Weber emphasizing that the legitimacy of formal organization does not derive from norms of rationality *per se*, but from their status in a specific type of society. Meyer and Rowan (1977: 345) then argue that societies such as ours have various established devices – 'building blocks . . . littered around the societal landscape' – for translating social into formal organizations. These blocks constitute the elements whose incorporation is a necessary condition for legitimating organizational activity. Many of them take a legal or para-legal form. In use, however, they act as what Meyer and Rowan (1977: 349) describe as 'vocabularies of structure . . . prudent, rational and legitimate accounts'. The parallel with the idea of 'vocabularies of motive' (Blum and McHugh 1971; Mills 1940) is intentional. Just as motives are used to make sense of individual action, so these structural references render action intelligible by placing it in a recognizably legitimate formal organization. These 'vocabularies of structure' thus help create trust in the product or service offered, as in the case of the credentials afforded by public schooling (Kamens 1977; Meyer and Rowan 1978).

'Legitimating myths' operate as general, albeit loose, constraints on formal organizational structures. However, they place major limits on members' actions. Options are restricted by the prospect of having to account for their choice within the framework of a given rhetoric. Because formal organizations must sustain an image of rational conduct to maintain their social legitimacy, members must be able to produce arguments that will be externally sanctionable and actions that are logically congruent with the means/end scheme thus depicted. The use of language, therefore, is a central document for this approach: 'people in a collectivity appraise their shared situation by talking about it . . . this talk is composed primarily of stylized expressions and the talk continues until it produces agreements' (Starbuck 1982: 22)

The 'new organization theory' retains the distinction between formal and social organization, but restates it as a difference in accounting practices rather than in substance. Although this approach seems able to avoid the problems created by placing priority on either aspect of organizational life, those who advocate it have failed to address critical methodological questions. Specifically, although language use is made into a central topic, new organizational theorists seem to lack any clear notion about how, in practice, it could be studied, except perhaps with the conventional methods of interactionist ethnography.

Yet traditional ethnography, as practised by negotiated order theorists and other interactionists, has been subject to an enduring weakness from the loose relationship between its data and its analyses. Although disciplined in various ways, the core of ethnographic methodology is an intuitive grasp of the nature of the organization that is then used to shape a persuasive narrative redescription for the reader. Analyses seldom attempt to reproduce members' constructions of the organization of their interactional setting and to display the inferential processes that make this possible for participants and intelligible to observers. Members' language remains relatively neglected, except where talk has an exotic character; for example, Becker et al.'s discussion of the term 'crock' (1961: 328-329). Yet, without such analyses, the ethnographer has no way to warrant his or her account other than the claim to have 'been there and seen'. And whole issues may be overlooked: the original formulation of negotiated order would in all likelihood have assumed a very different character had its methodology allowed recognition of the ways in which members themselves, on certain occasions, formalize organizations.[7]

If the ethnographic study of organization is to advance, then, as Goffman (1981, 1983) came to emphasize, it must respond to developments in the sociology of language, making the detailed examination of members' talk, from transcripts or near verbatim field notes, its hard ground for analytical inference.

Organizations, then, should be depicted as the product of members' actions in circumstances that are not entirely of their own making, although allowing scope for manipulation or manoeuvre. Organizational analysis should also be able to incorporate the distinctions that people observably make between different types of organization and adopt a methodology that uses direct reports of members' talk and action rather than observers' redescriptions as its basic data. The remainder of this chapter will attempt to specify how such requirements might be met in ethnographic research.

Ethnomethodological approaches to organization

Ethnomethodologists have long proposed that organizations are produced by the categorization practices used by members and observers to find an order in social action:

> the term 'an organization' is an abbreviation of the full term 'an organization of social actions'. The term 'organization' does not itself designate a palpable phenomenon. It refers instead to a related set of ideas that a sociologist invokes to aid him in collecting his thoughts about the ways in which patterns of social action are related. (Garfinkel 1956: 181)

These ideas included references to both ecological and cultural aspects of the action: territory, actors, relations and activities, on the one hand, and rules for proper conduct, on the other.

Strauss and his associates used Garfinkel's analysis of the uncertainty of rules to dismiss the cultural dimensions of organizations (1964: 313). All that remained was a domain of local understandings linked by ecological co-occurrence. Garfinkel and his students, however, consistently emphasized the constraining nature of rules. Although they might not govern action in a simple-minded fashion, actors necessarily oriented to them. Rules were not, as Strauss et al. (1964: 154) had it, 'symbolic cement', but the very framework that made coordinated action possible.[8] In Goffman's words:

> To utter something and to not disconfirm that we are sane requires that our saying be heard to draw appropriately on one array of presuppositions – that sustained by our hearers – and avoid being heard to make others . . . Responding to another's words, we must find a phrasing that answers not merely to the other's words but to the other's mind – so that the other can draw both from the local scene and from the distal wider worlds of his or her experience. (Goffman 1983: 48)

Bittner (1965: 249-250) had provided an early elaboration of such an approach, proposing that the official scheme of formal organizations could be treated as

> *a generalized formula to which all sorts of problems can be brought for solution . . .* [acquiring] *through this reference a distinctive meaning that they would not otherwise have.* Thus the formal organizational designs are schemes of interpretation that competent and entitled users can invoke in yet unknown ways whenever it suits their purposes.

This formula is made visible by three practices, employed by both members and observers, which Bittner terms 'compliance', 'stylistic unity' and 'corroborative reference'.

Compliance occurs when members act in such a way as to enable competent observers to identify their actions as organizationally relevant. Thus, the organizational scheme has 'some determining power over action that takes place under the scope of its jurisdiction' (1965: 250). Silverman (1973) provides several empirical examples in analysing selection interviews for a large corporation, specifying how candidates read interviewers' behaviour as evi-

dence of an underlying order; their actions were seen as 'obviously' determined by their status as selectors of new members.

Stylistic unity refers to the tendency for the sense of any action to be
determined not so much by the specific rule to which it is oriented as by the
entire order of which that rule is a part. Stylistic unity constitutes 'a principle of discipline . . . which works against centrifugal tendencies and
heterogeneity' (Bittner 1965: 252). Perhaps the best-known example of this
process is McHugh's (1968) discussion of the way subjects in a counselling
experiment made sense of the experience by inferring an underlying organization that enabled them to override deliberate inconsistencies in the advice
given.

Finally, *corroborative reference* points to the way in which the intrinsic
value of any individual action may be evaluated as part of a larger scheme.
This consideration 'not only persuades the participants of some correct or
corrected value of their duties, but can also be used as a potent resource for
enforcing prohibitions' (Bittner 1965: 254). In the military, for example,
trivial and absurd tasks – from whitewashing coal to cutting lawns with nail
scissors – are justified as inculcating a habit of unquestioning obedience to
orders thought to be invaluable in battle.

Notice the force of Bittner's language throughout these passages: 'determining power', 'a principle of discipline', 'enforcing prohibitions'. This
approach is a far cry from the amorphous oceans of negotiation, but it does
suffer from two particular limitations. First, what is a 'generalized formula'?
Are certain elements necessary? Take the stress on goals in the traditional literature: it is arguable that the ubiquity of goals actually reflects their
importance in the collection of and search for coherence in observed actions,
the essence of organization, as Garfinkel suggests. To warrant the ascription
of 'organization', joint action must be 'for' something: failing this, it could
not justifiably be considered as organized. Other possible elements in the formula, some of which may be sufficient rather than necessary, remain to be
identified. Possibilities include the following: the possession of a history and
a 'founder'; the possession of a formal name, rather than the mere nicknames
ascribed to less formal groups; the existence of formal, written rules; the official vesting of power to review, revise and superintend the workings of the
rules in certain positions; the formalization of membership in lists of current
members and visible signs of belonging; and, finally, formal means of reward
or sanction.

The second problem is the degree to which such formulas and supporting
practices are distinctive for formal organizations. In the first place, conversational analysis has shown that the maintenance of interactional
organization involves techniques for the identification of thematic relevance
that are cognate with those proposed by Bittner. Secondly, consider the
implications of variation in family organization. In ordinary families one
finds relatively little evidence of elaborated coordinating devices, as interaction is relatively dense, both ecologically and culturally, and material
interests are limited. Aristocratic families, however, with large kin networks,

fragmented interaction and substantial material interests, can take on much
of the appearance of a formal organization with an explicit scheme of interpretation. The family name and dynastic goals are elevated above those of
individual members; membership is closely regulated (only a few carefully
inspected candidates are permitted to join, whereas others are effectively
expelled); a formal hierarchy exists in which leaders meet to review current
activity, future policy and prospective takeovers or mergers; low-status tasks
(cooking, cleaning, security) are contracted out to permit selective attention
to other issues.

The analysis of any particular set of concerted actions, then, will necessarily be concerned with a great many processes that are common to all such
sets. There cannot, we suspect, be some totally separate branch of sociology
called 'organizational theory'. Nevertheless, the conceptual distinction
between social and formal organization plainly reflects and parallels a
common members' categorization. If we accept Bittner's proposals to analyse
organizations as constituted by reference to some sort of covering rubric or
'generalized formula', then we need to find a way of making warrantable distinctions within the general class of social organizations.

From 'licence' to 'charter'

One previous attempt to perform a similar task is Hughes's (1971: 287) discussion of occupational licence; 'An occupation consists in part in the
implied or explicit *license* that some people claim and are given to carry out
certain activities rather different from those of other people and to do so in
exchange for money, goods, and services.' Activities carried out under a
licence acquire thereby a distinctive meaning. They become work with an
exchange value rather than, say, forming part of reciprocal kinship ties.
Licences, and their companion devices, *mandates* (the occupation's claim to
define the proper conduct of its work) may be resources for enforcing compliance, stylistic unity or corroborative reference. Hughes's approach,
although resonant with Bittner's, provides a specific vocabulary for discussing concrete kinds of formulas that are used in sorting out and
coordinating a particular domain of action. Actions become describable as
occupation-relevant in so far as participants are or can be seen as orienting
towards a specific licence and, possibly, mandate.

Actions in formal organizations are subject to similar constraints and can
be analysed in the same fashion. Parallel to the licence and mandate of an
occupation, then, we propose the concepts 'charter' and 'mission' for
analysing action in formal organizations. A *charter* is the concept to which
organization members orient in their dealings with one another and with
non-members to establish the limits of legitimizable action. It refers to the
organization's notional contract with other institutions for the coordination
of a certain area of human action. In some sense, a charter can be said to represent the constraints on a member's freedom of action that he or she

experiences or depicts as exterior, objective and given. As Goffman (1968: 81) had discussed this phenomenon, 'each of these official goals or charters seems admirably suited to provide a key to meaning – a language of explanation that the staff, and sometimes the inmates, can bring to every crevice of action in the institution.'

Alongside charters, we may also find the members' own notion of 'what we are here for', the organization's *mission*. Although organization members may be subject to some pressure to demonstrate their orientation to a particular mission, mission is more likely to be experienced as a collective creation than as an external imposition. More relevantly, mission and charter may conflict, as when a version of the organization's mission includes a reformulation of its charter.[9]

All this talk of licences, mandates, charters and missions is in some respects metaphorical. We need not expect to find them embodied in written documents. None the less, the availability of written documents is important in distinguishing categories of occupations and organizations as, in modern societies, both are ultimately legal formations with a basis in statute. They exist through a framework of legality that regulates their goals and procedures and confers legitimacy on their actions. Law provides the most basic building blocks but, in exchange, requires documentation to be produced. The charters and licences that result represent various combinations of these elements, apparently reflecting the degree of collective interest in the activities involved (Strong and Dingwall 1983: 107-108).

Organizations and occupations cannot be sufficiently described solely by reference to their legal form, but there is an enormous difference between saying that such forms are, in principle, indefinitely negotiable and recognizing that they are, in practice, determinate.[10] Our argument is for the study of the ways in which that actual determinateness is accomplished. How are legal instruments articulated with members' everyday actions in such a way as to depict them as aspects of the same phenomenon? How are decisions made about what will count as charter-oriented action? How is 'the meaning' of charter institutionalized? What are the social bases of such chosen meanings? How are they used to constrain or influence members' actions? All these processes provide arenas for contest as each party – member, client or paymaster, as individuals or as groups – attempts to get its reading of the charter adopted as the only correct one. As Hughes (1971: 291) remarked about occupations:

> The power of an occupation to protect its license and to maintain its mandate and the circumstances in which licenses and mandates are attacked, lost, or changed are matters for investigation . . . Such work is the study of politics in the fundamental sense – that is, in the sense of studying constitutions. For constitutions are the relations between the effective estates which constitute the body politic. In our society, some occupations are among the groups which most closely resemble what were once known as estates.

The struggles within organizations over the interpretation of their charters are of comparable significance.

How do we look for charters?

Thus far, we have done no more than give a name to a concept, the referent of which we have characterized mainly in terms of formal documents. The real significance of concepts such as charters and licences is as orientations for action. The remaining two sections of this chapter will attempt to specify how and where to look for them.

We have already hinted that we regard language use recognized by speakers and hearers as organizationally relevant as the crucial data. We would justify this in two ways. First, such language use on many occasions is the most important datum for members themselves. Where a gap opens between charter and action, it is closed by accounting either in face-to-face interaction or in the production of reconciliatory documents. Charters define the range of legitimizable accounts. Secondly, the focus on language promises to strengthen the tie between data and analysis, a problem that has persistently bedevilled qualitative research. By concentrating on organizational documents and talk, whether recorded electronically or by hand, we should be able to move some way towards basing our work on data that can be publicly inspected and re-analysed by other investigators.

It is on the use of these data that we part company with the mainstream of ethnomethodological work, especially as it has developed in conversation analysis.[11] The essence of conversation analysis is its attempt to develop a rigorous description of the context-independent aspects of speech exchange. Although most conversation by analysis has focused on the question of what all conversations have in common – whether they take place in offices, shops, homes, schools or prisons – the same techniques can be used to look at differences between types of speech-exchange system or within a particular system in different contexts. That is, in accepting the idea of a transcontextual knowledge of principles for organizing speech-exchange, conversation analysis cannot rule out other kinds of transcontextual knowledge of social or cultural structures. Dingwall (1980b) has shown, in the case of a professional training school, how the solutions adopted to structural problems in talk identifiable from conversation analysis became resources for exhibiting the nature of the organization within which such talk occurred.

Organizationally relevant talk is organized by what Goffman variously referred to as 'rules of relevance and irrelevance' (1961b) or 'arrays or presuppositions' (1983). Organizational charters and, for that matter, occupational licences are the framing assumptions used to determine whether or not action is intelligible. They furnish a point of orientation, a special rhetoric, a vocabulary of motives and justifications, and a distinctive methodology for ascertaining 'facts'. In formal organizational settings only certain types of motive may be legitimately avowed or imputed, only certain justifications are acceptable as reasons for action, and only certain types of phenomena are admitted to constitute evidence for particular assertions.

The importance of this limited range of talk is twofold. First, and perhaps rather trivially, success is often a matter of thinking up 'good organizational reasons' for one's actions faster than one's opponents. In fact, however, much more is at stake than the ability of members to translate their own goals into organizational goals. The second point, then, is the way goals are embedded and used to deny the validity of certain justifications, motives or inferences. This control may be internal, superordinate over subordinate, or external, to the extent that the organization is collectively accountable to the outside bodies that granted the original charter. It is not too fanciful, for at least some members, to argue that the mode of discourse framed by the charter constitutes the limits of what is thinkable, let alone do-able, as organization-relevant action, even if the charter itself has effectively vanished behind that framing.

Where do we look for charters?

If the official mode of discourse does have this potentially constraining effect, we must then ask on what kinds of occasion can it be successfully invoked and accepted by the participants in a transaction. Obviously, where this only rarely occurs, action may be little affected by the constraints that charters impose. One extreme example here are the Italian bureaucracies set up by Mussolini, which still have a pay-roll and members but expect no work from them, appointment to such organizations being a political sinecure. Conversely, some organizations may be saturated by official purposes. For example, organizations that are specifically set up for the fulfilment of a radical ideology attempt to impose an 'official' mode of discourse on the whole of their members' lives.

The influence of charters on action depends, in essence, on three features. First, there is the specificity with which members conceptualize the charter in coordinating their activities. Where this is tightly defined, so that perhaps only one line of action is counted as falling under its rubric, the chances of legitimating alternative actions are small and members' choices are limited. A radical political organization may, for instance, hold that 'the only course of action open to a genuine revolutionary is . . .'. Those who would hold to other lines on a particular occasion, then, have no latitude to legitimate these as 'genuinely revolutionary' and, indeed, any attempt to do so will merely call into question their own status as members.

Secondly, there is the internal coherence of the charter. It may well contain contradictory elements that can be stressed in different contexts. The personnel department in a large corporation, for instance, may seek to justify its activities in both economic and welfare terms. Problems, of course, arise if the audiences for these justifications cannot be kept apart or if the charter is subjected to detailed external scrutiny. Nevertheless, it may well be a feature of successful organizations that their charters are sufficiently vague to be adapted to changing environmental circumstances.

Thirdly, of course, charters are much more important when members are heavily dependent on one another's cooperation for the success of their

joint action and, in effect, answerable for their compliance with the legitimate expectations of the other. We must, for instance, consider what
happens when A is accountable to B for actions that actually are carried out
by C. Charters are the device by which the efforts of these three actors are
tied together. The tightness of this bond, however, will be influenced by the
degree to which C's actions are, ecologically or culturally, visible to A and
the degree to which B demands that they comply with his or her expectations.

Obviously, this sort of ethnographic description is a substantial under-
taking and we have barely scratched its surface in this chapter. As we have
stressed, much of the time charters are effectively invisible. They are available
for consultation when problems arise, but these are comparatively rare. For
the most part, actors operate within the charter-legitimated mode of discourse without needing to reflect or elaborate upon it. In studying
organizations, one must recognize that the occasions on which charters surface are rare and unrepresentative of the mundane reality of the daily
activities of many members.

If we take public-sector organizations as an example, there clearly are at
lest four discernible elements in relating charters to action. First, the body to
which such organizations are accountable may itself attempt to influence
interpretation. Welfare bureaux, school boards and health care facilities are
the subject of various regulations, orders and directives, as well as of extra-
legal advice, circulars, memoranda, or requests from federal, state or county
authorities. Secondly, this stream of guidance is consulted by planners and
managers in order to determine how it may be implemented given locally
available staff, plant and resources and how it relates to their sense of local
priorities, especially as these latter are expressed by a locally representative
body. Thirdly, these local decisions are operationalized by supervisors in
defining task allocation and monitoring staff performance. Finally, all grades
of staff themselves make a variety of day-to-day decisions about priorities,
about the way they should construe the information available to them, and
the consequences they should derive for action. Similar elements seem likely
to be identifiable in private organizations.

More than one of these elements may be present on any particular occasion. A senior manager, for instance, receiving a federal directive must
obviously consider how responding to it will fit with the work on his or her
desk for that day and what the consequences will be in terms of his or her
accountability, just as much as lower-echelon staff must consider similar
issues in the context of supervisors' instructions. Nevertheless, these elements are likely to be differentially relevant at different points in an
organization. Lower-level staff may have few occasions on which it is necessary to discuss issues in terms of the organization's charter. Their work
setting, however, is structured in such a way as to pre-empt the relevance of
such discussions. Charter issues have been decided elsewhere, a task that may
considerably preoccupy senior managers in their deliberations. If one con-
centrates purely on the activities of lower-level personnel, one is in danger of

missing the coordinating and disciplining devices that bind their action together.

Many of the specific kinds of occasion that one might look to are those that are often dismissed as irrelevant, unworthy of attention or purely symbolic.

Official ceremonies: occasions on which the organization celebrates itself, such as university degree ceremonies, school graduations or, on a larger scale, coronations or presidential investitures. These are usually occasions for the symbolic evocation of the charter. Public discourse is almost totally confined to the official, which is why we sometimes tend to view such events as pious or platitudinous, although if we are strongly committed they may be deeply moving. Note that the lines of action prescribed by the frame of reference vary, as we stressed earlier, with the particular audience. There is therefore no one official mode of discourse, as events vary in their 'officiality'. Thus, ceremonies in the presence of guests may be very different from those to which only members are invited. Similarly, we may expect variations in the modes of discourse invoked in the situations discussed below, for in each of these the circumstances may be very different; for example, discussions in a university, senate or faculty compared with the bromides of degree ceremonies. Published examples of work on such settings might include Shils and Young's (1953) analysis of the British coronation of 1953 and Gluckman's (1958) discussion of a bridge opening in Barotseland.

Public relations events: those occasions when the organization puts its best face forward in an attempt to impress outsiders, usually when outside money or support is needed. Obviously, official ceremonies may also be used for this purpose, while public relations techniques may be used to ward off the accusations discussed later; but we are here concerned with events and techniques such as publicity films, press hand-outs, official visits by high-status outsiders, open days, interviews for new members, and advertising.

Formal policy-making events: meetings concerned with how the organization should function, with the allocation of resources; with the introduction of new techniques and aims; and with changes in formal rules. Such occasions are usually highly institutionalized with special venues, times, places and names. As they are more clearly thought of as 'political', an air of some scepticism reigns and each member's actions are potentially suspect. Individuals are thus forced to engage in continual motive revelation, but this is the most limited kind as the 'motives' they may openly reveal or ascribe are 'official' ones. Such meetings may produce decisions embodying formulations of charters that exert considerable influence on organizational structure.

Interdepartmental transactions: as action in many small sections within a large organization will seem pointless and lack any identity of its own, meaning can be given to the work by pointing out how such actions fit into the overall scheme. Similarly, as action in organizations occurs in highly compartmentalized areas, actions in one area may seem to contradict those in another; costs to A may be benefits to B. The charter may then be mobilized to provide another perspective besides the immediate context and can justify on 'organizational' what may seem wrong on 'sectional' grounds. Thus, management smooths over the complaints of particular sections by 'putting you in the picture'.

Assessments: routine occasions when organization members are called to account for their stewardship of the charter. A wide range of examples comes to mind: annual personnel appraisals, visits from auditors, surveys by management consultants. One of the most striking, perhaps, is examinations in educational institutions. The whole process of assessment is a neglected topic in both the sociology of education and the study of professional social-ization. As Dingwall (1977, 1986) has argued, however, it is critically important as a locale for debate over what instruction is for, what is to count as competent performance, and how this relates to a school's contract with society for the development of certain skills.

Routine handling of complaints: particular occasions on which some kind of account is explicitly or implicitly called for in response to questions from either within or outside the organization. Such accounts are called for on sev-eral different occasions:

1 Members of an organization who are officially or unofficially accused of breaking its rules may argue in their defence that they were only trying to implement the official charter of the organization in justification or at least mitigation of the offence.
2 Officials often redefine actions that are taken primarily on the basis of administrative or personal convenience in terms of the official charter of the organization in order to ward off clients' and relatives' complaints and to justify such action to themselves. (Goffman, 1961a)

Thus, much of the depersonalization that mental patients are forced to endure is justified on 'medical' grounds; similarly, many of the control strat-egies in schools are justified on the grounds of their 'educational' benefits. In what sense such action is conducive to the fulfilment of the charter is usually left vague.

It is important to note that Goffman is not arguing that such officials are necessarily lazy and cynical: they may genuinely believe in the justice of their claim. This analysis rests implicitly on two further arguments:

1 Ideologies may be exceptionally powerful, distorting agents, selecting only 'relevant' facts for the believer's attention and concealing others, hence 'taking in' even those with the best of intentions.
2 What is to count as following the charter is not determined by the char-ter itself, but by a further set of decisions about what will be socially accepted as charter-following. Especially where there is no generally accepted technology, a wide range of lines of action may be permitted, rendering the boundaries between the legitimate and the illegitimate exceptionally vague.

Informal use: finally, official goals crop up on all kinds of informal occasions. Goals are part of the fabric of organizational members' lives, and are commonly referred to in everyday talk, even if often in more cynical ways than is commonly found on more public occasions. Such informal talk about charters also requires examination.

Conclusion

In this chapter we have attempted to develop a programmatic statement for the ethnographic study of organizations. Given that the research monographs have, for a change, preceded the general formulation, we are not necessarily claiming that our own previous work (Dingwall 1977; Dingwall et al. 1983; Strong 1979) can necessarily stand as fully worked-out examples of the approach or that they meet the methodological standards we are now advocating. Nevertheless, we hope to have highlighted what we regard as fundamental deficiencies in the negotiated order perspective on organizations and pointed to the need to effect a reconciliation with work in organization theory, ethnomethodology and conversation analysis. Traditional ethnography remains important for identifying contextual features relevant to the analysis of recorded language. Nevertheless, our reports and findings must start from and return to the hard datum of language and the practical reasoning by which it is made into an intelligible document of a supposedly underlying reality.

Acknowledgements

This chapter was first published in *Urban Life*, 14(2): 205-231 (1985). We would like to acknowledge the advice of Peter Manning, as well as thanking Eric Batstone, John Heritage, Janine Nahapiet, David Silverman and Anselm Strauss for their comments on drafts of this chapter.

Notes

1 It must be said that this disillusionment is largely academic. As Worsley (1974) has observed in a discussion of racist theorizing, some ideas can display a remarkable resilience while their material base survives. The increasing reluctance of organization theory to sustain managerialist ideologies may be marked by the rise of economic studies of organizations (e.g. Williamson 1975) in a discipline that retains a touching faith in the rationality of human actions.

2 Although it is possible to identify earlier versions in the work of other Chicago-trained sociologists (Maines 1977: 243), the idea of negotiated order first appeared in a paper from Strauss's research team studying American psychiatric hospitals between 1958 and 1962 (Strauss et al. 1963), and subsequently formed a central theme of the monograph from that project (Strauss et al. 1964).

3 As both Strauss (1978: 110) and his critics (Day and Day 1977: 137n.) have observed, this model may, in fact, have been empirically accurate for the settings his team was investigating. American psychiatry was in a state of considerable flux at that time and the state hospital that

formed the principal research site was experiencing rapid and unplanned change. In that historical context, it is also easy to understand the approach's attraction to a generation of optimistic liberals. This may account for the relative neglect of those parts of *Psychiatric Ideologies*, especially the chapter on chronic wards, in which Strauss and his colleagues do give more weight to material constraints.

4 The origins of 'negotiation context' lie in the narrower notion of 'awareness context', which Strauss developed with Glaser during the study of terminal care following their work on psychiatric hospitals (Glaser and Strauss 1965).

5 Two such limitations can be noted here. First, researchers who have attempted to use these new concepts have almost without exception complained about the difficulty of applying them to specific situations (see the papers in October 1982 *Urban Life* as well as O'Toole and O'Toole 1981). Indeed, Strauss's article in the special issue (1982) seeks to provide conceptual clarification, especially of the idea of structural context. Secondly, one can note that, while the material conditions Strauss cites as making up the structural context are undeniably important, their explanatory power would appear to be limited, as emphasized by Starbuck (1982).

6 This extract is from field notes of a study of agency decision-making in child protection work reported in Dingwall et al. (1983).

7 Some of this may be explicable in terms of technological limitations: the classic interactionist ethnographies predate lightweight cassette tape-recorders. Its persistence, however, reflects a real failure to grasp the nature of the challenge posed by this material advance to existing standards of data collection and analysis.

8 This was a long way from being the most serious misunderstanding of ethnomethodology by symbolic interactionists, largely because they have failed to recognize the extent to which Garfinkel read Schutz and other phenomenologists in the light of Parsons's theory of action. For discussions of the intellectual roots of ethnomethodology, see Payne et al. (1981: 116–124) and Heritage (1984).

9 Introducing charter and mission as concepts distinct from licence and mandate also allows analysis of conflicts between organizations and occupations. In so far as members of strongly organized occupations orient to their licence, this may cut across their orientation to the charter of their employing organization. This is most evident in so-called bureau-professional settings (see Dingwall et al. 1983: 103–122).

10 For an elaboration of the basis of this position see Bloor's (1980) discussion of the debate on rule-use (in Douglas, 1971) between the ethnomethodologists, Zimmerman and Wieder, and the symbolic interactionist, Denzin.

11 We do so under the influence of arguments that Goffman elaborated in some of his last work (especially 1981, 1983) but that had been prefigured at least with the publication of *Encounters* in 1961. We have developed this argument in a previous paper (Dingwall, 1980b) and will only summarize it here.

11

Toward Ethnographies of Institutional Discourse: Proposal and Suggestions

Gale Miller

The purpose of this chapter is to offer an analytical framework for studying how talk and social context are inextricably intertwined and coterminous aspects of socially organized settings. The framework is informed by ethnomethodology (Garfinkel 1967; Heritage 1984; Mehan and Wood 1975; Zimmerman 1969), conversation analysis (Atkinson and Heritage 1984; Boden and Zimmerman 1991; Button and Lee 1987; Sacks et al. 1974), and Foucaldian discourse analysis (Arney and Bergen 1984; Dreyfus and Rabinow 1982; Foucault 1972, 1980; Lindstrom 1990). It is not intended to reconcile the many differences among the perspectives, but to develop complementary aspects of them.

Purpose and organization

The chapter is suggestive and programmatic. It suggests how ethnographers might take account of some of the issues and themes found in ethnomethodology, conversation analysis and Foucault's approach to discourse studies in doing their work. The suggestions are intended to broaden the empirical and analytical options available to ethnographers in organizing their studies, observing aspects of everyday life, and analysing their data. It also offers a more catholic vision of the ethnomethodological tradition and discourse studies than that advanced by some observers. For example, Maynard (1989) uses data collected in his study of plea bargaining to discuss the deficiencies of ethnographic observation and analytical advantages of video- and/or audio-taping social interactions.

Although I agree with much of Maynard's (1989) argument, I find it unduly restrictive because it gives short shrift to the ways in which ethnomethodological and conversation analytic concerns can be and have been developed through ethnographic research strategies and techniques. For example, Atkinson and Drew's (1979) and Holstein's (1993) studies of legal settings and proceedings show that even when it is impossible to video- and/or audiotape social interactions, theoretically informed observers can produce near transcripts that may be usefully analysed from a conversation analytic standpoint. The chapter is also concerned with how conversation analysis can be extended by combining it with ethnomethodologically informed ethnographic strategies and techniques and defining discourse as more than talk.

The chapter is programmatic because it discusses the major assumptions and concerns of the ethnography of institutional discourse perspective and some of the ways in which it may be applied and developed.[1] Ethnographies of institutional discourse combine ethnographers' interest in in-depth observations of diverse settings of everyday life, conversation analysts' construction and analysis of transcripts of naturally occurring talk within settings, and the Foucauldian focus on the formulation, dispersion and uses of knowledge within and across social settings. Whereas ethnomethodologically informed ethnographers, conversation analysts and Foucauldian discourse analysts disagree on many issues, they agree that social realities involve more than looking and seeing. Social realities are produced (or accomplished) by seeing and communicating from standpoints (or gazes) that are simultaneously ways of understanding and being in social worlds.

Ethnographies of institutional discourse take account of the ways in which interpretive and interactional activities are organized within institutional discourses, how oral and textual discourses are arrayed across settings, and the practical meanings that are produced within institutional discourses. Ethnographers of institutional discourse do so by analysing the ways in which setting members use resources available in settings to organize their activities and assign meanings to their own and others' actions. The perspective is not concerned with whether social realities are constructed from the bottom up or top down. Rather, it focuses on how setting members use institutional discourses to construct social contexts that structure, but do not determine, their mutual activities and reality claims (Silverman 1987).

I elaborate on the ethnography of institutional discourse perspective in the rest of the chapter by discussing how the analytical themes of the perspective may be developed through a combination of ethnographic and conversation analytic methodologies. The next section considers how Foucauldian, ethnomethodological and conversation analytic concerns are conceptualized and blended in the ethnography of institutional discourse perspective. Later sections focus on delimited aspects of the perspective and/or how it may be elaborated through qualitative studies of language use and reality construction in diverse social settings.

Issues in the ethnography of institutional discourse

Institutional discourses consist of the fundamental assumptions, concerns and vocabularies of members of settings and their usual ways of interacting with one another. Institutional discourses are shared and standardized frameworks for anticipating, acting in and reflecting on social settings and interactions. They allow and constrain setting members to organize their interactions as instances of standardized types of social relationship and produce conditions for responding to issues in predictable ways. Institutional discourses are also accountability frameworks to which setting members attend in organizing their behaviour in social settings and assessing and responding to others' behaviour.

Viewed one way, social settings and their institutional discourses are conditions of possibility for reality construction (Foucault 1977). Although reality-construction processes are never so determinate that interactants or observers may accurately predict how all practical issues will be interpreted within social settings, reality construction occurs under interactional and interpretive conditions that make some reality claims more available than others. Shumway (1989) compares Foucault's analysis of the social conditions of discourse with those of a dice game. He notes that, although no one can accurately predict the numerical outcome of each throw of the dice, it is possible to identify the range of numbers that may emerge on any single throw and analyse the players' practical interests in the numbers.

Certainly it is possible to take Shumway's metaphor too far, such as by forgetting that the possibilities for creating diverse social realities in social interaction are substantially greater than in a dice game. None the less, it is a useful image for analysing the practical circumstances associated with social settings and interactions. Like dice games, different settings and interactions are partly distinguished from one another by the limited possibilities that they are organized to produce. Also, one aspect of the meanings associated with any single throw of the dice or social interaction involves some players'/interactants' knowledge of the limited range of possibilities available to them.

This approach to institutional discourse may be elaborated to consider how organizational interests, power and dominance are aspects of, and practical achievements in, social settings (Foucault 1980). Organizational interests are organized and expressed in social settings as delimited concerns about and procedures for responding to practical issues. They are standardized (often mundane) work activities associated with settings. They include the interpretive and interactional procedures used by setting members to achieve organizationally preferred ends. Organizational interests may be studied by observing how organization members, particularly setting organizers, arrange and orient to the work activities associated with different social settings.

Setting organizers arrange for and sometimes direct the flow of activities within settings, such as by asking questions that others must answer, issuing directives to which others must respond, or otherwise acting in ways that require others to take account of their actions. Setting members produce discursive dominance by making some interactional resources available to themselves and others, and acting to make others less available. The production of the latter circumstance may involve explicit assessments of other possible formulations of and orientations to the issues at hand as inappropriate or undesired. It may also involve not acknowledging the possible availability of other – unstated – frameworks for organizing the issues at hand and interactants' positions in settings.

Setting members also produce social conditions to which others may respond by resisting. Setting members resist by acting in ways that setting organizers treat as uncooperative, defiant or otherwise inappropriate. Because their actions occur within concrete settings, however, resisters organize their actions by using the interpretive and interactional resources available to them in the settings. Thus resistance cannot be separated from the discursive contexts within which it is produced, and others may respond to it in ways that sustain organizationally preferred positions, relationships and realities.

Consider, for example, Gubrium's (1980) analysis of geriatric staff–patient meetings intended to produce mutually agreeable understandings of and orientations to patients' troubles and treatments. Staff members oriented to the meetings as potentially troublesome encounters in which they wished to appear as competent and knowledgeable professionals 'and not arbitrary or self-interested' (Gubrium 1980: 336). The meetings were organized as 'this-is-your-life routines' in which staff members described and summarized patients' organizational histories and present circumstances by reading selected entries in patients' charts.

For staff members, cooperative patients responded to their reading of the charts by noting factual errors in the charts, affirming that the charts were generally accurate descriptions of their circumstances, and sometimes elaborating on staff members' descriptions of their lives and troubles. Disputes emerged when patients objected to staff members' descriptions. Staff members treated these objections as disruptions of the expected and preferred interactional organization of the meetings and challenges to their professionalism. Gubrium (1980: 340) describes the emerging dispute in the following way:

> Should patients persist in objections, they may be glossed over as the briefing is completed over them . . . Should patients' disagreement grow beyond what is taken to be routinely acceptable, they are reminded that their behaviour is 'inappropriate'. They may even be told, with patronising firmness, 'Adults simply don't act that way', or 'We mustn't be so childish', or 'Let's try to be calm and more reasonable about this.' With the patient's persistence, the interaction of the patient and staff members may spiral into an exchange where the patient becomes increasingly enraged with staffers' diversion from what the patient takes to be the issue at hand and where staffers, in turn, increasingly become irritated by what they believe to be the patient's unrealistic, immature conduct. Should the patient refuse to calm down and cooperate in decorously completing the routine, the patient is led from the meeting, whereupon the staffing is completed.

Gubrium's analysis shows how power and resistance are inextricably intertwined in settings. Specifically, staff members produced power relations and social conditions for patient resistance by organizing the meetings as routine exchanges focused on assessing the accuracy of patients' files. Patients affirmed and maintained the power relations by responding in organizationally approved ways, or resisted by refusing to focus their attention and responses on the files. Gubrium also displays the interrelationships between power and resistance in discussing how staff members oriented to the meetings as potentially troublesome, and responding to 'defiant' patients in routine and predictable ways. Staff members used their responses to cast the patients' behaviour as irrational and defiant, and justify terminating the meetings. In this way, staff members achieved their practical interests in the settings and produced conditions that might be used to justify their organization of the meetings as 'this-is-your-life routines'.

In sum, ethnographers of institutional discourse synthesize Foucault's (1980) concern for specifying the conditions that shape what may be said and who can speak within socially organized settings with ethnomethodologists' and conversation analysts' interest in analysing the conditions associated with and the procedures through which reality claims are actually made. Such studies are enhanced by a combination of the deep immersion in social settings associated with ethnography and detailed conversation analyses of a limited number of video- and/or audiotapes of social encounters. They are not competing, but complementary, methodologies.

Ethnographic strategies and techniques provide analysts with information about social settings as conditions of possibility, and members' knowledge about how different settings are related in ways that may go unrecognized by the less frequent and intense observer. Such strategies and techniques allow the observer to learn about the 'background expectancies' associated with social settings (Garfinkel 1967). For example, Gubrium's (1980) analysis of staff–patient interactions in staff–patient geriatric meetings is enhanced by his familiarity with the diverse activities that make up everyday life in nursing homes, including how staff members' and patients' orientations to the meetings are related to more general practical concerns about their roles and options in other social settings.

Conversation and ethnomethodological analysis of social interactions are sources for understanding how the possibilities associated with social settings are interactionally organized and managed by setting participants, and how some potential reality claims come to be treated as truthful and linked to concrete social actions. Such analyses identify the methods used by setting members to produce reality claims. For example, Holstein's (1993) analysis of involuntary commitment hearings shows how the social reality of mental illness is constructed and contested within question–answer sequences. Attorneys ask questions and witnesses answer them.

In part, public defenders display the truthfulness of their claims that defendants do not warrant hospitalization by asking the defendants to respond to questions about their life circumstances and preferences. The public defenders' questions were distinctive because they were asked in ways that called for 'yes' or 'no' answers. District attorneys, on the other hand, asked questions about the same types of issues as the public defenders, but they used questioning methods that invited defendants to give lengthy responses, which the attorneys might use to claim that hospitalization of the defendants was warranted.

These issues are further considered in the next two sections, which focus on how institutions may be studied as situated conventions, and institutional discourses as talk and interpretation.

Institutions as situated conventions

I use the term *institution* to characterize conventions or practices associated with social settings. Such institutions range from shared and (somewhat) standardized greeting practices associated with diverse settings to the distinctive interpretive and interactional practices associated with a limited number of settings, such as doing classroom lessons (Mehan 1979) and conducting legal examinations (Atkinson and Drew 1979). Institutions exist in and through members' interactional and interpretive practices. They are observable and recurring activities through which members construct social settings, relationships and realities.

This approach to institutions is an alternative to those typically taken by ethnographers who analyse institutions as abstract structures (such as families, law and education) and/or kinds of formal organizations (such as churches, hospitals and social welfare agencies). Analysing institutions as situated conventions focuses attention on the practices that ethnographers and others take as signs of abstract structures and/or treat as components of formal organizations. Such analyses also show how social settings are shifting formations that are constructed and reconstructed as setting participants use interactional and interpretive conventions to organize the issues at hand and their mutual relations.

Consider, for example, the social expectation that greetings will be exchanged at the outset of interactions, and, particularly, that greetings that have been offered be returned by others. The expectation is an institutionalized aspect of diverse social contexts. On occasion, however, interactants use their knowledge of the expectation to initiate or continue conflict by strategically violating the exchange of greeting expectation. As Heritage (1984: 117-118) states, the exchange of greetings expectation is an institutional constraint that tends to bind interactants, but does not absolutely determine their behaviour:

> We are looking for a form of constraint which may influence persons to return greetings all their lives but who may yet still refuse to return one on this particular occasion . . . The actor who is determined to 'declare' or continue a quarrel can do so by visibly 'refusing' to return a greeting and leaving the other to draw the conclusion. Here not only is the norm not binding, it actually provides the vehicle for the declaration.

Thus social settings consist of more than territorial sites and their typical participants. Social settings are also organized as interpretive and interactional practices that may be used by participants to construct a variety of reality claims and social relationships. Such practices, and setting participants' possible uses of them, are aspects of the conditions of possibility associated with social settings, including possibilities for acquiescence and resistance. Indeed, acquiescence and resistance may be interrelated aspects of setting members; actions, as when one setting member accedes to the demands of another by declaring that he or she has no real choice in the matter.

An example is the following exchange between a state official and the local supervisor of a Work Incentive Programme (WIN). The exchange is part of an extended negotiation intended to establish mutually agreeable performance goals for the supervisor's staff. The exchange begins as a response to the supervisor's recommendation of a performance goal.

> State official: That puts you under your present performance. I can't support anything under your projected performance [for the current year]. You propose it [to the administrators at the state WIN office] and add an addendum justifying it if you want, but I can't support it.
> Local supervisor: Well, we might as well go with the [total number recommended by the state official] then.
> State official: Why?
> Local supervisor: Look . . . you're a powerful person in [the state WIN office]. You will affect how this plan is read, I know that. I can't propose something without your support and expect it to pass. That's silly.
> State official: Do you really think you won't make it?
> Local supervisor: Yes, but let's go with it, if that's what you'll support. (Miller 1991: 174)

Ethnographers and conversation analysts bring different but complementary strengths to the observation and analysis of institutions as situated conventions. Ethnographers' longer-term and more varied experiences in social settings are more likely to acquaint them with the variety of ways in which setting participants orient to and use the interactional and interpretive conventions available to them. For example, they are more likely than conversation analysts to observe occasions when interactants, who almost always return others' greetings, construct quarrels by refusing to return them.

Conversation analysis of social encounters provides highly detailed understandings of how participants use available interpretive and interactional resources to construct, sustain and change concrete social relationships and settings. They can show the various (often subtle) actions associated with the construction of quarrels, such as how the refusal to return a greeting is often associated with a distinctive interactant stance or gaze. Conversational data and analysis are also useful in analysing how interactants use available interactional and interpretive conventions to construct power relations (Foucault 1980) within which some reality claims are made more available and credible than others.

Consider, for example, Molotch and Boden's (1985) analysis of Senator Edward J. Gurney's interrogation of John Dean during the Senate Watergate hearings. Gurney sought to discredit Dean's testimony by using his position in the hearings' conversational structure to create grounds for doubting the objective and factual status of Dean's descriptions, explanations and other reality claims. Specifically, Gurney required that Dean testify by answering Gurney's questions, and offering literal – not impressionistic – descriptions of the events in question. The practical effects of Gurney's use of the hearings' conversational structure were to deny Dean any opportunities to provide contextual detail about his actions, and place Dean in a situation of being unable directly and adequately to answer questions that seemed to call for answers of simple and literal fact.

The following exchange is an example of how Gurney achieved his ends. It begins with Dean's answer to Gurney's questioning about whether Dean and President Nixon discussed the Watergate cover-up at a meeting on 15 September. Dean responded by stating that the president told him he was doing a good job, and his sense of what the president's comment meant.

> G: Did you discuss what Magruder knew about Watergate and what involvement he had?
> D: No, I didn't. I didn't get into any – I didn't give him a report at that point in time.
> G: Did you discuss cover-up money that was being raised and paid?
> D: No, sir.
> G: Did you discuss Strachan bringing wiretap information to Haldeman?
> D: No, I did not.
> G: Did you talk about coaching uh – uh Magruder on his perjured testimony in August?
> D: No, I did not.
> G: Well now how can you say that the President knew all about these things from a simple observation by him that 'Bob tells me you are doing a good job.'
> (Molotch and Boden 1985: 280)

Of course, Gurney was partly able to achieve his practical ends because congressional hearings involve a distinctive arrangement of speakership roles and other interactional resources, which potentially place committee members at a substantial advantage over the witnesses whom they question. Committee members and witnesses use such resources to construct power relations that make some claims to reality more available and/or credible than others. As Molotch and Boden (1985) show, conversation analytic techniques are especially useful in identifying and analysing how power relations are interactionally constructed in settings.

Institutional discourse as talk and interpretation

The analysis of institutions as situated conventions is linked to two different approaches to discourse. The first involves ethnomethodologists' and conversation analysts' focus on talk which they analyse as a socially organized and constitutive feature of social settings. For ethnomethodologists and conversation analysts, social settings are interactional arenas within which social realities are talked into being. They further analyse talk as context-sensitive and context-free. That is, speakers and interactants attend to both the distinctive features of social settings, and generally shared (institutional) expectations and practices in constructing social realities.

The interplay between the context-sensitive and context-free aspects of talk is central to Rawls's (1987: 139) analysis of the interaction order as a distinctive social domain that 'has an existence independent of either structures or individuals'. Her analysis focuses on the distinctive, cross-situational demands and concerns associated with the presentation of self in settings. Rawls further analyses the interaction order as a set of enabling conventions that interactants use to construct and sustain their social being in social settings that are partly organized to constrain interactants' reality-creating activities. Competent interactants orient to both aspects of social settings and interactions, including the practical difficulties that may arise in mediating between them.

For example, Maynard's (1991) conversation analysis of clinician–patient interactions shows that such interactants attend to both the general (egalitarian) expectations associated with ordinary conversation and the situation-specific conditions that encourage interactional asymmetry in some clinical settings. The latter conditions encourage clinicians to organize and direct the arrangement of talk sequences and topics to enhance their positions and interests in interactions and to discourage patients from voicing their concerns and pressing clinicians to respond to them.

Maynard's (1991) analysis addresses the complexity of talk in clinical settings by showing that clinician–patient interactions are not mere epiphenomena of organizational structures, needs and modes of control, but are simultaneously attentive to their contexts and the logic and orderliness of the interaction order. Such conversation analytic studies of talk may be elaborated and extended through ethnographic strategies that focus on how language is organized and used across settings. The latter studies might consider the diverse ways in which interactants attend to the interaction order and contingencies of particular settings as they move from encounter to encounter. They might also study how social settings are changed over time as interactants attend to new concerns and contingencies.

A second relevant approach to discourse focuses on the ways in which social settings are organized through members' interpretive practices. The approach is fundamental to many ethnographic studies of discourse and organizational process, particularly those that draw on aspects of Foucault's studies of discourse and power (Conley and O'Barr 1990; Gubrium 1992; Holstein 1993; Miller 1991; Silverman 1987). For example, in her ethnography of law and conflict in two New England towns, Merry (1990: 110) treats discourse as ideological language:

> Discourse here refers to systematic, impersonal modes of talking which govern the production of culture. A discourse is a specialized language, a particular jargon. It is usually signaled through particular phrases or modes of explanation but rarely spelled out. Every discourse . . . contains a more or less coherent set of categories and theories of action: a vocabulary for naming events and persons and a theory for explaining actions and relationships. Each discourse consists of an explicit repertoire of justifications and explanations and an implicit, embedded theory about why people act the way they do.

This approach to discourse involves treating different modes of talk and writing as interpretive conventions that have their own logic and orderliness. Speakers' and writers' uses of categories and vocabularies to describe issues and events necessarily involves making limiting assumptions about human nature and social reality, and using a limited range of logic in articulating and elaborating their perspectives. Douglas (1986) emphasizes this theme in arguing that life-and-death decisions are not made by individuals, but through institutional thinking. She uses the term 'institutional thinking' metaphorically and to highlight how fateful issues are organized, understood and responded to by using culturally shared and standardized categories that are related to unexplicated theories and logic.

For example, Loseke (1992) analyses the institutional thinking of staff members in a shelter for battered women by considering how staff members used culturally standardized images of the battered woman in organizing their relationships with women seeking admittance to the shelter, and to distinguish between applicants who were 'truly' battered women and 'inappropriate' applicants. Images of the truly battered woman were central to the staff members' interactions with shelter applicants. The interactions turned on staff members' interest in eliciting information from applicants about their life circumstances and reasons for seeking admittance to the shelter. Staff members used the information to assess applicants' requests and to justify their responses to the requests.

In sum, ethnographic studies based on interviews (such as Merry 1990) and analyses of organizational documents (such as Loseke 1992) are useful in identifying the categories and vocabularies used by setting participants in formulating and arguing for their positions on practical issues. Interview data are not so useful, however, when ethnographers of institutional discourse wish to analyse how setting participants interrelate, elaborate on and negotiate the practical meanings of such categories and vocabularies in social settings. For example, legal, psychiatric and other institutional categories and vocabularies may be articulated in social settings to construct diverse arguments and logic to justify very different decisions and actions.

Thus, although the metaphor of institutional thinking is useful for analysing patterns of interpretive practice associated with social settings, ethnographers of institutional discourse must also consider how such practices are artful and practical accomplishments of decision-makers. One way in which decision-makers artfully use institutional discourses is by making decisions that are responsive to diverse cross-situational and situation-specific contingencies, such as those analysed by Rawls (1987) and Maynard (1991). A concern for institutional thinking as artful practice and practical accomplishment, then, brings us back to the analytical and methodological emphases of ethnomethodology and conversation analysis.

These approaches to discourse focus on the concrete procedures used by setting participants to construct images of social reality interactionally and textually that others might treat as coherent and sensible. They also involve strategies and techniques for analysing how competing discourses are articulated and negotiated in settings, and how interactants' use of institutional categories and vocabularies is related to the interactional contingencies associated with the interaction order and social settings, including their social positions in the settings.

Although the ethnography of institutional discourse perspective may be applied and extended in various ways, two promising areas involve the relationship between institutional discourses and the social construction of settings, and the arrangement of institutional discourses within and across settings. The study and analysis of both issues are enhanced by using ethnomethodologically informed ethnographic and conversation analytic strategies and techniques. We turn to them in the next two sections.

Institutional discourses and the social construction of settings

Setting members construct social contexts for their actions by entering into institutional discourses that organize the issues at hand and members' orientations to them. Issues are organized by the assumptions, concerns and vocabularies used by setting members in constructing settings and their relationships within settings. On the other hand, setting members' assessments of the appropriateness of institutional discourses for concrete settings and issues involves defining the settings as appropriate contexts for some discourses and not others. Thus, an important issue in the ethnography of institutional discourse involves the ways in which setting members simultaneously construct social settings and enter into institutional discourses.

One way in which setting members construct social settings and enter into institutional discourses is by describing and instructing others on the assumptions, concerns, vocabularies and/or interactional patterns associated with settings. The instructions are frequently given by setting organizers and/or directors to setting members who are likely to be unfamiliar with the practices and expectations associated with settings. But entrance into institutional discourses is not always marked by instructions or other announcements. Indeed, it may occur in ways that leave some setting members unaware of some aspects of the social contexts within which their own and others' behaviours are interpreted.

For example, Whalen and Zimmerman's (1987) and Whalen et al.'s (1988) studies of citizen calls for help to emergency service organizations consider how dispatchers treat a variety of caller behaviours and circumstances as calls for help. Most striking are the ways in which dispatchers interpret ambient events as calls for help and respond in organizationally preferred ways. Ambient events include callers hanging up prior to making a request or describing events, silence, and such background sounds as dogs barking, fire alarms beeping, and human voices engaged in conversations separate from the calls.

Dispatchers treat ambient events as calls for help by assuming that callers know that both emergency and non-emergency telephone numbers are available to callers, and callers have knowingly selected an emergency number to call. Whalen and Zimmerman (1987) analyse the assumption as a 'prebeginning' of calls to emergency service organizations, and an aspect of the social contexts within which calls are received by dispatchers. Within this social context, dispatchers orient to a ringing telephone as an initiation of a call for help. They are also expected to maintain this organizationally preferred orientation until they have evidence that the call at hand is not a call for help.

From the ethnography of institutional discourse perspective, Whalen and Zimmerman's (1987) and Whalen et al.'s (1988) studies show how calls to emergency service organizations (including those involving ambient events) initiate callers' and dispatchers' entrance into an organizational discourse, the production of social conditions that link callers' and dispatchers' actions in recognized and unrecognized ways, and make them potentially accountable to one another. One way in which dispatchers hold callers accountable is by returning calls involving ambient events, questioning callers, and assessing whether the calls were truly calls for help. Once callers and dispatchers enter into the organizationally preferred discourse, their relationship may not be terminated until such an assessment is made.

In entering institutional discourses, then, setting members produce social conditions that make social action and interaction possible. The conditions make some social realities and relations readily available, and others less available. For example, Whalen and Zimmerman's (1987) and Whalen et al.'s (1988) studies of citizens' calls to emergency service organizations show how the calls initiated a process within which the callers were constructed as kinds of people (Hacking 1986; Loseke 1993). That is, entrance into this discourse produced conditions that made it likely that callers would be treated as citizens in need of emergency services.

Spencer's (1994) analysis of staff–client interactions in an agency that provided assistance to homeless persons shows that clients may also use entrance into institutional discourses to construct themselves as organizationally preferred kinds of people. In this case, potential clients used the open-ended question–answer format of intake interviews to describe themselves as appropriate clients for the agency. Applicants did so by responding to questions intended to elicit information about their life circumstances by emphasizing that they were not culpable for their homeless circumstances, were trying to improve their situations, and had no recourse to aid from family or friends.

The relationship between institutional discourses and their social settings becomes more complex when we consider how setting members move from one institutional discourse to another, while remaining in the same territorial location. In so doing, they may reconstitute themselves as setting members, their relationships with one another, and conditions of possibility for constructing social realities. The process partly involves attending to aspects of the interaction order and/or new situation-specific contingencies in new ways. It may also involve shifting from one interpretive and accountability framework to another.

For example, Conley and O'Barr (1990) analyse how small-claims court judges sometimes begin court proceedings by attempting to mediate disputes.

They do so by focusing on the relational contexts of the disputes and how the disputes might be resolved to the mutual satisfaction of the disputants. If the judges assess their mediation efforts as failing, they reconstruct the settings and members' positions in them by shifting to an adjudicative orientation and style. The orientation involves applying legal rules to the disputes and finding one or more disputants legally culpable. Thus social settings are potentially shifting formations. Setting members discursively constitute and reconstitute social settings by using available interactional and interpretive resources to organize and pursue their practical interests.

Arrangement of institutional discourses within and across settings

Anspach's (1987) analysis of hospitals as ecologies of knowledge is a beginning for exploring how institutional discourses are differentially positioned within and across settings. Specifically, Anspach studied conflict in the prognostic assessments made by physicians and nurses about newborn infants in intensive-care units. She reports that physicians who had little direct contact with the infants were more likely than nurses to emphasize information produced through diagnostic technology in making their assessments. Nurses differed from the physicians because they also used their interactions and experiences with the infants on the wards in formulating and justifying their assessments. The nurses sometimes used such interactions and experiences to explain and justify their pessimistic prognoses for infants who posed management problems on the wards, a concern that was largely irrelevant to the physicians' orientations to the issues at hand.

Anspach (1987) concludes that hospitals are ecologies of knowledge because physicians' and nurses' territorial and social locations in hospitals are sources for different kinds of knowledge about patients' circumstances. The locations are interpretive lenses or gazes (Foucault 1973) for assessing patients' needs, and associated with different organizational and professional interests in making life-and-death decisions about patients. Thus Anspach analyses conflict between physicians and nurses in prognostic meetings as expressions of their organizational locations and knowledge. Anspach's study may be extended to highlight three other important aspects of the social organization of institutional discourses and their uses in social settings.

First, Anspach's (1987) study shows how two or more institutional discourses may be associated with social settings and used by setting members to justify opposing orientations to practical issues. The discourses involved procedures for constituting others as kinds of people who warranted medical surveillance and intervention. The physicians used a discourse of technological and perceptual cues to constitute infants as clinical objects that might be observed and assessed for symptoms of disease. The nurses, on the other hand, used a discourse of interactional cues to constitute the infants as clinical subjects whose behaviours might be observed and assessed for their interactional appropriateness and the subjectivities embedded in them.

Ethnographers of institutional discourse might extend Anspach's (1987) approach to analysing how the knowledge claims made by physicians and nurses were interactionally organized. For example, they might ask how were the prognostic assessments organized as interactional sequences, and to what general and situation-specific interactional contingencies did the setting members orient? Such questions focus attention on the conditions of possibility for arguing that technological or interactional cues were relevant to the issues at hand, and how they were relevant. Further, whereas organizations may be analysed as ecologies of knowledge, each social setting is a somewhat distinctive domain for formulating and making knowledge claims (Lazega 1992a, Miller and Holstein 1993).

Ethnographers of institutional discourse might also extend Anspach's (1987) analysis by considering the practical implications of excluding infants' parents or other family members from the diagnostic meetings, such as by comparing meetings in which family members are present and absent. It is reasonable to expect that family members would bring different practical assumptions, concerns and interests to the decision-making process. Although they might take account of the technological, perceptual and interactive cues emphasized by nurses and physicians, family members might still describe and constitute the infants in new and different ways, perhaps in ways that challenge nurses' and physicians' assumptions about the legitimacy of medical surveillance and intervention.

Secondly, Anspach's (1987) study shows how institutional discourses are hierarchically positioned in social settings. She states that the discourse of technological cues was more valued by participants in the prognostic meetings. The greater valuing was partly related to the nurses' use of technological cues in describing and assessing infants' conditions. Thus, the nurses did not treat the meetings as occasions to choose between the preferred technological discourse and the less-valued interactional discourse. Rather, they used the discourse of interactional cues to build on or supplement knowledge produced through the discourse of technological cues.

From the ethnography of institutional discourse perspective, an important question involves the occasions when nurses, arguing within a discourse of interactional cues, were able to persuade others. Evidence of a hierarchical arrangement of discourses within a social setting is not a basis for assuming that the dominant discourse is hegemonic. The question directs attention to Foucault's (1972, 1973) emphasis on the gaps and discontinuities in discourses, and it is within such spaces that alternative – even subjugated – discourses may emerge and be taken seriously, if only for a short time.

Ethnographic and conversation analytic research strategies and techniques involve especially useful procedures for seeing and analysing occasions when dominant discourses are displaced by alternative discourses. For example, Buckholdt and Gubrium (1979), in their ethnographic study of a residential treatment centre for emotionally disturbed children, analyse how staff members sometimes displaced the dominant discourse of behaviourism with that of psychoanalysis. As in other organizations, decision-making in the treatment centre was complex and potentially open to several possible formulations of social reality.

Finally, Anspach's (1987) study shows how social settings and their institutional discourses may be interrelated. She analyses how the emphasis on technological cues in prognostic meetings was related to the hospital's record-keeping practices, which also emphasized technological over other cues. Documentary information produced in other settings, and in response to different practical concerns, was introduced into prognostic meetings when physicians and nurses read and discussed the infants' hospital records. Thus the hierarchical arrangement of discourses in the meetings was related to the discursive emphases in other organizational settings.

Analyses of the connection between different settings and their institutional discourses might also consider how setting members' assumptions, concerns and vocabularies anticipate and are responsive to the possible 'downstream consequences' of the members' actions (Emerson and Paley 1992). Such consequences are the conditions of possibility that setting members associate with other settings in which they or others may find themselves in the future. Analysis of setting members' descriptions of and orientations to downstream consequences is one way of studying how members construct and use knowledge about interorganizational processes and organizational contingencies as they enter institutional discourses, construct social settings and take actions within them (Emerson 1991).

Conclusion

Given the suggestive intent of this chapter, it would be inappropriate to conclude by enveloping the ethnography of institutional discourse perspective within a set of restrictive and determinate summary statements. Rather, I conclude by briefly discussing some additional issues and concerns that might be used to extend the perspective and organize qualitative research on social settings and their institutional discourses. I raise the issues by asking three questions, which focus on aspects of Foucauldian discourse studies and point to areas in which such studies may be blended with ethnomethodologically informed ethnography and conversation analysis. The questions do not exhaust, but merely hint at, the variety of issues that ethnographers of institutional discourse might study.

(1) *How are social settings and their institutional discourses related to non-discursive aspects of social settings?* Although Foucault (1972) emphasizes the ways in which kinds of people and power relations are discursively constructed, he also analyses the conditions of discourse as involving non-discursive, material aspects. The latter aspects of settings may be analysed as the conditions of possibility for discourses. They include the size of social settings' memberships, typical sites, and the material resources available to setting members in making and acting on their reality claims. The implications of non-discursive aspects of social settings for studying institutional

discourses are nicely articulated in the following personal communication from Donileen Loseke:

> What is and what is not possible is determined by more than preferred modes of discourse . . . I keep going back to the shelter for battered women as my example – it was only so big, there were only so many workers, given material resources there was much the workers could not do for their clients – they couldn't produce jobs, they couldn't produce low-cost housing, etc. . . . I would say that one 'reason' for the preferred psychological discourse was the practical, material impossibility of gathering 'real' resources for clients . . . The discourse is the 'way we do things'; by accepting and using the discourse, the 'way we do things' doesn't change much; the discourse is knowledge/power supporting whatever status quo might be; the discourse becomes social structure. (September 1993)

While attending to the non-discursive aspects of social settings, ethnographers of institutional discourse need to keep in mind that material conditions are also products of institutional discourses and social interaction. Money is not a simple independent variable that exists separate from setting members' interpretive activities that shape their behaviour and options. The availability of money and other resources are matters to which setting members may attend in a variety of ways, sometimes by stating that they have no choice but to continue things as they are and, other times, to argue that they have little left to lose. The latter response may be part of a rationale for challenging dominant institutional discourses and typical ways of acting in settings. Thus the relationship between discursive and non-discursive aspects of social settings is complex, and may vary across settings.

(2) *How are social settings and their institutional discourses organized as, and/or related to, textual realities?* This is a new issue for those qualitative researchers and analysts who have studied how organizational realities are textually organized and mediated (Bogdan and Ksander 1980; Gubrium and Buckholdt 1979; Kitsuse and Cicourel 1963; Smith 1984). For example, Anspach's (1987) study shows how the conditions of possibility for speech in social settings are shaped by textual formulations of social reality produced in other settings. Further, Molotch and Boden's (1985) analysis of the Watergate hearings shows one way in which social interaction in settings may be organized to negotiate the meaning of texts that describe activities occurring in other settings.

Such concerns may be extended by studying how textually produced and disseminated disciplinary knowledge is used within and shapes social settings. For Foucault (1977), disciplinary knowledge is knowledge that is produced within academic fields and used to monitor and manage persons' lives. Foucault's concern for disciplinary knowledge raises important questions about the ways in which aspects of the human sciences are disseminated across social settings and how members use them to assess and control their own and others' behaviour. Ethnomethodologically informed ethnography and conversation analysis are especially promising approaches to studying how disciplinary knowledge is organized within social settings and used to shape everyday life.

(3) *How is silence organized within social settings and their institutional discourses?* Foucauldian scholars seek to identify, amplify and legitimate devalued discourses associated with marginalized groups. Silence is significant for them because they assume that members of marginalized groups are discouraged from speaking or not allowed to speak at all in settings organized to further marginalize them (Miller 1995). These issues become analytically complex when analysts consider how silence may be associated with a variety of meanings in social settings and used to pursue diverse practical ends. For example, silence might signal resistance or assent to ongoing interactions. It is also used to inform others of one's intention to observe, but remain uninvolved in, their ongoing activities. Indeed, the latter use of silence is one way in which qualitative researchers position and define themselves in the settings that they study.

The research and analytical strategies of the ethnography of institutional discourse perspective are especially promising approaches to the study of silence in social settings. The ethnographer's sustained and in-depth involvement in social settings is a basis for observing and analysing the variety of ways in which silence may be organized and given practical meaning within settings. Further, conversation analyses of audio- and videotapes of social interactions might be used to display how silence is accomplished in social settings, and related to different bodily positionings, gazes, and forms of pre- and post-silence talk. Through such studies, ethnographers of institutional discourse might distinguish among different forms of silence and analyse occasions when silence is organized as resistance, and other times as assent, to dominant discourses.

Through studies of these and related issues, ethnographers of institutional discourse may develop comparative analyses of social settings and their discourses. They may also show how ethnomethodologically informed ethnography and conversation analysis are theory-building activities that have special relevance for the extension and elaboration of Foucauldian discourse studies.

Acknowledgements

This chapter was first published in the *Journal of Contemporary Ethnography*, 23(3): 280–306 (1994). I would like to thank Spencer Cahill, Jim Holstein, Doni Loseke, Courtney Marlaire and Jack Spencer for their comments on earlier drafts.

Note

1 The programme offered here complements that proposed by Drew and Heritage (1993) as the institutional interaction programme. The approaches are similar because both emphasize the importance of conversation analysis techniques in analysing institutional discourses/interactions. A major way in which the programme outlined here differs from that of Drew and Heritage is its explicit concern for combining aspects of conversation analysis with aspects of ethnographic field research and Foucauldian discourse analysis.

12

Ethnography and Justice

David L. Altheide and John M. Johnson

The social context of research and the importance of values and assumptions in research methods are receiving more attention from social scientists. Important questions have been raised about the complex relationships between the researcher, methodology, the human subjects in the setting and standards of knowledge and science. This is particularly true in the study of organizations (Schwartzman 1993) where an additional issue of 'relevance' and even 'critical analysis' has been raised (cf. Thomas 1993). However, each of these relationships has its own history, context and frames of reference, which are not easily integrated. Indeed, attempts to focus on these relationships often amount to efforts to bridge the frameworks and to find a common 'symbolic space' albeit not always successfully. We join this exploration to suggest that social justice as a framework may promote some integration and communication. Our basic argument is that many of the issues running through contemporary debates about research methods, conceptions of truth and validity and 'empowering' research have a common ground in a refined version of social justice which we will present.

The past three decades have witnessed a surge in social scientists' concerns with the foundations of knowledge, and particularly the role of the researcher in influencing results. Indeed, some of the major research developments, which in turn spawned some five decades of methodological and theoretical reflection, occurred in early organizational studies associated with the name 'Hawthorne studies'.

> The most influential behavioral science study of a business enterprise is still, even after 50 years, the Hawthorne study . . . The Hawthorne research is one of the creation myths of industrial psychologists and sociologists . . . The study began as a test of the scientific management principles . . . but it took a surprising turn and ended by disqualifying the major principles on which scientific management was based. In the process, the informal organization of workers was discovered, the human relations school was born. (Schwartzman 1993: 40–41)

A more general question has been raised about the nature of the reality we claim to be studying, as well as whether any method or approach is satis-factory to obtain knowledge.

Often referred to in scientific discourse as 'the validity issue', recent work has gone well beyond the useful cautions about 'reactivity', or how the research act might influence an optimal understanding of the objective truth under investigation. Another emphasis has been the place or fit of validity in research discourse. We (Altheide and Johnson 1994) have been among numerous researchers concerned with this important issue and offer some additional comments here about the nature of the issue and some possible resolutions. In the first section of this chapter, we attempt to put the current debate about validity within a broader context of social justice that is seldom articulated. At the core of many critiques about approaches to validity is a concern for power differentials and empowerment, which are also central to social justice issues. Some comments are offered to integrate validity issues with a reflexive theory of justice in order to suggest some ways that ethno-graphers might approach justice concerns as part of their work. In the second section, we address validity in ethnography. An overview of the context of recent discussions about validity and selected postmodern assumptions about knowledge and science is followed by a summary of our position on the problem of validity in social science and, particularly, ethnography.

Social reality and social justice

Several decades of methodological debate have moved justice concerns closer to methodological issues. All research attempts to present the truth(s) accepted by the investigator. This involves ontological and epistemological assumptions about reality, objectivity, methodology and professionalism. Of course, all of the above concepts are related, so that as one changes the others are likely to follow, albeit in less than predictable order. Another concept that resonates assumptions about truth is justice, although the latter is seldom considered in discussions of methodology *per se*, even though some investigators will acknowledge that social science should be concerned with promoting justice. Justice involves the attempt to apply truth to human expectations. We would define justice *as an emotional commitment to a standard, expectation and value of fairness, rightness and orderliness* (Solomon 1990). Justice is a cultural symbol of direction, order and com-mitment that the world (or the entire universe) is sensible and knowable. This sense of justice is acquired, tested and realized when it is absent in everyday life situations. It is a sense of justice, rather than an absolute stan-dard of justice, that is the domain of a reflexive theory of justice. It is for all these reasons that we draw on our broad understanding about the nature and complexities of justice in order to offer the following general definition of 'the study of justice': *the philosophical, historical and scientific investiga-tion of the nature, origin, process, implementation, use and consequences of certain standards and points of view referred to as 'justice'*. We argue that ethnography is both a way to study justice as well as to 'do justice'. Furthermore, we suggest that ethnographers are 'justice workers' in so far as they clarify the nature, process and consequences of human expectations which are manifested in everyday life as social definitions.

There are two senses in which ethnographers are implicated in social justice. First, and most straightforwardly, is when topics and problems are selected for investigation with the intent to change and improve the situation. This is the so-called 'underdog' emphasis, or the attempt to help correct a situation of unfairness. With exceptions, most ethnography resonates the values of the 'underdog' or the 'weak' suggested in Becker's (1967) important essay, 'Whose side are we on?' Behind this general idea is the firm belief that careful study will show that any imbalances of power, especially patterns of behaviour and interaction that are governed by unilateral and arbitrary dictates (usually by a few over many), are not desirable, and that there is often considerable misunderstanding (indeed, miscommunication!) between the parties involved in such asymmetric relationships. The second general slant involving justice and ethnography focuses on the processual and situated nature of social activities, including social routines as well as extraordinary events. The communication process, and particularly the way in which individuals become social and come to reflect their social world, suggest another important feature linking standards of justice to social reality. This involves the *definition of the situation*, or how one's experience, knowledge, language and intention provide meaning. A key point is that social order, including notions about justice, is implicated in who contributes to the definition of a situation, what criteria are brought to bear (and accepted) in defining a situation, and what the consequences of such definitions are. The implications of this become more apparent if we stress that virtually all criteria of membership, status, rights, inclusion and exclusion are central to the definition of the situation. Stated differently, from strictly a standpoint of participation and fairness, the justice process is extended when more people (or their representatives) can participate in defining a situation that will affect them.

Examples abound of the first impact of social justice in ethnographic research. Virtually all ethnographies contain clear asssertions about erroneous assumptions that were discovered in the study, including those which prevented people, roles and statuses from more fully participating in an activity under study, how their behaviour was informed by their fear of the 'others' assigned to monitor and control them, and the general unfairness by which people with power directly or indirectly guide and monitor selected experiences of those with less power. Indeed, Thomas's (1993) *Doing Critical Ethnography* explicitly focuses on topics that are arbitrary and unfair, suggesting that field workers can contribute to information about the arbitrary use of power in selected social relationships, and the relevance for the organizational context in which they are enacted. Numerous other studies, particularly those involving the poor, deviant and generally less powerful groups (for example, minority groups, drug addicts, homosexuals, street criminals, welfare recipients, the disabled, prisoners, and so on) present numerous portraits of individuals in social relationships that are asymmetrical, even oppressive. These reports delineate the consequences for the persons, the resulting interactions (for example, guard–prisoner relations), the organizational context, and society as a whole. An example is Wiseman's *Stations of the Lost* (1970). Carried out when 'public drunkenness' was a crime, this provocative study illustrates how 'street people' and chronic alcoholics adjusted and learned to 'exploit' the disorganized system of public and private agencies, including jails, designed to control them. As another example, various studies of prisons and prisoners make it clear that prison life is 'negotiated' within massive physical and symbolic constraints to the point that the oppressiveness of the prison structure is sometimes matched by the brutality of the informal 'inmate structure' (Thomas 1993).

The second category of justice studies overlaps with the first, but is generally characterized by an unveiling of irony, arbitrary decision-making, miscommunications that often result in maximum feasible misunderstanding and, in general, disregard of the views and perceptions of those in less powerful positions (*Journal of Contemporary Ethnography*, vols. 1–26; *Symbolic Interaction*, vols. 1–19). These studies show the weight of routine, ritual, taken-for-granted norms and 'sensible ways to act' for human safety, happiness and efficiency. A good example is the nature, significance and meanings of 'meetings' in organizations (Schwartzman 1989). Schwartzman's (1993: 40-41) review of ethnography in organizational studies stressed how perspective fundamentally altered the understanding of meetings to members in situations:

> staff and board members saw their world as a battleground and they became caught up in a battle for control, while at the same time viewing one another's activities as 'out of control'. In my view staff and board members saw the organization and their actions quite differently because they were seeing events, and trying to understand and interpret them, through different meetings (staff meetings versus board meetings). To explain these differences in terms of the different roles individuals occupied in the organization does not help us understand how these differences were experienced and generated in the daily actions of individuals in this context.

Such work often suggests dire consequences of the respective 'social organization' for the avowed goals of the organization, not to mention broader societal values. It is the irony of social life and social order that drives them, and the irony is seldom lost on the researchers' artful rendering of the implications for our everyday lives. Studies by Erving Goffman, especially *Asylums* (1961a) and *Behavior in Public Places* (1963b), illustrate the Janus-faced consequences of formal and informal social control in institutions and in routine everyday settings.

Basic to all these works is an implicit appeal to the reader to take serious notice, to be aware of not just what is interesting, but how the lives of people are being affected, and, particularly, how there are alternative ways to do things without such dire consequences. What is also very important in

this second category of ethnographic work is the awareness of what functionalist theorists referred to as 'unintended consequences'. Rules have
unintended consequences, usually paradoxical: drugs are banned, so they
are rampant in prisons; weapons are officially taboo, so they are routinely
made; heterosexual behaviour is essentially prevented and forbidden, so
homosexual brutality is ubiquitous. The ethnographers' reach for other
possibilities out of the foundation of irony and everyday patterns of social
interaction seems to be what appeals to many readers. When viewed
through ethnographic reflection, it is clear that things can be done in many
ways and some are less hurtful and more just than others. It is as though
getting the inside scoop, the 'right stuff', almost invariably is critical of
human suffering, deprivation and loss at the hands, assumptions and routines of others.

Any attempt to formulate a sound strategy for field investigations like
organizational studies, or a general perspective on what might be termed an
'ethnographic ethic', would surely have to consider the justice implications
of what has passed before in ethnography, as well as suggesting more explicitly what might follow, including the bold challenge to offer some rules of
thumb for guiding future ethnographic work. The ethnographic ethic calls
for researchers to articulate what influences members' communication and
participation in social activities and what the consequences are.

We argue that ethnographers are 'justice workers' in so far as they clarify
the nature, process and consequences of human expectations that are manifested in everyday life as social definitions. The ways in which the standard
of justice becomes incorporated into routine and everyday social life makes
the study of justice so important for ethnographers and for issues of validity.
Is everyone's perspective on a situation central to the social significance of the
experience and the situation? This would entail careful assessment in terms
of the accepted group definition of the situation and who was able to contribute to it. Moreover, how did the investigator decide on the appropriate
definition(s) and point(s) of view? *These are clear challenges not only for a
research ethics but for research approaches informed by an expansive view
of social justice in everyday life.* But an immense challenge comes with this
understanding of social life as process; namely, that social reality and ideas
of justice are closely tied together through language, habit and custom.

The suggestion is that the idea of an emotional commitment to everyday
life routines, which are commonly studied by ethnographers, implies standards that transcend a specific situation. Moreover, these standards also
contribute to a sense of order and meaning. Every culture that we have
studied has a way of explaining its origin, present and destiny, as well as a
way of accounting for other cultures. This is very important because it suggests that we actually learn about ourselves, our standards, morality and our
place in the world (if not the universe) by comparing 'us' with 'them'. For
example, in the language of every human group with which we are familiar,
the symbol or term for themselves ('us') draws a distinction between themselves and others, often translating themselves as 'human' or 'chosen', while

the others are not. A big part of this definition of self (or group) provides its members with an identity about who they are and who they are not.

Membership and the criteria of membership are very important for standards of justice and for ethnographers. It is for this reason that we see the study of justice as including, among its many aspects, the following kinds of question:

- what is (are) the standard(s)?
- what is its origin?
- to whom does it apply – who qualifies for the standard?
- what is the process or way of changing or modifying the standard?
- what are the consequences of the standard for all members of a social order?

The ways in which language, habits, routines and reality are intertwined with assumptions and underlying dimensions of social justice are not easily deciphered, but thinking about the problem in terms of 'social process' affords an opportunity for investigating the origin, criteria, application and change of standards of justice as they appear in language, thought, habits, routines and social institutions. A key concept that helps this process is membership, which refers to who belongs, or is eligible, and who is not. But membership is itself based on criteria of legitimacy or eligibility.

Membership is marked by symbols involving the time, place and manner of activities. When people share a common sense of time, place and manner, they can act in concert, smoothly and routinely. But this has another important consequence for social order and social justice. When we rely on membership criteria to help inform us about justice, orderliness and reality, part of the language and symbol systems we employ is brought to bear on developing one of the most important aspects of understanding social justice: members of social groups ('insiders') develop their sense of membership, identity and worth by contrast with, or learning about, the other groups, the outsiders. We learn who we are, what we stand for, what is right and just, by also learning what others do that is undesirable. On the one hand, membership involves common definitions involving the time, place and manner of activity: this also means that there are more than likely some common criteria and, ultimately, common or similar definitions of a situation. On the other hand, it is the 'other' or the non-group member, the 'outsider' in other words, who is implicated in our standards, identity, morality, justice and validity.

Social justice and injustice exist and are realized through social interaction in everyday life. When all is said and done, it is routine interaction that produces and sustains major problems involving social justice, such as inequality. One way to focus on hopes and ideas for enhancing social justice, including making certain changes, is to turn the question around and, rather than focus on 'how can we improve justice?', ask 'how is injustice and discrimination possible in a setting?' How is it experienced, interpreted, normalized and resisted? Part of our answer to this question requires that we spell out how we know that people in a given setting define any situation, including how to 'act unjustly'.

The problem is intriguing because it suggests that we must be able to experience, interpret or read a situation so that we know how to define it. But, a situation cannot be defined if it cannot be recognized. This leads to a major consideration in understanding social justice: social justice (and injustice) is made visible and intelligible. We know what it looks, sounds and even feels like. Social order is a communicated order, which means that the social distinctions between 'us' and 'them', 'me' and 'you', have a spatial and temporal dimension to them and, most importantly, they are visible. Social order and justice look a certain way to people: we learn how 'normal' relationships are conducted, look where certain people live and what their homes and dwellings look like, and, furthermore, we learn what 'outsiders' look like. It is the various ways in which social life is communicated that is especially intriguing to students of social justice, including where people live, what colour they are, what they sound like, how they dress and appear.

On justice and the ethics of ethnography

A justice perspective can help illuminate social worlds and identify a key dimension of social process, as well as contribute to researchers' conduct and criteria of 'good work', including validity. One answer is suggested in a recent formulation of the 'ethnographic ethic' and 'analytic realism'. 'An ethnographic ethic calls for retaining many long-standing and taken-for-granted canons of ethical ethnography, including the critical commitment to search for the members' understandings, contexts, etc., of the settings studied' (Altheide and Johnson 1994: 489).

A commitment to understand the contexts, definitions and meanings of the members requires the researcher systematically to check impressions and understandings. The ethnographic ethic calls for ethnographers to substantiate their interpretations and findings with a reflexive account of themselves and the process(es) of their research. This methodological stance is referred to as *validity-as-reflexive-accounting (VARA) as an alternative perspective*, which places the researcher, the topic and the sense-making process in interaction. Works and criteria suggested by Athens (1984), Dingwall (1992), Guba (1990), Hammersley (1990), Lincoln and Guba (1985) have been particularly helpful. The basic idea is that the focus is on the process of the ethnographic work (Athens 1984; Dingwall 1992). Accordingly, the ethnographic ethic draws attention to:

1 The relationship between what is observed (behaviours, rituals, meanings) and the larger cultural, historical and organizational contexts within which the observations are made (the *substance*).
2 The relationship between the observer, the observed and the setting (the *observer*).
3 The issue of perspective (or point of view), whether the observer's or the

member(s)', used to render an interpretation of the ethnographic data (the *interpretation*).

4 The role of the reader in the final product (the *audience*).

5 The issue of representational, rhetorical or authorial style used by the author(s) to render the description and/or interpretation (the *style*).

This view is consistent with the position of analytical realism, and the view that the social world is an interpreted world, not a literal world, always under symbolic construction (even deconstruction!):

> Analytic realism is an approach to qualitative data analysis and writing. It is founded on the belief that the social world is an interpreted world. It is interpreted by the subjects we study. It is interpreted by the qualitative researcher. It is based on the value of trying to represent faithfully and accurately the social worlds or phenomena studied. Analytic realism rejects the dichotomy of realism/idealism, and other conceptual dualisms, as being incompatible with the nature of lived experience and its interpretation. Like pragmatism, it cuts across conventional questions about ontology, truth and method, and instead redirects such concerns to the empirical world of lived experience. Analytic realism assumes that the meanings and definitions brought to actual situations are produced through a communication process. As researchers and observers become increasingly aware that the categories and ideas used to describe the empirical (socially constructed) world are also symbols from specific contexts, this too becomes part of the phenomena studied empirically, and incorporated into the research report(s). (Altheide and Johnson 1994: 489)

We regard many of the debates about validity in recent years to be very fruitful for promoting careful reflection on all scientific research, and particularly ethnography. We also regard many of the points that have been raised in this debate as more relevant for a discussion about research ethics in particular, and the role of ethnographers in condoning and promoting injustice. Indeed, some critics of ethnography associated with postmodernism have argued that the reflexive process which implicates researchers and the research process in findings precludes any systematic knowledge (Rosenau 1992). One alternative has been to deny the integrity of decades of ethnographic work as representing 'mere standpoints' or limited claims to knowledge, while arguing that the most any ethnographer can hope to accomplish is to present the 'voices' or 'perspectives' of people being studied to an audience. Such alternatives, which unabashedly affirm the assumptions that create them, are promoted as reasonable responses to the alleged 'crisis of representation' in the social, cultural and interpretive sciences.

While the veracity of many of these claims has been challenged elsewhere (Snow and Morrill 1995), particularly the more bizarre claims which include assertions that an 'unconscious oedipal desire' underlies sociological observations (Dickens 1995), their relevance for arguments about validity require some attention here. The postmodern world, and the intellectuals and researchers who inhabit it, are presumed to be more or less fully captured by a social reality enmeshed in capitalism, hegemony, racism, sexism and so on (Denzin and Lincoln 1994, 1995). And while some critiques of ethnography lament the injustices in the world, the Enlightenment rationale for systematic research is trashed for letting the injustices happen (Denzin 1996), as though the most oppressive forms of capitalism, brutality and techno-control are consistent with the Enlightenment, pragmatism and the ethnographic project!

One of the strongest criticisms of the insensitivity of ethnographic work has been lodged by those loosely affiliated with the even looser moniker of 'postmodernist'. Space limitations restrict us to Thomas's (1993: 23) succinct overview:

> Postmodernists claim that modernism is dead. Modernism's characteristics include (a) belief in the power of reason and the accumulation of scientific knowledge capable of contributing to theoretical understanding; (b) belief in the value of centralized control, technological enhancement, and mass communication; (c) adherence to established norms of testing validity claims; (d) acceptance of the Kantian view of the possibility of establishing universalistic value statements; and (e) belief in the possibility of progressive social change. In response, postmodernists offer an ironic interpretation of the dominance of a master technocratic or scientific language that intrudes into realms once considered private, the politics of techno-society, and the sanctity of established civil and state authority.

As noted, a concern with injustice, and especially the use of power, runs through many of the critiques. With some exceptions, the avowed anti-authoritative stance of many postmodern critics, along with their commitment to include any and all minority group standpoints, suggests that the discourse transcends any notion of methods not also joined to popularized versions of 'empowerment' and 'liberation'. Power is clearly implicated, but since symbolic interactionists and most qualitatively oriented researchers have seldom set forth a conceptually informed statement of power (Prus 1995), subsequent referrals often lack clarity, and in many instances smack of an unquestioned acceptance of structural definitions which may equate power with 'resources' or some other notion.

Many academics seem to accept abstract and absolutist notions of justice (Johnson 1995). Indeed, reading a plethora of critiques about ethnographers and validity suggests that removing the authority of ethnographers to make statements about a social setting is a kind of levelling of 'authority rights' to make everyone's view equal. This form of 'symbolic enrichment' becomes an entitlement of equality: everyone has the right to their own story and every story has equal footing, leaving it to the reader to interpret the text. Notwithstanding the elliptical treatment of justice and injustice in such claims, we want briefly to join power to justice, and approach the issue more directly by suggesting that justice concerns may be incorporated within the ethnographic ethic. We offer some initial reflections on ways of conceiving justice so that it may inform ethnographic work and its guiding ethics.

It is the way the ethnographic ethic is constituted as justice through analytical realism and interpretive validity that we want to address. The ethnographic ethic is consistent with a much broader concern for developing a 'reflexive theory of justice', which 'needs to be processual, emotional, developmental, gendered, personal, interactional, and interpretive' (Johnson 1995: 199). Justice is a cultural symbol of direction, order and commitment that the world (or the entire universe) is sensible and knowable. This sense of justice is acquired, tested and realized when it is absent in everyday life situations. It is a sense of justice, rather than an absolute standard of justice that is the domain of a reflexive theory of justice. So conceived, justice is viewed primarily as an emotional struggle of the self 'to live with virtue in our social and communal lives' (Johnson 1995: 199), realized through social interaction with others in our affective communities, including the contexts, experiences and meanings from which the self emerges.

Ethnographic research embraces a reflexive view of justice as a topic and as a resource (see Douglas 1971; Jorgensen 1989; Shaffir and Stebbins 1991). As a topic, any research endeavour is an assertion that communication and understanding are intersubjectively possible, and, we emphasize, realizable. (We also believe that the underlying utility of all research is that it is beneficial, but this argument will not be made here.) As researchers, we are fundamentally committed to what is possible. This is an ethical issue for all research, one we have incorporated within the ethnographic ethic. Truth runs against deception here: if a researcher is deceived, there may indeed have been communication, but, clearly, less than complete intersubjective understanding and analysis have been accomplished. All research risks the possibility of being negated; that is, of being deceived or misdirected so that intersubjective understanding does not occur. Research implies a commitment to avoiding the multiple sources of distortion that have been identified above, as well as the sources to be discovered through future reflections. The process, including the way situations are defined, meanings are developed and selves are managed, is central for justice.

The research authority is a moral authority but it differs from many others in the conception of how its focus and topic of study are constituted. Ideologues of all stripes, be they Nazis, capitalists or any one of the dozens of 'ists', do not have the authority of truth, independently of how a project is carried out, interpreted, presented and evaluated by a community (an audience) also committed to truth. *The kind of truth we speak of involves a feeling, an irrational commitment to 'truth as justice'.* From this standpoint, ignorance is an enemy of justice.

We reject the assumption of equal capacity and authority to provide an adequate understanding of social life compatible with the ethnographer/ social scientist's commitment to provide a descriptive account of the members' social world and to conceptually relate how this world is a feature of basic communication and interaction processes. Anyone can offer an understanding, of course, but all interpretations are assessed by an audience. The assessment implies standards, and it is this essential audience involvement and response that constitutes its own discourse of representation and comparison.

Within the framework of knowing, we propose, there is not only the possibility of error, but also ignorance. We believe that there has been a serious confusion of injustice with ignorance. So central have justice concerns been to the ethnographic and broader social science reflections, that those who believed that the underdogs, the minorities and the dispossessed have been ill served by social science have advocated an inclusive position that renders all claims to be equal, all authorized knowers to be on the same footing. Ironically, this opening up of 'knowledge space' can also deny errors and outright ignorance. The social scientists' purview, like most specialists, is that of expertise, suggesting that we know certain things about the world-as-viewed-by-us that others do not; others, in fact, may be uninformed, unaware and not capable in certain situations of seeing and appreciating what we do *vis-à-vis* our disciplinary perspective.

Just as any competent ethnographer enters a setting to be investigated with a standpoint of 'ignorance about their world', so too are most people ignorant of the ethnographic perspective. The guiding principle of validity in whatever form it appears is, after all, the issue of truth. This takes on critical dimensions when empirical research and basing a research account on actual instances, observations and comments are invoked. Notwithstanding the lucid reflections by researchers who remind us that any research report is done by particular authors, the guiding assumption behind empirical research is that it is 'someone else's story' as 'told by us' (van Maanen 1988). Indeed, it is partly for this reason that researchers are advised to attempt to separate the empirical materials from analysis and interpretation (Dingwall 1992). Accordingly, to conduct empirical research is a commitment to an audience and reflexive justice.

As a *resource*, ethnographers and researchers in general are implicated in the communities, activities and selves that they investigate. Every ethnographic report involves implicit and explicit materials and claims relevant to the struggles, activities, contexts and meanings suggested by the reflexive view of justice noted above. Any statement made about the 'other' will include a reference to their activities, points of view, meanings and understandings. All such statements have implications for their views of justice. Schwartzman's (1993: 41) lucid comments about meetings in organizational contexts resonates this point:

> Individuals also use meetings to read and/or see their places in particular social systems. We say that an individual is or is not a powerful person, but often we only 'know' this based on how we read and interpret events in a meeting. This was certainly the case for participants at Midwest, where there were very few ways outside of meetings for individuals to negotiate and/or determine their status and social ranking, and where their status was frequently in flux. In some cases it was only by astutely 'reading' meetings . . . that an individual might learn about his or her place in the status system of the Center.

The ethnographic ethic, of course, is not a substitute for 'ethics in research', including what we should study and how we should study it. Indirectly, the ethnographic ethic is very important for larger ethical considerations, although not definitive. This is because virtually any topic or approach to a problem that violates basic human rights and respect for human dignity – the sovereignty of body and mind – would also intrude on the research process and invalidate the findings. For example, most research ethics issues involve notions of 'privacy'; if an investigator – with or without informed consent – violates privacy (meaningful temporal and spatial parameters of human subjects), that research will be compromised not only ethically, but also substantively. At least for social science topics, the meaning, setting and action central to the definition of the situation will be compromised, and the data collected will reflect these changes, so that while the investigator may claim to be studying X, he/she is really studying Y. This suggests the importance of the definition of the situation.

One interactionist position on power we offer rests on social definitions. Analytical realism celebrates the notion of multiple voices and different perspectives without caving into solipsism or naïve relativism. All interpretations of people's interpretations are not equally valid and sustainable in the face of varieties of data. Data exist in the field – for example, organizations – where people make their way. As suggested by Charmaz and Mitchell (1996: 286), words, while important, are not omnipotent:

> Postmodernists have reified descriptive language into a hidden power that commands and controls the intersubjective, while veiling sovereign dictates of a metonymic tyranny. From our perspective, words are both limited and useful; they are neither magic nor nonsense. Symbolic interactionists can tell a reasoned tale without retreat into scientific autism, and an interesting one without regress to arty irrationalism.

Notwithstanding the problems with methodologically navigating this world under constant construction, interpretations and understandings can be checked independently of blatant acts of power. From this slant, *power is the ability to define a situation for self and others.* The process, origins, adjustments and consequences of social definitions are the subject matter of most social analysis. Most cogent analyses of social life provide a coherent statement about how the time, place and manner of activities is reflexive, contextual and processual. Social life is temporal, clocked by the rhythm of everyday life. The meanings, routines, relationships, expectations, norms, habits and taken-for-granted activity have an origin; that origin, many studies suggest, is often a point of conflict, even violence. Ultimately, new habits and routines appear, as suggested by the classicists and others, including Schutz (1967), Berger and Luckmann (1966) and the symbolic interaction of George Herbert Mead (1934) on which many of their ideas were based. Social stability and change is recognized, explained and resisted through symbolic communication. It is the way in which situations are defined, and how these definitions may or may not transcend situations to become 'internalized' and 'reified', that draws attention to power and justice.

Conclusion

This overview of some recent issues involving validity in ethnographic work has raised additional questions about relationships between research and justice. Our aim is to contribute to the debate about ethnographic work as well as offer another standard by which to conduct and assess this work. A quick summary of this point suggests that a reflexive theory of justice is implicated in issues about ethnography, validity and researcher authority. Some notion of a standard or criterion is implied by any statement about the adequacy of research, including how one ought to proceed. Basically, analytical realism recognizes the interpreted quality of the social world and locates the researcher within this interpreted world. While absolute truth and certainty are never guaranteed, the foundations of interpretation are drawn on to suggest that the researcher can give an account of how certain problems and issues that inform most interpretations are reflexively a feature of the report. The commitment to this perspective, and particularly interpretive validity, is a feature of an *ethnographic ethic*, or an assertion about the basic communicative ecology surrounding an empirically based research report (for example, relationships and perspectives of the observer *vis-à-vis* subject matter, subjects, the reader/audience and rhetorical styles).

A more focused and sociologically informed *reflexive theory of justice* is oriented to felt experience and emotions in specific and local contexts. Critical to concerns about validity and justice is the definition of the situation and the role of power. We suggest that interpretive validity is constituted in the merging of power and justice in the everyday life contexts of subjects, ethnographers and the perspectives they share and that are unique to each. We further suggest that many critiques of validity reflect an emotional dis-ease with what is so important, yet missing, from an informed research ethic. It is justice that is missing, and we offer a reflexive theory of justice as integrating knowledge with enquiry, advocacy and responsibility.

The upshot is that social justice is more complicated than is suggested by the mere differences and ways of adjusting them that have captured most utilitarian views of justice. Most importantly, ethnographic research is tied to a reflexive notion of justice as a topic and as a resource. The ethnographic ethic celebrates 'good faith' and is thereby limited in what it prescribes and, by implication, what is proscribed. We recommend that ethnographers be well versed in the complex interaction process, and particularly the nature and process of power in defining situations in order to clarify further how justice is constituted, communicated and experienced in everyday life.

13

One Branch of Moral Science: an Early Modern Approach to Public Policy

P. M. Strong

Unlike our immediate ancestors, or some of our colleagues in other disciplines, or indeed (for those of us who are middle-aged) some of our earlier selves, sociologists – qualitative and quantitative alike – work in an ethically incoherent world in which there is no clear disciplinary morality which connects our research to public policy. To say this is not to yearn for some lost golden age, or to assume that there ever was or ever could be a completely coherent disciplinary ethic on which all could agree. It is merely to note that modern sociology now mostly lacks what it has had on some occasions in the past: a powerful sense of moral purpose and commitment to public policy. We commonly feel and are now often treated as marginal.

This feeling is not just a matter of which political party is in power but a sense of the times – that either they are out of joint or, worse, that we ourselves are. Not only are we often critics from the side-lines rather than players in the main debates but, more revealingly, many of us aspire to no higher status. Indeed, the very term 'policy' has long seemed squalid and second-rate in some prestigious sociological circles, for it implies a commitment to a world which some of us do not really like and wish we could do without: a world which we can, perhaps, intellectually understand – or so we may think – but to which we cannot join ourselves in any ethically comfortable fashion.

This chapter tries to resolve such problems: first, by providing a model of the contemporary policy arena in liberal societies, so that we can see how our own experiences are matched by many others; then, by sketching out the foundations of a new disciplinary public ethic – a liberal metaphysics which may not appeal to all, but is a good deal more effective and more durable than the alternatives currently on offer. Of course, not all the dilemmas that face modern sociologists when they consider public policy can be settled here. As in all branches of human action, there are inherent controversies and conflicts of interest in the policy arena; some must be left to the skill, judgement and conscience of the individual actor; others can only be managed rather than permanently resolved. None the less, some of the problems that cause us the most public agony do seem capable of resolution; they are not, in fact, as difficult as they might at first appear.

To say this is not to diminish the solution that I shall propose. It is, instead, merely to be humble: to acknowledge that my solution is not really mine at all, that the approach of early modern moral science, whose cause I shall advocate, is now several hundred years old, has found wide acceptance in some other disciplines, and is, indeed, part of our own genealogy, even if it has long passed from our collective memory. For, to understand, feel at ease and act effectively in a modern, liberal society, sociology needs to appreciate liberalism in a much deeper fashion than has been conventional for several generations.

Such an ethical realignment does not mean rejecting the sociological tradition. This is, and will continue to be, a valuable and distinctive source of insight into the human condition. But it does mean abandoning the relatively recent idea that if the heroic sociological morality fashionable for most of this century has failed, then we are doomed, or even honoured, to be the permanent member of the awkward squad – to be a discipline whose unique contribution is not to join in but to stand on the sidelines and sneer. It also means abandoning the arrogant notion, more common perhaps amongst grand theorists than among empirical researchers, that modern sociology, by itself, can provide the explanation for most human social problems.

To see where we might go and what we might learn from liberalism, we need to stand back and view ourselves in much broader and much longer perspectives than we are currently prone to do. This chapter summarizes two such prospects. The first examines our relationship with the contemporary policy process in liberal societies, drawing not just on sociology, but also on the vision of these matters in parts of policy history, political science and political philosophy, disciplines which have made a much deeper study of some aspects of the science–policy relationship and have rather better resources for grasping the essentials of the modern liberal world.

Relocating our place in the historical tradition of liberal thought, the task of the chapter's second section, requires a bigger imaginative leap. A core part of my argument here consists of a brief sketch of the new moral science produced in the early modern period of European history, the period from the sixteenth to the eighteenth centuries which saw the birth of the modern world. This vital era has been seriously neglected by modern sociological thinkers, for both the name 'sociology' and the academic discipline itself date from the nineteenth century, and this late academic origin has had a peculiarly distorting effect upon our self-understanding. Far too many sociological theoreticians, even those like Alexander, Giddens and Turner who proclaim that the subject of sociology is modernity, go back no further than the theorists of the nineteenth century who, great though they undoubtedly were, were also, as we are too, latecomers to the modern world. For that world began, not with the Industrial or French Revolutions, but two hundred years earlier and it is to the first great theorists of the modern world, to Machiavelli, Montaigne, Hobbes, Montesquieu, Smith and the like, that we must also look if we wish to comprehend fully the world in which we live.

This new appreciation also means a new course of reading. For the absence of any serious appreciation of early modern thought has been mas-sively reinforced by the way in which we, like most other occupations, depend on home-grown, amateur histories of our discipline – presentist, 'Whig' affairs which, in our case as in psychology's, rarely look further back than the nineteenth century, often fail to place even nineteenth-century writ-ers in any adequate historical context and, thus, have fundamentally misleading effects upon the theory we produce and the moral and political judgements we make. Instead, to understand our past properly, we must study, not just the classical early modern texts themselves, but the profes-sional, not the amateur, historians of ideas; and we must study them, not just out of whimsical, antiquarian curiosity, but for a much deeper understand-ing of the liberal world in which we still live. For the version of liberalism we are taught as sociologists, though it has powerful, critical points to make, is the product of a later, oppositional, somewhat deviant branch of the main-stream tradition, a branch which needs to understand the tree from which it has grown.[1]

Scientific research and the policy process

Let us begin, however, by considering the contemporary relationship between policy and scientific research. Like most human beings, qualitative socio-logical researchers exaggerate both their problems and their unique qualities. In fact, we have a good deal in common, not just with quantitative colleagues in our own discipline, but with all other scientific researchers in liberal soci-ety. First, in common with almost all other scientists, we share three fundamental beliefs which stem from the scientific revolution of the early seventeenth century: a secular materialism which excludes supernatural causation; a vision of science as a collective, public endeavour; and a post-sceptical epistemology which asserts that, though much may be doubted, there is still sufficient certainty in our perception of the world on which to base a science.

Secondly, however, neither materialism, nor collective endeavour, nor sci-entific method guarantees complete certainty or certain public approval, either within or outwith science. As a result, we also share a common policy dilemma. There is no direct process by which research necessarily informs or transforms policy in any dramatic, rational or linear fashion. Instead, the relationship is, for the most part, little different from any other form of human social relationship and is shaped by the same contrary mix of reason, emotion, interest, exchange, altruism, representation and low cunning. Thus, it would seem that in every shade of government, powerful interests may block, distort or ignore well-established scientific findings so far as it suits them to do so. Moreover, in so far as research does affect policy, this is nor-mally due to a slow process of diffusion, commonly, if perhaps optimistically, described by modern commentators as 'enlightenment'. Most often, a slow crab-like process of increasing influence is the norm, not dramatic, Pauline mass conversion. Moreover, as Kuhn and his successors have shown, similar processes seem to take place within science itself. Even here there seems relatively little room for purely 'rational' debate.

Thirdly, in such diffusion, networks are fundamental. At both a national and local level, the key policy worlds are often backstage arenas where a small number of key players represent different interests. Many policy shifts commonly occur primarily through a slow transformation of opinion within these, and national attempts to transform local policy are often best conducted through targeting influential figures within the local policy arenas, rather than through general campaigns. Moreover, diffusion through such networks is often shaped by imitation and fashion rather than by any more rational assessment – 'if others are doing it we must not be left behind' – and, equally, through powerful currents of collective emotion in which 'science' and its 'findings' take on a decidedly religious air. The behaviour of network members is also powerfully influenced by the constraints and opportunities in their environment. Key players, whether politicians, managers or research entrepreneurs, use research in a way that often appears self-interested, cynical and imperialistic to others, though it may sometimes be viewed rather differently by the actors themselves.

Fourthly, the representation of our science to outsiders, whether it be qualitative sociology or quantum physics, and whether that representation occurs in public or private debate, also has its own characteristic forms: forms that are heavily determined by the occasions of scientific utterance and the means and needs of communication and not simply by scientific theory and data. Thus, not only is there a distinctive rhetoric of science within academic publications, but the mass-media representation of science is fundamentally shaped by journalistic genres, by internal press criteria of what constitutes a tellable story to a mass audience. Likewise, the diffusion of scientific doctrines through private policy networks depends heavily on sound bites and on dogma, on readily intelligible, and thus repeatable, slogans and stories as much on scientific adequacy.

At the same time, if the basic tenets of science – and much of the policy process – are common to all of its forms, there are still important differences between the social and the natural sciences, differences which produce distinctive relationships to public policy. These differences take a contrary form. On the one hand, the social world is, by and large, a far more complex field of determination, prediction and intervention than is true of most natural science arenas. In consequence, professional social scientists, quantitative and qualitative alike, possess less epistemic authority as a social class and play, at least at the technical level, a smaller part in relevant debate than their natural science colleagues. Individual gurus and sometimes particular disciplines and sub-disciplines may, of course, exert considerable influence in particular historical periods but, overall, lay theory and perception are more powerful here than is now normally true of the natural sciences. As a result, 'critique' is an intrinsic feature of all social science and not just the property of a special school within it.

This important bunch of properties is, however, mediated by an opposite and equally important set. Although the laity may claim much greater understanding of the social than of the natural world, the understandings they do claim are powerfully shaped, though not wholly determined, by social science traditions – traditions which, of course, reach them through the distorting mirrors of representation discussed earlier. Moreover, unlike modern natural science, social science remains an integral branch of politics and of ethics. Social science began as, and in fundamental respects continues to be, a 'moral science', an attempt to create an ethically justifiable public policy on a secular and materialist basis. Thus, although all science can potentially be used by power, social science has a special relationship to it. It began as advice to the powerful (Machiavelli's *The Prince* is the paradigm case), and has, for the most part, been closely linked to power ever since (as rationalization, discipline or the civilizing process according to taste). And, even where social science is in opposition, it still continues to make a powerful, if implicit, claim to power.

Finally, there are, therefore, many good grounds for doubting whether the Millian and Habermasian ideal of a rational critical sphere, comprising both systematic private deliberation and rigorous, informed and public debate, can ever be fully realized. The world is not a seminar, and even seminars do not have the properties that they were once ideally ascribed. But having said this, we must also recognize – and this is my first fundamental, liberal point – that there is still a crucial difference between policy formation in liberal and authoritarian societies. Mill and Habermas do have a powerful point. The human social world is not and never can be constructed solely through collective reason. But societies which offer serious and methodical scope for the expression of collective reason – societies, that is, with a liberal public sphere – do offer the opportunity for critical debate and, with all its interests and intrinsic irrationalities, this demonstrably can and does make a difference on some crucially important occasions, even if it does not do so on others. There are clear and systematic differences in societies with and without a liberal public sphere, including, of course, the very existence of most forms of critical social science.

The moral science tradition and our place within it

So far, I have suggested that the problems faced by qualitative researchers in relation to policy are far from unique; that though we may sometimes feel that our case is not heard and that others discriminate against us or distort what we have to say, such feelings are common right across the sciences – are, in fact, the everyday product of intrinsic features of policy formation.[2] I have also made two further, perhaps more important, points: on the one hand, that though the policy process may be far from perfect, perfection is not to be looked for in this life – that policy formation is constructed from the same fallible human materials as every other social process; and, on the other hand, that despite these fallibilities, the liberal version of the policy process offers more space for the operation of collective reason than any other.[3] What I now want to show is that these last two claims are intimately connected: that the liberal tradition is premised on human fallibility, recognizes that we can never transcend it, but tries instead to make the best of what we have got.

This position lies at the heart of the public ethic which modern sociology now needs to embrace. To grasp fully what that ethic is and where we currently stand in relationship to it, I need to say more about the early modern period when that ethic was first pronounced. The new moral science, proposed by writers such as Hobbes, was based on a novel approach to the public realm. This was a secular, chastened, pluralist, materialist and experimental morality which, breaking with the dominant classical and medieval ideals of consensus and virtue, set its sights a good deal lower. Drawing on other aspects of their intellectual inheritance, in particular, on the disenchanted historical analysis and collective psychology of Thucydides and Tacitus, on the pessimistic Stoical tradition of post-republican Rome and on the sinful view of fallen humanity found in Stoicism's Christian successors, the moral scientists of the early modern period argued that this much more glum approach to human behaviour was not only more realistic, but could also – and this was their real innovation – be systematically used in ways that its original inventors had never imagined; could be used, in fact, on Baconian lines, for systematic, secular, human amelioration. Through sustained investigation and experiment, human ingenuity could learn to exploit the worst as well as the best aspects of human behaviour to our mutual, collective advantage. For, once we knew and recognized what the worst was, then it became possible to base realistic, practical, effective public policy upon it.

By contrast, it was ethically irresponsible and socially unproductive collectively to aspire to the moral heights. This was a reasonable pursuit for saints, but not for societies, for such attempts inevitably failed, sometimes with catastrophic consequences. We should aim, instead, for much lower and more achievable targets; targets on which it was possible to establish, if not unanimity, then at least a fair measure of collective agreement. Our public policy goal should therefore be, not the *summum bonum*, the greatest good, but the more pragmatic avoidance of the *summum malum*, the systematic circumvention of the greatest human evils such as tyranny, famine and civil war. The provision of liberty, food and security might not be everything but this was, still, a fundamental framework within which many other things might flourish. Moreover, once such a framework had been established within a society, its members could and should be left to do pretty much as they pleased. There was little possibility of reaching any more tightly focused consensus on the good life and a great deal of danger in attempting to do so.

This fundamental ethical and governmental innovation was associated with two further radical intellectual breaks. The dominant traditions in classical and medieval thought had stressed the ethical and social priority of the *polis*, or community, of a single authoritative, collective standard. But the new *summum malum* doctrine minimized any such collective agreement and substituted, instead, the ethics of effectiveness and of the lowest common denominator. For, in its stress on the need to deal realistically with egoism, the new ethic placed the individual, not the collectivity, at the heart of social arrangements and moral standards. The community now became what you could get individuals to agree on and actually carry out, not an ultimate source of good, while the state was a backstop which supplied the necessary framework for the individual pursuit of life, liberty and happiness; a 'mortal God', certainly, at those times when it was necessary to awe an unruly populace into the ways of peace, but not a sovereign moral and intellectual authority.

Theorizing about the fundamental constitution of the social world was also radically transformed. In the new secular, materialist vision, both individuals and the communities in which they lived were simply machines. Human social life, in fact, was a matter of artifice – or, in more modern terminology, of social construction – not a product of some divine order. The *polis* or community did not fulfil a transcendent end or *telos*, as it had done for Plato, Aristotle and St Augustine; rather it should be made to serve the ends that its members wished it to serve, and should be rearranged, where mechanically possible, to further those individual needs and purposes.

In breaking so fundamentally with the classical and medieval *summum bonum* tradition, the new seventeenth-century moral science was, thus, mechanical, rational, egoistic, individualistic and egalitarian in its orientation. But this extreme form of the reaction against the Platonic, Aristotelian and Catholic past, did not last long. By the eighteenth century, many leading moral scientists began to stress the need for organic and collective perspectives to complement the seventeenth century's vision. In Scotland, the heart of Enlightenment liberal moral science, a new synthesis began to be created, one which was still firmly premised on the *summum malum* position invented a century before, but which recognized that a purely mechanical, individualistic and egoistic model of human behaviour, though enormously powerful, needed serious qualification. Human society was a natural phenomenon as well as an artificial one; there was a role for sympathy as well as self-interest; the stress on egalitarianism needed to be complemented by noting the stratification which also accompanied most human activities.

This synthesis of old and new was in its turn, however, rapidly upset. The French and Industrial Revolutions, the associated rise of a far more powerful state than early modern liberalism had ever envisaged and the development, by the late nineteenth century, of a remodelled university system with massively increased academic specialization, fragmented the older versions of moral science into new, isolated, self-enclosed disciplines. 'Economics' grew out of the seventeenth-century vision; 'sociology' was born from the revived emphasis on the collective aspects of social life, and came to specialize almost solely in these. This separate, collective focus had three powerful effects on the discipline we now inhabit:

1 We possess a much more comprehensive account of the effects of social structure and of culture: 'society', a radically new notion in the seventeenth century, has been made visible in myriad ways.

2 At the same time, the middle-class radicals' rejection of the aristocratic interest in etiquette and micro-social behaviour and the new awareness of the properties of the collectivity – both consequences of the Industrial and French Revolutions – produced a fundamental split between micro and macro theory; a split which would have been incomprehensible to theorists of the seventeenth or eighteenth century who drew automatically on both; a split that we are only now trying to start to mend in any systematic fashion.

3 Finally, the separate, collective focus has had powerful but temporally variable consequences for the discipline's relationship to public ethics and policy. At first, with Hegel, Marxism, normative functionalism and the revival of Plato (the dominant theorist in early twentieth-century British sociology), *summum bonum* morality made a highly successful return. Here, so it seemed, was a public ethic which provided a solid basis for sociological involvement in matters of policy: an ethic which had a powerful appeal to many liberal – and other – governments in the latter half of the nineteenth century and the first half of this century, as they struggled with the potentially frightening implications of industrialization, mass society, militarization and the new world of nation-states.

However, with the massive post-war success and stability of liberal government, the nineteenth-century forms of *summum bonum* morality have lost much of their appeal both within and outside the discipline. And, with this faith gone, the alternative ethical vision in sociology, the Nietzschean strand represented by Weber and Foucault, has come to dominate most of the more fashionable forms of sociological theory.[4] This particular vision bears some striking resemblances to the sceptical and post-sceptical morality of the early modern period.[5] It, too, argues that there is no *summum bonum*; it, too, recognizes the enormous variety of formal moral belief even within any one society; and it, too, stresses the fundamental role of power and self-interest in human life. There is, however, a crucial difference. Unlike their early modern ancestors, the Nietzschean strand in modern sociology sees these features of our existence as largely inevitable, not as things that can potentially be turned to public advantage. In this bleak, structuralist vision, all of us are used by an impersonal and decentred system – a machine world, an iron cage whose disciplining bands bind ever tighter – not a mechanism which presents a challenge to human ingenuity.[6] Such nihilism offers little place for a public ethic for research practice: room for critique but not for constructive comment or collaboration. Thus it is that theoretical sociology, once a flourishing part of moral science, is now in some danger of becoming a largely amoral tradition.

Of course, quite regardless of these shifts in metaphysical fashion, empirical sociologists have continued to conduct research in a vast range of areas relevant to public policy. This is where most of the research money is, and getting research money drives most modern academic departments, at least in the more elite parts of higher education. So public policy research continues for quantitative and qualitative sociologists alike. But it does so in ways which often lack any real sense of disciplinary mission and which are constantly and often savagely internally critiqued, both by the Nietzschean members of the community and by the radicals of varying kinds who cling to the fragments of the more millenarian versions of the *summum bonum* tradition. As a result, there is considerable unease among some sociologists about many forms of policy research, and a profound sense of estrangement from the main discipline among many of those who do conduct such enquiry.[7]

Conclusion

What should be done? Perhaps nothing should be. Moral nihilism has an important ethic of its own. Standing aside and doubting is and will remain a valuable part of social science. It cannot, however, provide a satisfactory moral and practical foundation for many of the forms of research which sociologists do and should undertake. As a result, there has been a growing demand for a new sociological morality and a seemingly wide range of suggestions has been made over the past two decades. But, on close inspection, almost all still cling to the *summum bonum* past, exhuming ancient variants of the tradition to see if this or that version might offer some present help. A variety of such warmed-up remains is now on offer, most with their more unattractive elements cosmetically treated or discreetly removed. Neo-functionalism, a much weaker form of normative functionalism, has attracted some adherents. Others have followed Taylor in an attempt to create a new communitarianism. Yet other communitarians have turned with Macintyre and Bauman (the latter in a nominally postmodernist ethics) to an essentially religious faith. None of these, however, seems a particularly plausible candidate for a revived public ethic. At first sight, the American pragmatist tradition, as revived by Selznick, looks a more likely bet, since it has always rejected *summum bonum* foundations. However, it still suffers, even in its new form, from inadequate attention to the problem of human evil, a problem that liberal moral science puts at the very heart of its programme.

My own belief is that none of these moves will prove particularly effective. They have been tried before and failed. If sociology is to regain and hold on to its formerly prominent place on the public stage, we must look beyond faith and beyond the nineteenth century and start to place our trust, once again, in the *summum malum* tradition; a tradition with which we once broke, but with which we must now learn to be reconciled. For, if the *summum bonum* tradition has floundered, the *summum malum* tradition has not. Following in the footsteps of Machiavelli and Bacon, the great early modern theorists searched for social mechanisms that would enable us to outride Fortuna, that would lessen, even if they could never abolish, the many evils that beset the human condition; that would provide a robust, durable framework inside which humanity, in all its different forms, might flourish. The aim of liberalism is merely to do better, not to be the best. It has favoured, instead, the incremental and the controlled, cautious experiment. That hope has, by and large, been granted. Liberalism has proved durable and those who have been fortunate enough to live inside liberal societies have prospered in comparison with both their ancestors and their contemporaries in other forms of society.

Such an observation, though common enough, is often seen as smug by the many critics of liberalism in the sociological tradition. However, when we rightly observe that liberal society had and still has many obvious and glaring faults, we should not forget that it itself is an open and experimental doctrine that encourages both criticism and invention in order to do better next time. And, when we respond that some of its evils are essential and inbuilt, we must also remember that its more fundamental faults were wryly foreseen by its key early theoreticians. Liberalism is a worldly, unheroic doctrine. Hobbes, the founder of modern liberalism, saw only too well that the state of nature would continue to thrive between nation-states and that even within them, though its very worst excesses might be abolished, a low-level, insidious state of nature would continue to inform a great deal of individual human action.[8] Ferguson and Smith both recognized that the liberal, commercial society, while it had many advantages over the old heroic, aristocratic society, was also 'a society of strangers': that there were and would continue to be important losses as well as gains.

Of course, some liberal thinkers can and do become complacent.[9] We should remember, instead, what the great early modern theorists of the *summum malum* tradition still have to tell us. Modern science, the modern state and their associated welfare order have removed some important elements of the uncertainty and tragedy that so powerfully shaped every human life until relatively recently, but such success is only a thin veneer. Tragedy and evil are and will always remain part of the human condition and only a systematic *summum malum* public ethic pays serious attention to the hard thought and hard choices that the human condition inevitably requires.

A reconciliation between sociology and the *summum malum* tradition would give us a firm basis on which to face up to such facts; a firm ethical base on which we might stand without falling prey to either the despair of the Nietzschean tradition, or the utopianism of the Platonic and Socialist dream. It would provide a clear and coherent purpose to our current involvement in public policy. It would, moreover, teach us to pay systematic attention to effectiveness and efficiency, as well as to humanity and equity, and require us, also, to think of invention as well as description. All this could be done without abandoning the many things we have learned from the collective vision of the past century and a half. Though some sociologists, such as Coleman, have sought to look outside sociology and refound it solely on the rational, egoistic tradition, such a move is both unnecessary and profligate, for it abandons the many important lessons that the collective tradition still has to teach. If we seek a model, we must look instead to the eighteenth-century Scottish synthesis and try to build along the lines suggested there. Though it obviously contains much with which any of us would now quarrel, its broad outline is a most valuable template. It makes room for the micro as well as the macro; gives space for the individual, rational and mechanical as well as the organic, collective and emotional aspects of social life; and, above all, pays more attention to *summum malum* than to *summum bonum* arguments; as, indeed, any public ethic must do which wishes to engage systematically with policy in a modern liberal society.[10]

Acknowledgements

This chapter has grown out of a study of the British public debate over AIDS policy and what that, in turn, reveals about policy formation in a liberal society. I would like to thank the Nuffield Provincial Hospitals Trust both for their generous funding of the study and for the intellectual openness which has given me the opportunity to engage in these more general reflections. I must also thank Nick Black, Virginia Berridge and Gill Walt, my colleagues in other policy disciplines, for what I have learnt from them; and my partner, Anne Murcott, who has tolerated, listened to, and sometimes commented sharply upon, innumerable verbal formulations of some of the ideas in this chapter. I must also thank Nick Black for his patient support in his other capacity as grant-holder. My greatest intellectual debt is to Graham Burchell, from whom I have no doubt pinched even more than I am currently aware of and distorted that which I think I have understood.

Editors' note

Philip Strong died on 11 July 1995 while this manuscript was still in advanced draft. Following discussions with his partner and literary executor, Anne Murcott, it was agreed that the text was substantially that which he would have wished to see published and that his main further addition would have been to provide a bibliography. Rather than guess at his intentions in this respect, and possibly misdirect the reader, we have chosen to publish the text exactly as it was left in a computer file dated 16 April 1995 (the manuscript carries the date of 19 March 1995). This also has the advantage of emphasizing his gifts as an essayist for whom the sweep of the argument was sometimes more important than the detail.

Notes

1 A nice example of this systematic neglect of the early modern tradition is the way in which the debate over 'the Hobbesian problem of order' – one of sociology's more fundamental concerns – proceeds with little or no attention to what Hobbes actually said, or to the great wealth of modern Hobbes scholarship.

2 Moreover, although it may be the case that some are more discriminated against than others, and that qualitative researchers are sometimes at the bottom of the heap, we need to remember, not only that some qualitative sociologists have had a very significant policy influence, but that in other areas, such as history, management and political science, qualitative researchers have very considerable prestige.

3 For the detailed arguments as to why this is so, see the classic statements by Mill and Habermas. As most commentators have noted, Habermas's analysis of the properties of the liberal public sphere is seriously historically flawed. His ideal model, however, does represent an important addition to Mill. Both perhaps need supplementing by Dahl's powerful summary of the virtues of democracy and Oakeshott's subtle substitution of the term 'conversation' for that of 'debate'.

4 The extent to which Foucault was wholly Nietzschean can be disputed. He showed a good deal of interest in liberalism in his later, mostly unpublished, lectures. Nietzsche himself might have argued that sociological Nietzscheanism represents, merely, the profoundly frustrated theological aspirations of the discipline: the children of the 1960s have seen both Parsons and Marx dethroned and now fear that ethical meaning has gone out of human life; indeed, may never have been there to begin with. This would explain why writers such as Giddens and Turner combine a dominant Nietzschean motif with a strain of wistful *summum bonum* yearning; a yearning which Nietzsche would surely have condemned as weakness.

5 Not surprisingly, perhaps, since Nietzsche's precursor, Schopenhauer, drew directly on the early modern tradition.

6 This moral pessimism may also stem from the distinctive national traditions on which modern sociology has rested. Liberalism, with its base in Anglo-American society, has been a largely optimistic vision. The Nietzschean perspective has been based on the much more pessimistic German experience of modernity.

7 Many such sociologists belong, instead, to a 'virtual' discipline: the imagined ideal sociology with which they would like to associate but can never actually find.

8 Consider, for example, the unpleasant truths contained in the following eloquent and profound passage: 'The comparison of the life of man to a race, though it holdeth not in every point, yet it holdeth so well for this our purpose that we may thereby both see and remember almost all of the passions [which Hobbes has just discussed]. But this race we must suppose to have no other goal, nor no other garland, but being foremost. And in it:

> To endeavour is appetite.
> To be remiss is sensuality.
> To consider them behind is glory.
> To consider them before is humility.
> To lose ground with looking back, vain glory.
> To be holden, hatred.
> To turn back, repentance.
> To be in breath, hope.
> To be weary, despair.
> To endeavour to overtake the next, emulation.
> To supplant or overthrow, envy.
> To resolve to break through a stop foreseen, courage.
> To break through a sudden stop anger.
> To break through with ease, magnanimity.
> To lose ground by little hindrances, pusillanimity.
> To fall on the sudden is disposition to weep.
> To see another fall, disposition to laugh.
> To see one out-gone whom we would not is pity.
> To see one out-go we would not, is indignation.
> To hold fast by another is to love.
> To carry him on that so holdeth, is charity.
> To hurt oneself for haste is shame.

Continually to be out-gone is misery.
Continually to out-go the next before is felicity.
And to forsake the course is to die (Hobbes 1994: 59–60).

9 See Hampshire for a powerful critique of contemporary forms of liberal complacency from a *summum malum* position. Hampshire, it might be noted, was in charge of the Gestapo section in British counter-intelligence during the Second World War.

10 Although we are obviously still a long way from such a modern synthesis, those of us in the qualitative tradition have a head start over some of our more quantitative colleagues. For, in Erving Goffman, we possess a scholar who successfully combined both the Durkheimian and the Hobbesian traditions.

Conclusion: the Moral Discourse of Interactionism

Robert Dingwall

This conclusion is the product of an unfinished conversation with Phil Strong. It does not necessarily express the specific views of other contributors but it is intended to explain the turn to moral concerns in interactionist writing and the impatience of all of us with the postmodern repudiation of their possibility. The nature of the project may become clearer if I outline some of that conversation and why it has led me to this way of thinking.

Like many students of my generation, I was not trained to consider sociology as a moral discipline. Some of my teachers presented it as a scientific study, many of whose laws turned out to have an uncanny resemblance to the policies of Fabian socialism. Others presented it as a critique of morality, demonstrating that all restraints on behaviour were arbitrary, repressive and generally in the interests of monopoly capitalism. I first met Phil when I went to Aberdeen as a PhD student in the early 1970s. In those days Aberdeen was a social democratic utopia, a prosperous city run by an enlightened professional class whose programme we tended to celebrate rather than reflect upon. I moved to Oxford in 1977 and our careers parted for a while until Phil also took up a post in the same university.

By this time, Margaret Thatcher was Prime Minister. Phil was one of the few to recognize the significance of this development and began to explore two problems. One was that the British working class did not seem to be in the collective grip of some mass delusion or manipulation by the tabloid press. If the Conservatives had a thumping majority, this was because they had plucked some chord that British sociologists had failed to notice. The other problem was that the 'attack' on social science by that administration was not an act of intellectual spite or vandalism. It was actually an acknowledgement of the importance of disciplines like sociology in articulating an intellectual foundation for government. The Conservative project included a serious attempt to reconstruct thinking about social policy and to draw attention to issues and authors neglected for a generation. The past 17 years have seen the continuation of this engagement with the task of winning minds as well as hearts.

Most sociologists have either ignored or dismissed this phenomenon and clung to a 1960s politics of protest on behalf of every minority. Phil insisted that we had to understand the project, to consider where it came from and why it was so potent. Mrs Thatcher's declaration that there was no such thing as society was a statement about the nature of order in the modern world. Its genealogy lay in the distinctive intellectual contours of that world's creation.

Our joint response is represented by 'Romantics and Stoics' (Strong and Dingwall 1989). In that paper, we began to set out our dissatisfaction with the sociology we had learned as young men and to signal our growing interest in theorists of spontaneous order. How could the study of everyday life add up to a study of the modern world? How was local order constitutive of and constituted by global order? How did the empirical and the moral plug together? These discussions took us both into unfamiliar intellectual waters. Although they were themes in some of G.H. Mead's writing, they were less prominent than in fellow pragmatists like William James or John Dewey. Alfred Schutz had a lot to say about the analysis of the everyday world that we live in but very little to say on the question of the kind of world that we might *want* to live in. Both Goffman and the ethnomethodologists have a powerful sense of the moral nature of order without ever making it a specific topic. The Romantics represented the movements that we were beginning to reject; the Stoics the tradition in which we developed an abiding interest.

The Stoic trace is a key lead to follow in this story. The Stoics were the first social constructionists, arguing against the essentialist models of Aristotle and Plato. For them, the world had no forms to be discovered, merely immanent possibilities for being made. Our everyday world was substantially created by our active perception of it. The corollary of this was that it was a world for which we were morally responsible. A world for free men – and women – required its citizens to have a particular kind of understanding of the duties that went with citizenship. Stoic thought was a great influence on the high culture of republican Rome. Its ideals persisted to challenge the corruption of the imperial period. Stoicism also had a profound impact on early Christianity. However, it fades from the scene with the Empire. Indeed, the Dark Ages can be seen as a period of Stoic oblivion. The Catholic Church found Aristotelian essentialism more congenial to its intellectual project. Aristotle's natural forms became the world fixed by God.

Stoic thinking was eventually rediscovered during the sixteenth and seventeenth centuries, particularly on the mainland of Europe. It came out of the turmoil of the Reformation and the wars over religion and economic rivalry fought between the major powers for much of that period. It was part of the rise of early modern science and its empirical challenge to the certainties of Aristotelian learning.

Two great questions came to be asked, both of which ultimately pointed to Stoic answers. On the one hand, there was the question of what kind of life men and women could lead amid this confusion. This is a recurrent theme of Montaigne's work and is re-echoed by people like the Dutch legal philosophers Hugo Grotius and Justus Lipsius. In the midst of anarchy, famine, despair, people can still live moral lives, much as Marcus Aurelius had tried to do while the Roman Empire decayed around him. Understandably, perhaps, this seems to have been more of a predicament for mainland Europeans, who were the principal victims of apparently endless warfare. The other question preoccupied the English rather more. On the mainland, at the risk of heroic oversimplification, the wars went on but the systems were unchanged. The English more or less kept out of the wars and changed the system instead. What kind of society could they build if they had removed the divine capstone of monarchy. This, of course, is Hobbes's question: if we all pursue our own interests, what is to prevent anarchy? In the end there seemed to be only two choices: either we erected a government and tried to prevent it from oppressing us or we tried to establish a moral foundation which led us to act in ways which rendered government irrelevant.

This is the theory of spontaneous order that, under the right environmental conditions, people will recognize their interests and 'naturally' do the right thing. The result will be a society which is more open, more flexible, more just and less oppressive than any which relies primarily on external regulation or government action to achieve the same objectives. Spontaneous order avoids the costs and distortions of government, has fewer problems of legitimacy and higher levels of compliance than any legal code can produce. People behave well because they choose to rather than because they are afraid of some sanction, whose application is always likely to be random and arbitrary.

A pivotal figure in this story is Adam Smith, whose appropriation by economists as a progenitor in the modern division of social scientific labour has had disastrous effects for our understanding of the history of Anglophone sociology. There is an argument that many of the difficulties that we have in establishing the place of sociology in British academic life result from its turn towards the Romantic theorizing inspired by the French Enlightenment and away from the Stoic analysis of the Scottish Enlightenment. In a sense, we are practising a discipline that has no roots in its own national intellectual culture. The founders of American sociology did not share this neglect. They took some of it at second hand from Herbert Spencer but also drew directly on Smith himself. Albion Small wrote several times of the need to reclaim Smith's work as the foundation of modern sociology, subordinating economic analysis to a moral science of society. Cooley's theory of the 'looking-glass self', which is the foundation of all interactionist sociologies, derives both its central metaphor and much of the detail of its analysis from Smith, who, in turn, draws it from Stoic sources. Small also argues that Smith's sociological vision was more strongly followed by the elements of the German and Austrian economic traditions, which produced the work of people like Schutz. Although the Americans have had their own Romantic turns in recent years, the resilience of the Scottish Enlightenment traditions remains apparent. I suspect that this has something to do with the greater legitimacy that the discipline enjoys in American academic life.

In a recent book on the history of social research methods in the USA,

Jennifer Platt (1996) has argued that post-war American sociology was both more homogeneous and more divided from its predecessors than its folk-history has proposed. On her account, there is a decisive break between the First Chicago School of the 1920s and 1930s and the Second Chicago School of the late 1940s and 1950s. The pre-war generation did not have an explicit and self-conscious methodological position and, in particular, made much less use of direct qualitative data-gathering than is traditionally supposed. It is only after the Second World War that symbolic interactionism was elaborated as a distinctive theoretical position by Blumer and the methodology of participant observation was defined, mainly by Hughes and Becker. Platt contends that this was done as part of the same movement towards scientism that produced structural functionalism and the modern survey. In other words, the supposed antagonisms of the 1950s were actually alternative responses to the same shifts in the disciplinary environment. After the Second World War, everyone was trying to produce a more scientific sociology: they simply operationalized this goal in different ways.

While Platt may overstate her case in some respects, this analysis does make sense of the way in which interactionist theories of social action have become stripped of the explicit moral dimension that Smith gave them. Let me try to illustrate this with a description of one of the basic ideas of all interactionist thought about communication: the three-turn structure of conversation.

According to this analysis, human communication works as follows. At the first turn in any interaction, I produce some set of symbols. For the present purpose, let us call these symbols words. Words are a sequence of sounds that my body is capable of generating. Those sequences, however, have no inherent meaning. The human body can generate many more sounds and sequences than are actually used in any particular language. I may intend to convey some particular meaning by their production but their meaning is actually given by your response. It is only because you and I both understand this sequence of sounds in the same way that joint action is possible. How do I know that you have understood me in roughly the way that I intended? Alternatively, how might I find out that you have misunderstood me and do something about it? Well, clearly, this is not a matter of telepathy. If we were a telepathic species then we would not need language in the sense that we currently understand it. The only evidence that we have is the response of the hearer of the sounds that we have produced. This is the second turn in the sequence. Of course, it need not be a direct vocal response: it may be an action or it may be an indirect response by the production of some piece of talk that builds on my first in a way that marks understanding. However, it may also be a response that shows incomprehension: either the wrong action is produced or there is a piece of talk that does not seem to connect with mine or there is an explicit request for clarification. So the turn passes back to me. In this third turn, I can either repair the apparent misunderstanding or, if this is unnecessary or I choose to let it pass, I can move on in a way that now makes your turn in second position into a turn in the first position. It is now for me to display my comprehension of your turn. Your next turn responds to mine as a turn in the third position. And so on. Social interaction is founded upon this revolving structure.

This position is bound up with a number of consequences. One, clearly, is a particular view of language as a set of tokens. It is in this that we see a Stoic legacy. Words are not given to us by nature. They are not Aristotelian forms or Platonic essences. They are arbitrary collections of sounds assigned in an apparently arbitrary way to phenomena. However, the arbitrariness is only apparent. If the correspondence were truly arbitrary, then communication would be impossible. As Wittgenstein (1972) showed so elegantly, it is not possible to have a private language: language is a social system, a set of conventions about the relationship between sounds and phenomena which is shared between members of a group. In my first turn, I am showing you which set of conventions I am proposing that we adopt by choosing to speak English rather than French or whatever. There are a variety of important methodological consequences that flow from this about our ability to communicate private experience when the only means available is a social one. What can any form of interview or questionnaire – formal, informal, structured, semi-structured – tell us about private experience? Might it not be that all that these can tell us is about the uses of language to express private experience that are conventional within some group?

This issue has been well rehearsed previously. Here, I wish to focus on a more neglected aspect, the implications of an incorrect use of the conventions. Suppose you respond to me in a way that breaches these conventions? I may just let it go if it happens once, but if it happens consistently then I will be led to doubt either my own ability or yours to function as a competent user of these conventions. The classic examples of this, of course, are Garfinkel's breaching experiments: going home and behaving as if you were a lodger, trying to bargain over prices in a supermarket, playing noughts and crosses to idiosyncratic rules. However, as later writers have stressed, the observation of the conventions is a moral obligation. The analysis, though, goes little further than this statement. What sort of a moral obligation is it? What does it mean to talk about a moral obligation in this context? There is also a related and neglected question: why should we interact with each other at all? In their technical concern for understanding face-to-face interaction, many interactionist sociologies have not stopped to ask about the significance of the phenomenon itself. We have made a lot of progress in recent years with the 'how?' questions without really addressing the 'why?' questions.

This is where Smith's contribution becomes critical. Smith gives us an early sketch of the three-turn structure in *The Theory of Moral Sentiments* when he introduces the metaphor of the looking-glass self. We learn what kind of people we are by studying others' reactions to us.

> We suppose ourselves to be the spectators of our own behaviour and to endeavour to imagine what effect it would, in this light, produce on us. This is the only looking-glass by which we can in some measure, with the eyes of other people, scrutinize the propriety of our own conduct. (Smith 1976: 112)

The nature of our engagement with social interaction is an index of the sort of person that we are.

Smith starts by broadly accepting Hobbes's position that all human beings are ultimately driven by the pursuit of self-interest. This is the one part of his system that is lodged firmly in nature. We are simply made that way. However, unlike Hobbes, Smith then shows how self-interest can be the foundation of social order rather than leading to anarchy. He does not need the fictions of a state of nature or a social contract. Rather, self-interest leads men and women to cooperate and coordinate their activities because the result is to make everyone better off. People serve each other because it is in their interest to do so.

Smith describes the process involved in this as 'sympathy'. It is the imaginative placing of oneself in another's situation, taking the role of the other. By this means we formulate our projects for action and evaluate the behaviour of others. In the process, it becomes a force for moderation. Since we cannot fully understand another's emotions, or expect them to understand ours, this rational behaviour restrains our passions. Joy, grief, anger, revenge are constrained to be expressed in such ways and to such a degree as another will think them proportionate. Since others can only imagine the passion, rather than experience it directly, their sense of it will be muted and our anticipation of this becomes a device for muting its expression. If we fail to do this appropriately, then we risk losing the approval of others, which is the key to our relations with them. The withdrawal of others' approval is the key sanction in Smith's model of social order.

So Smith draws a picture of a world in which order can arise spontaneously from the micro-relations between ordinary men and women: a world where human behaviour is generally marked by temperance, decency, modesty, moderation, industry, self-command and frugality. However, he also saw the threats to this from the extension of the market. In a large-scale society, face-to-face relations might not be a sufficient basis on their own for order. Without the desire for approval, our relations with others might be driven by utility rather than propriety, maximizing short-term gains rather than long-term benefits. Moral behaviour was only possible in contexts that favoured it.

It was here that he saw a positive role for government. Generally, Smith was not over-impressed with government, possibly because he spent much of his life close to it. He was hostile to salaried public bureaucracies where the absence of market pressures led to a lack of incentive for effort and innovation. He therefore preferred to use market solutions to market failures, where possible. Smith accepted, for example, that the criminal could not be expected to be honest in a context where honesty was not possible. Crime would not be solved by laws or prisons but by providing full employment at high wages. He recognized the way in which markets tended to pull people apart and the need to provide positive opportunities for individuals to come together in smaller, secondary associations which bridged different classes and circumstances. Again, he considered how government might encourage a rich civic life which offered people meaningful opportunities for self-expression and for a sense of mutual obligation to one another. He also wrote at some length about the cultural role of government in ensuring the education of all classes and, in particular, creating opportunities to counter the stultifying effects of repetitive labour on the lower classes. Smith's ideal government was one that created the conditions for moral actions rather than made laws to substitute for them.

Smith's world was also one that was supportive of diversity. He recognized that moral obligations and moral pressures spiralled out from any individual. There were those that were a condition of membership in primary groups which became progressively more general and more attenuated as people moved through secondary associations to nations and to the world community. Our obligations to the Chinese were much weaker than to our own neighbours. However, this decentring was a source of strength and vitality in a society: it encouraged a range of differences within an overall framework of interpersonal morality. This framework was not optional. It represented the necessary conditions for human intercourse.

This is obviously a very brief sketch. However, I want to use it to sustain one conclusion. The study of social interaction is not merely a technical enterprise. It is not an obsession with the trivia of everyday life. It is the most fundamental study of the foundations of social order. As such, it stands beyond an ephemeral concern with this government policy or that political initiative. In our studies of the way we talk to each other, we are studying the very conditions that make society possible. We are also, I suggest, encouraged to see these as matters over which we have very little choice. These are preconditions for mutual society: if we allow them to perish, whether from neglect, indifference or transient gain, then we are attacking something far more basic than a particular form of delivering welfare or organizing health care. If we have a mission for our discipline, it may be to show the timeless virtues of compromise and civility, of patient change and human decency, of a community bound by obligations rather than rights. Perhaps we should stop aiming to be legislators for humankind and settle for being its looking-glass. Our work might be the mirror in which others see their actions reflected and are challenged to consider whether they are worthy.

Sociology cannot confine itself to describing the world in which we live or to seeking to remake it according to some utopian blueprint. It must question all grand designs, wherever they come from. Unlike the postmodernist, however, it cannot use this scepticism to ignore ordinary lives and what it takes to live them. Microsociology is not just the natural history of everyday life: it is the dissection of what it might take to live a moral life. If we may not believe in great projects, we can believe in better lives and perhaps they might cumulatively add up to a better world. The Enlightenment project is not yet dead – but perhaps it needs a new inspiration from Edinburgh rather than Paris!

Acknowledgements

An earlier version of this chapter was presented at the conference, 'Sociology and Health: a Multidisciplinary Celebration of the Life of Philip M. Strong', London, 11 July 1996.

References

Adler, P.A. and Adler, P. (1987) *Membership Roles in Field Research*. London: Sage.

Albrow, M. (1968) 'The study of organizations – objectivity or bias?', in J. Gould (ed.), *Penguin Social Sciences Survey*. Harmondsworth: Penguin.

Altheide, D.L. (1995) *An Ecology of Communication*. Hawthorne, NY: Aldine de Gruyter.

Altheide, D.L. and Johnson, J.M. (1980) *Bureaucratic Propaganda*. Boston: Allyn and Bacon.

Altheide, D.L. and Johnson, J.M. (1994) 'Criteria for assessing interpretive validity in qualitative research', in N.K. Denzin and Y.S. Lincoln (eds), *Handbook of Qualitative Research*. Newbury Park, CA: Sage. pp. 485–499.

Anspach, R.R. (1987) 'Prognostic conflict in life and death decisions', *Journal of Health and Social Behavior*, 28: 215–231.

Anspach, R.R. (1993) *Deciding Who Lives*. Berkeley: University of California Press.

Ardener, E. (1989) *The Voice of Prophesy and Other Essays* (ed. M. Chapman). Oxford: Basil Blackwell.

Arney, W.R. and Bergen, B.J. (1984) *Medicine and the Management of Living*. Chicago: University of Chicago Press.

Athens, L. (1984) 'Scientific criteria for evaluating qualitative studies', in N.K. Denzin (ed.), *Studies in Symbolic Interaction 5*. Greenwich, CT: JAI Press.

Atkinson, J.M. (1977) 'Coroners and the categorization of deaths as suicides: changes in perspective as features of the research process', in C. Bell and H. Newby (eds), *Doing Sociological Research*. London: Allen and Unwin. pp. 31–46.

Atkinson, J.M. and Drew, P. (1979) *Order in Court*. London and Atlantic Highlands, NY: Macmillan and Humanities Press.

Atkinson, J.M. and Heritage, J. (eds) (1984) *Structures of Social Action*. Cambridge: Cambridge University Press.

Atkinson, P. (1995a) *Medical Talk and Medical Work: the Liturgy of the Clinic*. London: Sage.

Atkinson, P. (1995b) 'Some perils of paradigms', *Qualitative Health Research*, 5: 117–124.

Babbie, E. (1994) *The Practice of Social Research*. Belmont: Wadsworth.

Barr, A. and Rogers, S. (1989) *A Survey of Met and Unmet Health Need in the Wycombe Health Authority Area*. Oxford: Oxford Regional Health Authority Operational Research Unit.

Baruch, G. (1981) 'Moral tales: parents' stories of encounters with the health professions', *Sociology of Health and Illness*, 3: 275–296.

Bechhofer, F. (1974) 'Current approaches to empirical research: some central ideas', in J. Rex (ed.), *Approaches to Sociology*. London: Routledge and Kegan Paul.

Becker, H.S. (1953) 'Becoming a marihuana user', *American Journal of Sociology*, 59: 235–242.

Becker, H.S. (1958) 'Problems of inference and proof in participant observation', *American Sociological Review*, 23: 652–660.

Becker, H.S. (1963) *Outsiders*. New York: Free Press.

Becker, H.S. (1967) 'Whose side are we on?' *Social Problems*, 14: 237–248.

Becker, H.S., Geer, B., Hughes, E.C. and Strauss, A.L. (1961) *Boys in White*. Chicago: University of Chicago Press.

Benford, R.D. (1987) 'Framing activity, meaning and social movement participation: the nuclear disarmament movement'. PhD dissertation, University of Texas.

Benford, R.D. (1993) 'You could be the hundredth monkey: collective action frames and vocabularies of motive within the nuclear disarmament movement', *Sociological Quarterly*, 34: 195–216.

Benford, R.D. and Hunt, S.A. (1992) 'Dramaturgy and social movements: the social construction and communication of power', *Sociological Inquiry*, 62: 36–55.

Benson, J.K. (1971) 'Models of structure selection in organizations: on the limitations of rational perspectives'. Paper presented at the 66th Annual Meeting of the American Sociological Association, Denver.

Benson, J.K. (1977a) 'Organizations: a dialectic view', *Administrative Science Quarterly*, 22: 1–21.

Benson, J.K. (1977b) 'Innovation and crisis in organizational analysis', *Sociological Quarterly*, 18: 5–18.

Benson, J.K. and Day, R.A. (1976) 'On the limits of negotiation: a critique of the theory of negotiated order'. Paper presented at the 71st Annual Meeting of the American Sociological Association, New York.

Berg, B.L. (1995) *Qualitative Research Methods for the Social Sciences*, 2nd edn. Boston: Allyn and Bacon (1st edn, 1989).

Berger, P.L. and Luckmann, T. (1966) *The Social Construction of Reality: a Treatise in the Sociology of Knowledge*. New York: Doubleday.

Berkowitz, S.D. (1982) *An Introduction to Structural Analysis*. Toronto: Butterworth.

Bittner, E. (1965) 'The concept of organization', *Social Research*, 32: 239–255.

Bittner, E. (1967) 'Police on Skid Row', *American Sociological Review*, 32: 699–715.

Blau, P.M. (1955) *The Dynamics of Bureaucracy*. Chicago: University of Chicago Press.

Blau, P. and Scott, W.R. (1963) *Formal Organizations: a Comparative Approach*. London: Routledge and Kegan Paul.

Bloor, D. (1976) *Knowledge and Social Imagery*. London: Routledge.

Bloor, M. (1976) 'Bishop Berkeley and the adeno-tonsillectomy enigma: an exploration of variation in the social construction of medical disposals', *Sociology*, 10: 43–61.

Bloor, M. (1980) 'An alternative to the ethnomethodological approach to rule use? A comment on Zimmerman and Wieder's comment on Denzin', *Scottish Journal of Sociology*, 4: 249–263.

Bloor M. (1981) 'Therapeutic paradox: the patient culture and the formal treatment programme in a therapeutic community', *British Journal of Medical Psychology*, 54: 359–369.

Bloor M. (1983) 'Notes on member validation', in R. Emerson (ed.), *Contemporary Field Research: a Collection of Readings*. Boston: Little, Brown. pp. 156–172.

Bloor, M. (1991) 'A minor offence: the variable and socially constructed character of death certification in a Scottish city', *Journal of Health and Social Behavior*, 32: 273–287.

Bloor, M. (1994) 'Scrutiny and routine: medical decision-making and death certification practice', in M. Bloor and P. Taraborrelli (eds), *Qualitative Studies in Health and Medicine*. Aldershot: Avebury.

Bloor, M., McKeganey, N. and Fonkert, D. (1988) *One Foot in Eden: a Sociological Study of the Range of Therapeutic Community Practice*. London: Routledge.

Blum, A.F. and McHugh, P. (1971) 'The social ascription of motives', *American Sociological Review*, 36: 98–109.

Blumer, H. (1969) *Symbolic Interactionism*. Englewood Cliffs, NJ: Prentice-Hall.

Boden, D. and Zimmerman, D.H. (eds) (1991) *Talk and Social Structure*. Berkeley: University of California Press.

Bogdan, R. and Ksander, M. (1980) 'Policy data as a social process', *Human Organization*, 39: 302–309.

Borgatti, S. (1991) *UCINET 4*. Department of Sociology, University of Southern Carolina, Columbia, SC.

Bowler, I.M.W. (1990) 'Midwives, mothers and the maternity system: the role of cultural difference in the creation of inequality'. Unpublished M.Litt. thesis, University of Oxford.

Bowler, I.M.W. (1993) '"They're not the same as us": Midwives' stereotypes of South Asian descent maternity patients', *Sociology of Health and Illness*, 15: 157–178.

Bowler, I.M.W. (1994) 'Midwifery: independent practice in the 1990s?', in M. Bloor and P. Taraborrelli (eds), *Qualitative Studies in Health and Medicine*. Aldershot: Avebury.

Bowler, I.M.W. (1995) 'Further notes on record-taking and making in maternity care: the case of South Asian descent women', *Sociological Review*, 43: 36–51.

Brint, S. (1992) 'Hidden meanings: cultural content and context in Harrison White's structural sociology', *Sociological Theory*, 10: 194–208.

Bryman, A. (1988) *Quantity and Quality in Social Research*. London: Unwin Hyman.

Buchanan D.R. (1992) An uneasy alliance: combining qualitative and quantitative research methods', *Health Education Quarterly*, Spring: 117–135.

Bucher, R. (1970) 'Social process and power in a medical school', in N.Z. Mayer (ed.), *Power in Organizations*. Nashville: Vanderbilt University Press.

Buckholdt, D.R. and Gubrium, J. (1979) *Caretakers*. New York: University Press of America.

Bulmer, M. (1984) *The Chicago School of Sociology: Institutionalization, Diversity and the Rise of Socoiological Research*. Chicago: University of Chicago Press.

Burke, K. (1945) *A Grammar of Motives*. Berkeley: University of California Press.

Burke, K. (1950) *A Rhetoric of Motives*. New York: Prentice Hall.

Burke, K. (1968) 'Dramatism', in D.L. Sills (ed.), *The International Encyclopedia of the Social Sciences, volume 7*. New York: Macmillan. pp. 445–451.

Burt, R.S. (1982) *Toward a Structural Theory of Action*. New York: Academic Press.

Burt, R.S. (1991) *STRUCTURE 4.2*. Center for the Social Sciences, Columbia University, New York.

Buttney, R. (1987) 'Sequence and practical reasoning in accounts episodes', *Communication Quarterly*, 35: 67–83.

Button, G. and Lee, J.R.E. (eds) (1987) *Talk and Social Organisation*. Clevedon, UK: Multilingual Matters.

Carey, J.T. (1975) *Sociology and Public Affairs: The Chicago School*. Beverly Hills, CA: Sage.

Charmaz, K. (1983) 'The grounded theory method: an explication and interpretation', in R. Emerson (ed.), *Contemporary Field Research*. Boston: Little, Brown.

Charmaz, K. and Mitchell, R.G. (1996) 'The myth of silent authorship: self, substance and style in ethnographic writing', *Symbolic Interaction*, 19: 285–302.

Chenitz, W.C. and Swanson, J.M. (1986) *From Practice to Grounded Theory*. Menlo Park, CA: Addison-Wesley.

Cicourel A.V. (1964) *Method and Measurement in Sociology*. New York: Free Press.

Cicourel, A.V. (1968) *The Social Organization of Juvenile Justice*. New York: John Wiley.

Cicourel, A.V. (1973) *Cognitive Sociology: Language and Meaning in Social Interaction*. Harmondsworth: Penguin.

Cicourel, A.V. and Kitsuse, J.I. (1963) *The Educational Decision-Makers*. New York: Bobbs-Merrill.

Clavarino, A., Najman, J. and Silverman, D. (1995) 'Assessing the quality of qualitative data', *Qualitative Inquiry*, 1: 223–242.

Clifford, J. and Marcus, G.E. (eds) (1986) *Writing Culture*. Berkeley: University of California Press.

Coffey, A., Holbrook, B. and Atkinson, P. (1996) 'Qualitative data technologies and representations', *Sociological Research Online*: <http://kennedy.soc.surrey.ac.uk/socresonline/1/1/4.html>.

Conley, J.M. and O'Barr, W.M. (1990) *Rules vs. Relationships*. Chicago: University of Chicago Press.

Cornwell, J. (1984) *Hard Earned Lives: Accounts of Health and Illness from East London*. London: Tavistock.

Currer, C. (1983) *The Mental Health of Pathan Mothers in Bradford: a Case Study of Migrant Asian Women*. Coventry: University of Warwick.

Davies, C. (1979) 'Organization theory and the organization of health care: a review of the literature', *Social Science and Medicine*, 13: 413–422.

Day, R. and Day, J.V. (1977) 'A review of the current state of negotiated order theory: an appreciation and a critique', *Sociological Quarterly*, 18: 128–144.

Denzin, N. (1989a) *The Research Act: a Theoretical Introduction to Sociological Methods*, 3rd edn. Englewood Cliffs, NJ: Prentice Hall (1st edn, 1970).

Denzin, N. (1989b) *Interpretive Interactionism*. London: Sage.

Denzin, N. (1991) 'Back to Harold and Agnes', *Sociological Theory*, 9: 278–285.

Denzin, N. (1996) 'Post-pragmatism' (review of H. Joas, *Pragmatism and Social Theory*), *Symbolic Interaction*, 19: 61–75.

Denzin, N. and Lincoln, Y. (eds) (1994) *Handbook of Qualitative Research*. London: Sage.

Denzin, N. and Lincoln, Y. (1995) 'Transforming qualitative research methods: is it a revolution?', *Journal of Contemporary Ethnography*, 24: 349–358.

Dickens, D. (1995) 'Whither ethnography?', *Symbolic Interaction*, 18: 207–216.

DiMaggio, P. (1992) 'Nadel's paradox revisited: relational and cultural aspects of organizational structure', in N. Nohria and R.G. Eccles (eds), *Networks and Organizations*. Boston, MA: Harvard Business School Press.

Dingwall, R. (1977) *The Social Organisation of Health Visitor Training*. London: Croom Helm.

Dingwall, R. (1980a) 'Ethics and ethnography', *Sociological Review*, 28: 871–891.

Dingwall, R. (1980b) 'Orchestrated encounters: a comparative analysis of speech-exchange systems', *Sociology of Health and Illness*, 2: 151–173.

Dingwall, R. (1986) 'The certification of competence: assessment in occupational socialization', *Urban Life*, 15: 367–393.

Dingwall, R. (1992) '"Don't mind him – he's from Barcelona": qualitative methods in health studies', in J. Daly, I. McDonald and E. Wallis (eds), *Researching Health Care: Designs, Dilemmas, Disciplines*. London: Routledge. pp. 161–175.

Dingwall, R. and Durkin, T. (1993) 'Deconstructing defence'. Paper presented at the Annual Meeting of the Law and Society Association, Chicago.

Dingwall, R. and Durkin, T. (1995) 'Time management and legal reform', in A.A.S. Zuckerman and R. Cranston (eds), *Reform of Civil Procedure*. Oxford: Oxford University Press.

Dingwall, R. and Strong, P.M. (1985) 'The interactional study of organizations: a critique and reformulation', *Urban Life*, 14: 205–231. [Reprinted as Chapter 10 in this volume]

Dingwall, R., Durkin, T. and Felstiner, W.L.F. (1990) 'Delay in tort cases', *Civil Justice Quarterly*, 9: 353–365.

Dingwall, R., Eekelaar, J.M. and Murray, T. (1983) *The Protection of Children: State Intervention and Family Life*. Oxford: Basil Blackwell.

Donovan, J. (1986) *We Don't Buy Sickness, It Just Comes*. Aldershot: Gower.

Douglas, J.D. (1971) *Understanding Everyday Life*. London: Routledge & Kegan Paul.

Douglas, J.D. (1976) *Investigative Social Research: Individual and Team Field Research*. Beverley Hills, CA: Sage.

Douglas, J.D. and Rasmussen, P. with Flanagan, C.A. (1977) *The Nude Beach*. Beverley Hills, CA: Sage.

Douglas, M. (1986) *How Institutions Think*. Syracuse: Syracuse University Press.

Drew P. and Heritage, J.C. (eds) (1992) *Talk at Work*. Cambridge: Cambridge University Press.

Dreyfus, H.L. and Rabinow, P. (1982) *Michel Foucault*. Chicago: University of Chicago Press.

Durkin, T. (1990) 'Comparing propensities to sue'. Paper presented at the Annual Meeting of the Law and Society Association.

Durkin, T. (1994) 'Constructing law'. PhD dissertation, University of Chicago.

Emerson, R.M. (1969) *Judging Delinquents*. Chicago: Aldine.

Emerson, R.M. (1981) 'Observational field work', *Annual Review of Sociology*, 7: 351–378.

Emerson, R.M. (1983) *Contemporary Field Research*. Boston: Little, Brown.

Emerson, R.M. (1991) 'Case processing and interorganizational knowledge', *Social Problems*, 38: 198–212.

Emerson, R.M. and Messinger, S.L. (1977) 'The micro-politics of trouble', *Social Problems*, 25: 121–134.

Emerson, R.M. and Paley, B. (1992) 'Institutional horizons and complaint-filing', in K. Hawkins (ed.), *The Uses of Discretion*. Oxford: Oxford University Press. pp. 230–248.

Emerson, R.M. and Pollner, M. (1988) 'On the uses of members' responses to researchers' accounts', *Human Organization*, 47: 189–198.

Evans-Pritchard, E.E. (1940) *The Nuer: a Description of the Modes of Livelihood and Political Institutions of a Nilotic People*. Oxford: Oxford University Press.

Felstiner, W. and Dingwall, R. (1988) *Asbestos Litigation in the United Kingdom*. Chicago and Oxford: American Bar Foundation and Oxford Centre for Socio-Legal Studies.

Fielding, N. (1982) 'Observational research on the National Front', in M. Bulmer (ed.), *Social Research Ethics: an Examination of the Merits of Covert Participant Observation*. London: Macmillan.

Filmer, P., Phillipson, M., Silverman, D. and Walsh, D. (1972) *New Directions in Sociological Theory*. London: Collier Macmillan.

Finch, J. (1984) 'It's great to have someone to talk to: the ethics and politics of interviewing women', in C. Bell and H. Roberts (eds), *Social Researching: Politics, Problems, Practice*. London: Routledge and Kegan Paul.

Fine, G.A. (1991) 'On the macrofoundations of microsociology: constraint and the exterior reality of structure', *Sociological Quarterly*, 32: 161–177.

Fine, G.A. (1992) 'Agency, structure, and comparative contexts: toward a synthetic interactionism', *Symbolic Interaction*, 15: 87–107.

Fine, G.A. and Ducharme, L.J. (1995) 'The ethnographic present', in G.A. Fine (ed.), *A Second Chicago School?* Chicago: University of Chicago Press.

Fine, G.A. and Kleinman, S. (1983) 'Network and meaning: an interactionist approach to structure', *Symbolic Interaction*, 6: 97–110.

Fish, S. (1980) *Is There a Text in This Class?* Cambridge, MA: Harvard University Press.

Fish, S. (1989) *Doing What Comes Naturally*. Durham, NC: Duke University Press.

Fontana, A. and Frey, J.H. (1994) 'Interviewing: the art of the science', in N. Denzin and Y. Lincoln (eds), *Handbook of Qualitative Research*. London: Sage.

Forrest, B. (1986) 'Apprentice-participation: methodology and the study of subjective reality', *Urban Life*, 14: 431–453.

Foucault, M. (1972) 'The discourse on language', in *The Archaeology of Knowledge and the Discourse on Language*, trans. A.M. Sheridan Smith. New York: Harper and Row. pp. 215–238.

Foucault, M. (1973) *The Birth of the Clinic*, trans. A.M. Sheridan Smith. New York: Pantheon.

Foucault, M. (1977) *Discipline and Punish*, trans. A.M. Sheridan Smith. New York: Pantheon.

Foucault, M. (1980) *Power/Knowledge*, ed. and trans. C. Gordon. New York: Pantheon.

Frake, C. (1961) 'The diagnosis of disease among the Subanun of Mindanao', *American Anthropologist*, 63: 113–132.

Frankenberg, R. (1966) *Communities in Britain*. Harmondsworth: Penguin.

Freidson, E. (1976) 'The division of labour as social interaction', *Social Problems*, 23: 304–313.

Freidson, E. (1986) *Professional Powers*. Chicago: University of Chicago Press.

Galliher, J.F. (1980) 'Social scientists' ethical responsibilities to superordinates: looking upward meekly', *Social Problems*, 27: 298–308.

Gantley, M., Davies, D.P. and Murcott, A. (1993) 'Sudden infant death syndrome: links with infant care practice', *British Medical Journal*, 306: 16–19.

Garfinkel H. (1956) 'Some sociological concepts and methods for psychiatrists', *Psychiatric Research Reports*, 6: 181–195.

Garfinkel H. (1967) *Studies in Ethnomethodology*. Englewood Cliffs, NJ: Prentice Hall.

Gau, D. and Diehl, A. (1982) 'Disagreement among general practitioners regarding the cause of death', *British Medical Journal*, 284: 239–244.

Geertz, C. (1983) *Local Knowledge*. New York: Basic Books.

Georgiou, P. (1973) 'The goal paradigm and notes toward a counter-paradigm', *Administrative Science Quarterly*, 18: 291–310.

Giddens, A. (1976) *New Rules of Sociological Method*. London: Hutchinson.

Gilbert, G.N. and Mulkay, M. (1983) 'In search of the action', in G.N. Gilbert & P. Abell (eds), *Accounts and Action*. Aldershot: Gower.

Gilbert, G.N. and Mulkay, M. (1984) *Opening Pandora's Box*. Cambridge: Cambridge University Press.

Gilson, R.J. and Mnookin, R.H. (1985) 'Sharing among human capitalists: an economic inquiry into the corporate law firm and how partners split profits', *Stanford Law Review*, 37: 313–392.

Gladwin, T. (1964) 'Culture and logical process', in W. Goodenough (ed.), *Explorations in Cultural Anthropology*. New York: McGraw-Hill.

Glaser, B. (1978) *Theoretical Sensitivity: Advances in the Methodology of Grounded Theory Analysis*. Mill Valley, CA: The Sociology Press.

Glaser, B. (1992) *Emergency vs Forcing: Basics of Grounded Theory Analysis*. Mill Valley, CA: The Sociology Press.

Glaser, B. and Strauss, A. (1965) *Awareness of Dying*. Chicago: Aldine.

Glaser, B. and Strauss A. (1967) *The Discovery of Grounded Theory*. Chicago: Aldine.

Glaser, B. and Strauss, A. (1968) *Time for Dying*. New York: Aldine.

Gluckman, M. (1958) 'Analysis of a social situation in modern Zululand', *Rhodes-Livingstone Papers*, 28.

Goffman, E. (1959) *The Presentation of Self in Everyday Life*. New York: Doubleday.

Goffman, E. (1961a) *Asylums*. New York: Anchor.

Goffman, E. (1961b) *Encounters: Two Studies in the Sociology of Interaction*. Indianapolis: Bobbs-Merrill.

Goffman, E. (1963a) *Stigma: Notes on the Management of Spoiled Identity*. Englewood Cliffs, NJ: Prentice Hall.

Goffman, E. (1963b) *Behavior in Public Places*. New York: Free Press.

Goffman, E. (1968) *Asylums*. Harmondsworth: Penguin.

Goffman, E. (1974) *Frame Analysis: an Essay on the Organization of Experience*. Boston: Northeastern University Press.

Goffman, E. (1981) *Forms of Talk*. Oxford: Basil Blackwell.

Goffman, E. (1983) 'Felicity's condition', *American Journal of Sociology*, 83: 1–53.

Gold, R.L. (1958) 'Roles in sociological field observations', *Social Forces*, 36: 217–223.

Goodenough, W. (1964) 'Cultural anthropology and linguistics', in D. Hymes (ed.) *Language in Culture and Society*. New York: Harper and Row. pp. 36–39.

Griffiths, V. (1984) 'Feminist research and the use of drama', *Women's Studies International Forum*, 7: 511–519.

Gross, E. (1969) 'The definition of organisational goals', *British Journal of Sociology*, 20: 277–294.

Guba, E.G. (1990) 'Subjectivity and objectivity', in E.W. Eisner and A. Peshkin (eds), *Qualitative Inquiry in Education: the Continuing Debate*. Peshkin, NY: Teachers College Press. pp. 74–91.

Gubrium, J.F. (1980) 'Patient exclusion in geriatric settings', *Sociological Quarterly*, 21: 335–348.

Gubrium, J.F. (1989) 'Local cultures and service policy', in J.F. Gubrium and D. Silverman (eds), *The Politics of Field Research*. London: Sage. pp. 94–112.

Gubrium, J.F. (1992) *Out of Control*. Newbury Park, CA: Sage.

Gubrium, J.F. and Buckholdt, D.R. (1979) 'The production of hard data in human service institutions', *Pacific Sociological Review*, 22: 115–136.

Gusfield, J. (1981) *Drinking-Driving and the Symbolic Order*. Chicago: University of Chicago Press.

Hacking, I. (1986) 'Making up people', in T.C. Heller, M. Sosna and D.E. Wellbery (eds), *Reconstructing Individualism*. Stanford, CA: Stanford University Press. pp. 222–236.

Halfpenny, P. (1979) 'The analysis of qualitative data', *Sociological Review*, 27 (4): 799–825.

Hammersley, M. (1990) *Reading Ethnographic Research*. New York: Longman.

Hammersley, M. (1992a) *What's Wrong with Ethnography: Methodological Explorations*. London: Routledge.

Hammersley, M. (1992b) 'On feminist methodology', *Sociology*, 26: 187–206.

Hammersley, M. and Atkinson, P. (1995) *Ethnography*. London: Routledge.

Handel, W. (1979) 'Normative expectations and the emergence of meaning as solutions to problems: convergence of structural and interactionist views', *American Journal of Sociology*, 84: 855–881.

Health Education Authority (1994) *Health and Lifestyles: Black and Minority Ethnic Groups in Britain*. London: Health Education Authority.

Heinz, J. and Laumann, E. (1994) *Chicago Lawyers*. Chicago: American Bar Foundation.

Heritage, J. (1984) *Garfinkel and Ethnomethodology*. Cambridge: Polity Press.

Heritage, J. (n.d.) 'Recent developments in conversation analysis', *Warwick Papers in Sociology*. Coventry: University of Warwick.

Hill, M.R. (1993) *Archival Strategies and Techniques*. London: Sage.

Hindess, B. (1973) *The Use of Official Statistics in Sociology*. London: Macmillan.

Hobbes, T. (1994) *Human Nature and De Corpore Politico*. Oxford: Oxford University Press.

Holstein, J. (1993) *Court-ordered Insanity*. Hawthorne, NY: Aldine.

Holstein, J. and Gubrium, J. (1995) *The Active Interview*. Thousand Oaks, CA: Sage.

Holstein, J. and Staples, W.G. (1992) 'Producing evaluative knowledge: the interactional bases of social science findings', *Sociological Inquiry*, 62: 11–35.

Homans, H. (1980) 'Pregnant in Britain: a sociological approach to Asian and British women's experiences'. Unpublished PhD thesis, University of Warwick.

Hughes, E.C. (1945) 'Dilemmas and contradictions of status', *American Journal of Sociology*, 50: 353–359.

Hughes, E.C. (1958) *Men and their Work*. Glencoe, IL: The Free Press.

Hughes, E.C. (1971) *The Sociological Eye*. Chicago: Aldine.

Hunt, S.A. (1991) 'Constructing collective identity in a peace movement organization'. PhD dissertation, University of Nebraska.

Hunt, S.A., Benford, R.D. and Snow, D.A. (1994) 'Identity fields: framing processes and the social construction of movement identities', in E. Larana, H. Johnstone and J. Gusfield (eds), *New Social Movements: from Ideology to Identity*. Philadelphia: Temple University Press. pp. 185–208.

Johnson, J.M. (1995) 'In dispraise of justice', *Symbolic Interaction*, 18: 191–206.

Johnson, J.M. and Waletzko, L. (1992) 'Drugs and crime', in J.A. Holstein and G. Miller (eds), *Perspectives on Social Problems 8*. Greenwich, CT: JAI Press.

Johnson, W.T. (1976) 'Researching the religious crusade: a personal journal', in M.P. Golden (ed.), *The Research Experience*. Itasca, IL: F.E. Peacock. pp. 230–240.

Jorgensen, D. (1989) *Participant Observation*. Newbury Park, CA: Sage.

Jowell, T., Larrier, C. and Lawrence, R. (1990) 'Action project into the needs of carers in black and minority ethnic communities in Birmingham'. Unpublished report to the King's Fund, London.

Junker, B. (1960) *Field Work*. Chicago: University of Chicago Press.

Kamens, D.H. (1977) 'Legitimating myths and educational organization: the relationship between organizational ideology and formal structure', *American Sociological Review*, 42: 208–219.

Kitsuse, J.I. and Cicourel, A.V. (1963) 'A note on the uses of official statistics', *Social Problems*, 11: 131–139.

Krueger, A.E. (1978) 'The organization of information in criminal legal settings: a case study of prosecutorial decision-making in Los Angeles'. PhD dissertation, Department of Sociology, UCLA.

Kuper, A. (1973) *Anthropologists and Anthropology: the British School 1922–1972*. Harmondsworth: Penguin.

Laumann, E. and Knoke, D. (1987) *The Organizational State*. Madison: University of Wisconsin Press.

Lazega, E. (1992a) *The Micropolitics of Knowledge: Communication and Indirect Control in Workgroups*. New York: Aldine de Gruyter.

Lazega, E. (1992b) 'Analyse de réseaux d'une organisation collégiale: les avocats d'affaires', *Revue Française de Sociologie*, 33: 559–589.

Lazega, E. (1995) 'Les échanges d'idées entre collègues: concurrence, coopération et flux de conseils dans un cabinet américain d'avocats d'affaires', *Revue Suisse de Sociologie*, 21: 61–84.

Lazega, E. and van Duijn, M. (1997) 'Position in formal structure, personal characteristics and choices of advisors in a law firm: a logistic regression model for dyadic network data', *Social Networks*.

Liebow, E. (1967) *Tally's Corner*. Boston: Little, Brown.

Lincoln, Y.S. and Guba, E.G. (1985) *Naturalistic Inquiry*. Beverly Hills, CA: Sage.

Lindstrom, L. (1990) *Knowledge and Power in a South Pacific Society*. Washington, DC: Smithsonian Institution Press.

Lofland, J. (1970) 'Interactionist imagery and analytic interruptus', in T. Shibutani (ed.), *Human Nature and Collective Behavior*. Englewood Cliffs, NJ: Prentice Hall. pp. 35–45.

Lofland, J. and Lofland, L.H. (1995) *Analyzing Social Settings: a Guide to Qualitative Observation and Analysis*, 3rd edn. Belmont, CA: Wadsworth (1st edn, 1971).

Loseke, D.R. (1992) *The Battered Woman and Shelters*. Albany: State University of New York Press.

Loseke, D.R. (1993) 'Constructing conditions, people morality and emotion', in G. Miller and J.A. Holstein (eds), *Constructionist Controversies*. Hawthorne, NY: Aldine.

Lyman, S.M. and Scott, M.B. (1970) *A Sociology of the Absurd*. New York: Appleton-Century-Crofts.

Lyman, S.M. and Scott, M.B. (1975) *The Drama of Social Reality*. New York: Oxford University Press.

Lynch, M. and Bogen, D. (1994) 'Harvey Sacks's primitive natural science', *Theory, Culture and Society*, 11: 65–104.

Maanen, J. van (1988) *Tales of the Field*. Chicago: Chicago University Press.

McCall, G.J. and Simmons, J.L. (1966) *Identities and Interactions*. New York: Collier Macmillan.

McHugh, P. (1968) *Defining the Situation: the Organization of Meaning in Social Interaction*. Indianapolis: Bobbs-Merrill.

McIver, S. (1991) *An Introduction to Obtaining the Views of Users of the Health Service*. London: King's Fund.

McIver, S. (1994) *Obtaining the Views of Black Users of the Health Service*. London: King's Fund.

Maines, D.R. (1977) 'Social organization and social structure in symbolic interactionist thought', *Annual Review of Sociology*, 3: 235–259.

Maines, D.R. (1988) 'Myth, text and interactionist complicity in the neglect of Blumer's macrosociology', *Symbolic Interaction*, 11: 43–58.

Malinowski, B. (1922) *Argonauts of the Western Pacific*. London: Routledge and Kegan Paul.

Manis, J.G. and Meltzer, B.N. (eds) (1972) *Symbolic Interaction: a Reader in Social Psychology*. Boston: Allyn and Bacon.

Marlaire, C.L. (1990) 'On questions, communication and bias: educational testing as "invisible" collaboration', in G. Miller and J.A. Holstein (eds), *Perspectives on Social Problems*, vol. 2. Greenwich, CT: JAI Press.

Marlaire, C.L. (1992) 'Professional idealizations and clinical realities', in G. Miller (ed.), *Current Research on Occupations and Professions*, vol. 7. Greenwich, CT: JAI Press. pp. 59–76.

Marlaire, C.L. and Maynard, D.W. (1990) 'Standardized testing as an interactional phenomenon', *Sociology of Education*, 63: 83–101.

Marsden, P.V. (1990) 'Network data and management', *Annual Review of Sociology*, 16: 435–463.

Marsh, C. (1982) *The Survey Method*. London: Allen and Unwin.

Maynard, D. (1989) 'On the ethnography and analysis of discourse in institutional settings', in J.A. Holstein and G. Miller (eds), *Perspectives on Social Problems*, vol. 1. Greenwich, CT: JAI Press. pp. 127–146.

Maynard, D. (1991) 'Interaction and asymmetry in clinical discourse', *American Journal of Sociology*, 97: 448–495.

Maynard, D. and Clayman, S. (1991) 'The diversity of ethnomethodology', *Annual Review of Sociology*, 17: 385–418.

Mead, G.H. (1934) *Mind, Self and Society*. Chicago: University of Chicago Press.

Mead, M. (1923) *Coming of Age in Samoa*. New York: Morrow.

Mechanic, D. (1962) 'Sources of power of lower participants in complex organizations', *Administrative Science Quarterly*, 7: 349–364.

Mehan, H. (1979) *Learning Lessons*. Cambridge, MA: Harvard University Press.

Mehan, H. and Wood, H. (1975) *The Reality of Ethnomethodology*. New York: Wiley.

Melia, K.M. (1981) 'Student nurses' accounts of their work and training: a qualitative analysis'. PhD thesis, University of Edinburgh.

Melia, K.M. (1987) *Learning and Working: the Occupational Socialization of Nurses*. London: Tavistock.

Melia, K.M. (1996) 'Rediscovering Glaser', *Qualitative Health Research*, 6: 368–378.

Meltzer, B.N., Petras, J.W. and Reynolds, L.T. (1975), *Symbolic Interactionism*. London: Routledge & Kegan Paul.

Merry, S.E. (1990) *Getting Justice and Getting Even*. Chicago: University of Chicago Press.

Messinger, S.L., Sampson, H. and Towne, R.D. (1962) 'Life as theater: some notes on the dramaturgic approach to social reality', *Sociometry*, 25: 98–110.

Meyer, J.W. and Rowan, B. (1977) 'Institutionalized organizations: formal structure as myth and ceremony', *American Journal of Sociology*, 83: 340–363.

Meyer, J.W. and Rowan, B. (1978) 'The structure of educational organizations', in M.W. Meyer et al. (eds), *Environments and Organizations*. San Francisco: Jossey-Bass. pp. 78–109.

Milgram, S. (1963) 'Behavioral study of obedience', *Journal of Abnormal and Social Psychology*, 67: 371–378.

Miller, G. (1991) *Enforcing the Work Ethic Program*. Albany: State University of New York Press.

Miller, G. (1995) 'Dispute domains', *Sociological Quarterly*, 36: 37–59.

Miller, G. (1997) Building bridges: the possibility of analytic dialogue between ethnography, conversation analysis and Foucault', in D. Silverman (ed.), *Qualitative Analysis: Issues of Theory and Method*. London: Sage. pp. 24–44.

Miller, G. and Holstein, J.A. (1993) 'Disputing in organizations', *Mid-American Review of Sociology*, 17: 1–18.

Miller, G. and Holstein, J.A. (1995) 'Dispute domains: institutional contexts and dispute processing', *Sociological Quarterly*, 36: 37–59.

Miller, G. and Holstein, J.A. (1996) *Dispute Domains and Welfare Claims*. Greenwich, CT: JAI Press.

Miller, L. (1993) 'Claims-making from the underside', in G. Miller and J.A. Holstein (eds), *Constructionist Controversies*. Hawthorne, NY: Aldine. pp. 153–180.

Mills, C.W. (1940) 'Situated actions and vocabularies of motive', *American Sociological Review*, 5: 439–448.

Mills, C.W. (1959) *The Sociological Imagination*. New York: Oxford University Press.

Mitchell, J.C. (1983) 'Case and situational analysis', *Sociological Review*, 31: 187–211.

Molotch, H. and Boden, D. (1985) 'Talking social structure', *American Sociological Review*, 50: 573–588.

Moore, M.W.B. (1974) 'Demonstrating the rationality of an occupation', *Sociology*, 8: 111–124.

Morgan, D. (1988) *Focus Groups*. Sage Qualitative Methods in the Social Sciences no. 16. Beverly Hills, CA: Sage.

Mouzelis, N. (1995) *Sociological Theory: What Went Wrong?* London: Routledge.

Nadel, S.F. (1957) *Theory of Social Structure*. London: Cohen and West.

Natanson, M. (ed.) (1963) *Philosophy of the Social Sciences*. New York: Random House.

Nelson, R.L. (1988) *Partners with Power: the Social Transformation of the Large Law Firm*. Berkeley: University of California Press.

Nohria, N. and Eccles, R.G. (eds) (1992) *Networks and Organizations*. Boston, MA: Harvard Business School Press.

Oakley, A. (1981) 'Interviewing women: a contradiction in terms', in H. Roberts (ed.), *Doing Feminist Research*. London: Routledge and Kegan Paul.

Olesen, V.L. and Whittaker, E.W. (1968) *The Silent Dialogue*. San Francisco: Jossey-Bass.

O'Toole, R. and O'Toole, A.W. (1981) 'Negotiating interorganizational orders', *Sociological Quarterly*, 22: 29–41.

Payne, G., Dingwall, R., Payne, J. and Carter, M.P. (1981) *Sociology and Social Research*. London: Routledge and Kegan Paul.

Peräkylä, A. and Silverman, D. (1991) 'Reinterpreting speech-exchange systems: communication formats in AIDS counselling', *Sociology*, 25 (3): 627–651.

Perinbanayagam, R.S. (1982) 'Dramas, metaphors and structures', *Symbolic Interaction*, 5: 259–276.

Perrow, C. (1961) 'The analysis of goals in complex organizations', *American Sociological Review*, 26: 854–866.

Platt, J. (1983) 'The development of the participant observation method', *Journal of the History of the Behavioural Sciences*, 19: 379–393.

Platt, J. (1994) 'The Chicago School and firsthand data', *History of the Human Sciences*, 7: 57–80.

Platt, J. (1996) *The History of Sociological Research Methods in America 1920–1960*. Cambridge: Cambridge University Press.

Prus, R. (1995) 'Envisioning power as intersubjective accomplishment'. Paper presented for the Study of Symbolic Interaction, Washington DC, August 20–21 1995.

Raffel, S. (1979) *Matters of Fact: a Sociological Inquiry*. London: Routledge and Kegan Paul.

Ragin, C. (1994) *Constructing Social Research*. Thousand Oaks, CA: Pine Forge Press.

Rawls, A.W. (1987) 'The interaction order sui generis', *Sociological Theory*, 5: 136–149.

Reinharz, S. (1992) *Feminist Methods in Social Research*. New York: Oxford University Press.

Reitz, K.P. and White, D.R. (1989) 'Rethinking the role concept: homomorphisms on social networks', in L.C. Freeman, D.R. White and A.K. Romney (eds), *Research Methods in Social Network Analysis*. New Brunswick: Transaction.

Rhodes, P.H. (1994) 'Race of interviewer effects in qualitative research: a brief comment', *Sociology*, 28: 547–558.

Richards, T. and Richards, R. (1994) 'Computers and qualitative analysis', in N. Denzin and Y. Lincoln (eds), *Handbook of Qualitative Research*. Thousand Oaks, CA: Sage.

Rivers, W.H.R. (1913) 'Report on anthropological research outside America'. in W.H.R. Rivers, A.E. Jenks and S.G. Morley (eds), *The Present Condition and Future Needs of the Science of Anthropology*. Washington DC: Gibson Brothers.

Roberts, H. (ed.) (1981) *Doing Feminist Research*. London: Routledge and Kegan Paul.

Roethlisberger, F.J. and Dickson, W.J. (1939) *Management and the Worker*. Cambridge, MA: Harvard University Press.

Rosenau, P.M. (1992) *The Phenomenology of the Social World*. Evanston, IL: Northwestern University Press.

Roth, J.A. (1963) *Timetables*. Indianapolis: Bobbs-Merrill.

Rushing, W. (1964) *The Psychiatric Professions*. Chapel Hill: University of North Carolina Press.

Sacks, H. (1992) *Lectures on Conversation*. Oxford: Basil Blackwell.

Sacks, H., Schegloff, E.A. and Jefferson, G. (1974) 'A simplest systematics for the organization of turn-taking for conversation', *Language*, 50: 696–735.

Sanders, W.B. (1977) *Detective Work*. New York: Free Press.

Sarat, A. and Felstiner, W. (1995) *Divorce Lawyers and their Clients*. New York: Oxford University Press.

Schutz, A. (1964) *Collected Papers*, vol. 1 (ed. M. Natanson). The Hague: Martinus Nijhoff.

Schutz, A. (1967) *Collected Papers*, vol. 2 (ed. M. Natanson). The Hague: Martinus Nijhoff.

Schutz, A. (1970) *Reflections on the Problem of Relevance* (ed. R. Zaner). New Haven: Yale University Press.

Schwartzman, H.B. (1989) *The Meeting: Gatherings in Organizations and Communities*. New York: Plenum.

Schwartzman, H.B. (1993) *Ethnography in Organizations*. Newbury Park, CA: Sage.

Scott, M.B. (1968) *The Racing Game*. Chicago: Aldine.

Scott, M.B. and Lyman, S.M. (1968) 'Accounts', *American Sociological Review*, 33: 46–62.

Scott, M.B. and Lyman, S.M. (1970) 'Accounts, deviance and social order'. in J.D. Douglas (ed.), *Deviance and Respectability*. New York: Basic Books. pp. 89–119.

Shaffir, W.B. and Stebbins, R.A. (eds) (1991) *Experiencing Fieldwork*. Newbury Park, CA: Sage.

Shah, L., Harvey, I. and Coyle, E. (1993) *The Health and Social Care Needs of Ethnic Minorities in South Glamorgan. Phase I: a Qualitative Study*. Centre for Applied Public Health Medicine, University of Wales College of Medicine.

Shaw, A. (1988) *A Pakistani Community in Britain*. Oxford: Basil Blackwell.

Shils, E.A. and Young, M. (1953) 'The meaning of the coronation', *Sociological Review*, 1: 62–81.

Shumway, D.R. (1989) *Michel Foucault*. Boston, MA: Twayne.

Silverman, D. (1973) 'Interview talk: bringing off a research instrument' *Sociology*, 7: 31–48.

Silverman, D. (1987) *Communication and Medical Practice*. Newbury Park, CA: Sage.

Silverman, D. (1989) 'The impossible dreams of reformism and romanticism', in J.F. Gubrium and D. Silverman (eds), *The Politics of Field Research: Sociology beyond Enlightenment*. London: Sage. pp. 30–48.

Silverman, D. (1993) *Interpreting Qualitative Data: Methods for Analyzing Talk, Text and Interaction*. London: Sage.

Silverman, D. (1996) *Discourses of Counselling: HIV Counselling as Social Interaction*. London: Sage.

Silverman, D. (1997) 'Towards an aesthetics of research'. in D. Silverman (ed.), *Qualitative Research: Issues of Theory and Method*. London: Sage.

Silverman, D. and Gubrium, J.F. (1994) 'Competing strategies for analyzing contexts of social interaction', *Sociological Inquiry*, 64: 179–198.

Smigel, E. (1969) *The Wall Street Lawyer: Professional Organizational Man?*, 2nd edn. Bloomington: Indiana University Press (1st edn, 1964).

Smith, A. (1976) *The Theory of Moral Sentiments*. Oxford: Clarendon Press (first published 1759).

Smith, D.E. (1984) 'Textually mediated social organization', *International Social Science Journal*, 36: 59–75.

Smith, D.E. (1990) *The Conceptual Practices of Power*. Boston: Northeastern University Press.

Snow, D.A. (1980) 'The disengagement process: a neglected problem in participant observation research', *Qualitative Sociology*, 3: 100–122.

Snow, D.A. and Benford, R.D. (1988) 'Ideology, frame resonance and participant mobilization', *International Social Movement Research*, 1: 197–217.

Snow, D.A. and Morrill, C. (1993) 'Reflections on anthropology's ethnographic crisis of faith', *Contemporary Society: a Journal of Reviews*, 22: 8–11.

Snow, D.A. and Morrill, C. (1995) 'A revolutionary handbook or a handbook for revolution?' *Journal of Contemporary Ethnography*, 24: 341–348, 358–362.

Snow, D.A., Benford, R.D. and Anderson, L. (1986) 'Fieldwork roles and informational yield: a comparison of alternative settings and roles', *Urban Life*, 14: 377–408.

Snow, D.A., Zurcher, L.A. and Peters, R. (1981) 'Victory celebrations as theater: a dramaturgical approach to crowd behavior', *Symbolic Interaction*, 4: 21–41.

Snow, D.A., Zurcher, L.A. and Sjoberg, G. (1982) 'Interviewing by comment: an adjunct to the direct question', *Qualitative Sociology*, 5: 285–311.

Solomon, R.C. (1990) *A Passion for Justice: Emotions and the Origins of the Social Contract*. Reading, MA: Addison-Wesley.

Spencer, J.W. (1994) 'Homeless in River City: client work in human service encounters', in G. Miller and J.A. Holstein (eds), *Perspectives on Social Problems*, vol. 6. Greenwich, CT: JAI Press.

Starbuck, W. (1982) 'Congealing oil: inventing ideologies to justify acting ideologies out', *Journal of Management Studies*, 19: 3–27.

Stern, P.N. (1994) 'Eroding grounded theory', in J. Morse (ed.), *Critical Issues in Qualitative Research Methods*. Thousand Oaks, CA: Sage. pp. 212–223.

Stimson, G. (1986) 'Place and space in sociological fieldwork', *Sociological Review*, 34: 641–656.

Stimson G. and Webb, B. (1975) *Going to See the Doctor*. London: Routledge and Kegan Paul.

Strauss, A. (1978) *Negotiations: Varieties, Contexts, Processes and Social Order*. San Francisco: Jossey-Bass.

Strauss, A. (1982) 'Interorganizational negotiation', *Urban Life*, 11: 350–367.

Strauss, A. (1987) *Qualitative Analysis for Social Scientists*. New York: Cambridge University Press.

Strauss, A. and Corbin, J. (1990) *Basics of Qualitative Research: Grounded Theory Procedures and Techniques*. Newbury Park, CA: Sage.

Strauss, A. and Corbin, J. (1994) 'Grounded theory methodology: an overview', in N. Denzin and Y. Lincoln (eds), *Handbook of Qualitative Research*. London: Sage. pp. 273–285.

Strauss, A., Schatzman, L., Bucher, R., Ehrlich, D. and Sabshin, M. (1963) 'The hospital and its negotiated order', in E. Freidson (ed.), *The Hospital in Modern Society*. New York: Free Press.

Strauss, A., Schatzman, R., Bucher, R., Ehrlich, D. and Sabshin, M. (1964) *Psychiatric Ideologies and Institutions*. New York: Free Press.

Strong, P.M. (1979) *The Ceremonial Order of the Clinic*. London: Routledge.

Strong, P.M. and Dingwall, R. (1983) 'The limits of negotiation in informal organizations', in G.N. Gilbert and P. Abell (eds), *Accounts and Action*. Farnborough: Gower.

Strong, P.M. and Dingwall, R. (1989) 'Romantics and Stoics', in J.F. Gubrium and D. Silverman (eds), *The Politics of Field Research: Sociology beyond Enlightenment*. London: Sage. pp. 49–69.

Stryker, S. (1980) *Symbolic Interactionism: a Social Structural Version*. London: Benjamin/Cummings.

Stryker, S. and Statham, A. (1985) 'Symbolic interaction and role theory', in L. Gardner and E. Aronson (eds), *Handbook of Social Psychology*, 3rd edn, vol. 1. New York: Random House.

Suchman, L.A. (1987) *Plans and Situated Actions: the Problem of Human–Machine Communication*. Cambridge: Cambridge University Press.

Sudnow, D. (1965) 'Normal crimes', *Social Problems*, 12: 255–276.

Sudnow, D. (1967) *Passing On*. Englewood Cliffs, NJ: Prentice Hall.

Tesch, R. (1991) 'Computers and qualitative research'. Presentation to Breckenridge Qualitative Computer Conference.

Thomas, J. (1993) *Doing Critical Ethnography*. Newbury Park, CA: Sage.

Thompson, E.P. (1967) 'Time, work-discipline and industrial capitalism', *Past and Present*, 38: 56–97.

Turner, R.H. (1956) 'Role-taking, role standpoint and reference group behavior', *American Journal of Sociology*, 61: 316–328.

Turner, R.H. (1962) 'Role-taking: process versus conformity', in A. Rose (ed.), *Human Behavior and Social Process*. Boston: Houghton Mifflin.

Voysey, M. (1975) *A Constant Burden: the Reconstitution of Family Life*. London: Routledge and Kegan Paul.

Warren, C.A.B. (1974) *Identity and Community in the Gay World*. New York: John Wiley.

Warren, C.A.B. (1988) *Gender Issues in Field Research*. London: Sage.

Warren, C.A.B. and Rasmussen, P.K. (1977) 'Sex and gender in field research', *Urban Life*, 6: 349–369.

Wasserman, S. and Faust, K. (1994) *Social Network Analysis: Methods and Application*. Cambridge: Cambridge University Press.

Webb, B. (1946) *My Apprenticeship*, 2nd edn. London: Longman (1st edn, 1926).

Webb, E. (1966) 'Unconventionality, triangulation and inference', in *Proceedings of the 1966 Invitational Conference on Testing Problems*. Princeton, NJ: Educational Testing Service. pp. 34–43.

Webb, S. and Webb, B. (1975) *Methods of Social Study*. Cambridge: Cambridge University Press (first published 1932).

Weber, M. (1947) *The Theory of Social and Economic Organization*. New York: Free Press.

Weitzman, E. and Miles, M. (1995) *Computer Programs for Qualitative Data Analysis*. Thousand Oaks, CA: Sage.

Whalen, J., Zimmerman, D.H. and Whalen, M.R. (1988) 'When words fail', *Social Problems*, 35: 335–362.

Whalen, M.R. and Zimmerman, D.H. (1987) 'Sequential and institutional contexts in calls for help', *Social Psychology Quarterly*, 50: 172–185.

White, H.C. (1992) *Identity and Control: a Structural Theory of Social Action*. Princeton, NJ: Princeton University Press.

White, H.C., Boorman, S.A. and Breiger, R.L. (1976) 'Social structure from multiple networks. I: Blockmodels of roles and positions', *American Journal of Sociology*, 81: 730–780.

Whyte, W.F. (1981) *Street Corner Society: the Social Structure of an Italian Slum*, 3rd edn. Chicago, IL: University of Chicago Press (1st edn, 1943).

Williamson, O.E. (1975) *Markets and Hierarchies: Analysis and Antitrust Implications*. New York: Free Press.

Wilson, J. (1973) *Introduction to Social Movements*. New York: Basic Books.

Winch, P. (1958) *The Idea of a Social Science and its Relationship to Philosophy*. London: Routledge and Kegan Paul.

Wiseman, J.P. (1970) *Stations of the Lost: the Treatment of Skid Row Alcoholics*. Englewood Cliffs, NJ: Prentice Hall.

Wittgenstein, L. (1972) *Philosophical Investigations*. Oxford: Basil Blackwell.

Worsley, P. (1974) 'The state of theory and the status of theory', *Sociology*, 8: 1–18.

Wyckoff, W.A. (1971) *A Day with a Tramp and Other Days*. New York, Benjamin Blom (first published 1901).

Zimmerman, D.H. (1969) 'Record-keeping and the intake process in a public welfare agency', in S. Wheeler (ed.), *On Record*. New York: Russell Sage. pp. 319–354.

Zuo, J. and Benford, R.D. (1995) 'Mobilization processes and the 1989 Chinese democracy movement', *Sociological Quarterly*, 36: 131–156.

Zurcher, L.A. and Snow, D.A. (1981) 'Collective behavior: social movements', in M. Rosenberg and R.H. Turner (eds), *Social Psychology: Sociological Perspectives*. New York: Basic Books. pp. 447–482.

Subject Index

Author Index